Wellington's Regiments

WELLINGTON'S REGIMENTS

The Men and their Battles from Roliça to Waterloo 1808–1815

IAN FLETCHER

SPELLMOUNT

Staplehurst

TO
Debbie and Jack

British Library Cataloguing in Publication Data:
A catalogue record for this book is available
from the British Library

Copyright © Ian Fletcher 1994

ISBN 1-873376-06-5

First published in the UK in 1994 by
Spellmount Limited
The Old Rectory
Staplehurst
Kent TN12 0AZ

1 3 5 7 9 8 6 4 2

The right of Ian Fletcher to be identified
as the author of this work has been asserted by him
in accordance with the Copyright, Designs
and Patents Act 1985

Typeset and designed by M Rules
Printed in Great Britain by
Butler & Tanner Ltd, Frome, Somerset

CONTENTS

INTRODUCTION

It is nearly 180 years since the Duke of Wellington fought his last battle, Waterloo, the battle that brought the curtain down on a momentous period in world history. It marked the end of the military careers of both Wellington, arguably the greatest general Britain has ever produced, and Napoleon, probably the greatest commander the world has ever seen. But the close of the Napoleonic Wars in 1815 also brought to an end one of the greatest chapters in the history of the British Army, a chapter begun in the summer of 1808 when the army took its first nervous steps in Portugal and ending with its triumphant march into Paris some seven years later. Wellington's army marched virtually undefeated from the coast of central Portugal to the green fields of southern France in six years of hard fighting, gaining a reputation as one of the finest armies ever to leave Britain's shores, a reputation confirmed by those British regiments present at Waterloo in June 1815.

The majority of Wellington's regiments have long since been disbanded or have been amalgamated with one another. In recent years, however, this steady process has increased in pace and today's politicians have succeeded where numerous French marshals failed. Scores of great regiments have been decimated in the face of both political and economic adversity and Wellington himself is probably gazing down from Valhalla with some dismay at the size of today's British Army. Hence the motivation behind Wellington's Regiments; a tribute to a once great army before it all but disappears.

Strictly speaking, Wellington's army in the Peninsula was an Anglo-Portuguese one, for several Portuguese brigades served with distinction alongside their British counterparts, as did several battalions of the King's German Legion. At Waterloo Wellington's army contained even fewer British battalions, only one third of the Anglo-Dutch army being British, the rest being Dutch, Belgian, Brunswick and Hanoverian regiments. However, this book, whilst paying tribute to these regiments, and the Portuguese in particular, is not about Wellington's 'foreign' regiments. It is concerned only with the regiments of the British Army. Also, it does not look at the tremendous services of the other branches of Wellington's army, such as the artillery and engineers, without whom life in the Peninsula and at Waterloo would have been virtually impossible. I make no apologies for these omitions but it is the cavalry and infantry who take centre stage in this book.

The writing of this book involved scores of letters to the descendants of Wellington's regiments – except for the Foot Guards on whom I had already carried out much research for a previous book – an exercise which proved to be a useful and enlightening survey of regimental museums and associations. The degree of co-operation varied enormously; some regiments, in spite of financial constraints and under-manning, sent reams of photocopied records and illustrations whilst others, including some of the more prominant regiments, did not bother to respond at all. The reader may discover for himself the regiments included in this latter category by a diligent inspection of the following acknowledgments.

First and foremost I have to thank Colonel Peter Walton and Major James Falkner, of the Army Museums Ogilby Trust, for allowing me the freedom to plunder its collections, without which this book would probably not have been possible and to the National Trust for Scotland. Thanks also go to Dawn Waring for her superb, meticulously researched paintings that form one of the plate sections in this book, and on Dawn's behalf I would like to thank Michael Barthorp and Philip Haythornthwaite for their expert assistance. On the regimental side I have to thank, in no particular order, the following people who found the time to respond to my enquiries; Colonel H.B.H. Waring OBE, of The Queen's Own Royal West Kent Regiment; Major (Retd) A.J. Maher MBE, of The Queen's Lancashire Regiment; Colonel H.J. Lowles CBE, of The Worcestershire and Sherwood Foresters Regiment; Captain (Retd) P.H.D. Marr, of The Fusiliers Museum of Northumberland; Colonel J.P. Wetherall, of The Museum of the Northamptonshire Regiment; Christine Beresford, of the Regiments of Gloucestershire Museum; D.W. Scott, of The York and Lancaster Regimental Museum; Lieutenant Colonel R.B. Merton, of The King's Royal Hussars; Rena McRobbie, of RHQ The Argyll and Sutherland Highlanders; Major (Redt) M. Wright, of The Royal Irish Fusiliers Regimental Museum; Lieutenant Colonel S.W. McBain, of RHQ The Royal Scots; Adrian Lewis, of Blackburn Museum and Art Galleries; Major R.J. Jeffreys MBE, of Home Headquarters, The Light Dragoons; Major (Retd) C.P. Bowes-Crick, of The Royal Regiment of Fusiliers; Major (Retd) S.G.B. Matthews, of The Royal Hampshire Regiment Museum; Major W.H. White DL, of The Regimental Museum, The Duke of Cornwall's Light Infantry; Stuart Eastwood, of The Regimental Museum of The Border Regiment and The Kings Own Royal Border Regiment; Major J. Carroll, of Dorset Military Museum; Kate Thaxton, of Norfolk Museums Service; Andrew J.L. Davies, of the Museum of Lincolnshire Life; J.P. McGourty, of The Cameronians (Scottish Rifles) Regimental Museum; Major (Retd) R.D.W. McLean, of The Museum of the Staffordshire Regiment; G. Archer Parfitt, of The Shropshire Regimental Museum; Major (Retd) J.McQ. Hallam, of The Lancashire Headquarters The Royal Regiment of Fusiliers; Gareth Stephen Gill, of the Regimental Museum, 1st The Queen's Dragoon Guards; Major G.E.M. Stephens MBE, of The Royal Inniskilling Fusiliers Regimental Association and Regimental Museum; Major J.S. Knight, of the Queen's Royal Hussars; T.F.J. Hodgson, of The Royal Museum and Art Gallery, Canterbury; Major (Retd) W. Shaw MBE, of RHQ The Royal Highland Fusiliers; Dr Stephen Bull, of Lancashire County Museum Service; Nick Forder, of the Museum and Art Gallery, Derby; Peter Donnelly, of the King's Own Royal Regiment Museum, Lancaster; Norman Holme, of the Regimental Museum, The Royal Welch Fusiliers; Major D.J.H. Farquharson, of Home Headquarters, 16th/5th The Queen's Royal Lancers; Bryn Owen FMA, of The Welch Regiment Museum; Major R.W. Smith, of Home Headquarters, The Queen's Royal Irish Hussars; Lieutenant Colonel D.R. Roberts BEM, of RHQ The Devonshire and Dorset Regiment; Lieutenant Colonel (Retd) A.A. Fairrie, of RHQ, Queen's Own Highlanders (Seaforth and Camerons); Captain (Retd) C. Harrison, of RHQ, The Gordon Highlanders; Major (Retd) P.J. Ball, of The Regimental Museum, The Duke of Edinburgh's Royal Regiment (Berkshire and Wiltshire); Ian Hook, of the Essex Regiment Museum; Captain (Retd) C. Boardman, of RHQ, The Royal Dragoon Guards; Brigadier J.K. Chater, of The Royal Regiment of Fusiliers, Warwick; Brigadier (Retd) J.M. Cubiss CBE MC, of RHQ The Prince of Wales's Own Regiment of Yorkshire.

WELLINGTON'S ARMY

I n October 1807, Napoleon Bonaparte, Emperor of the French,
sent 30,000 French troops under the command of Marshal Andoche Junot to occupy
Portugal following its refusal to implement
his so-called 'Continental System', an
European embargo of British goods designed
to strike at the heart of Britain's economic
foundations. The Portuguese Royal Family
subsequently fled to Brazil after first appoint-
ing a Council of Regency to rule in its place.
Barely five months later, in March 1808,
Napoleon despatched a further 100,000
troops, this time into Spain, following which
he set up his brother Joseph as King of
Spain. Both nations appealed to Britain for
help and so was begun the Peninsular War,
known in Spain as the War of Independence.

When Napoleon sent his legions south
across the Pyrenees he had little idea of the
repercussions his invasion of the Iberian
Peninsula were to have for him and his empire.
Indeed, 'The Spanish Ulcer', as the war in the
Peninsula was to become known, ultimately
proved to be a turning point in the history of
Europe and was a major factor that led to his
final downfall in 1815. In Spain and Portugal
what appeared to be yet another Napoleonic
conquest turned into a bitter conflict, fought
not only between the armies of France,
Britain, Spain and Portugal but also between
the French invaders and the populations of
both of the Iberian nations who waged a savage guerrilla war on their oppressors. The war
was a massive drain on French arms, armour
and, more important, manpower for thousands
of French troops were tied down in the
Peninsula who could otherwise have been

Wellington and his
Peninsular generals, painted
several years after the war.

The Duchess of Richmond's Ball, June 15th 1815. In spite of the salubrious surroundings depicted here the ball was actually held in the workshop of a Brussels' coachbuilder. Many of Wellington's officers, called away hastily during the Ball, fought at Quatre Bras the following day still wear their silk stockings and dancing pumps.

engaged elsewhere in Europe as Napoleon's armies waged a succession of wars against the Allies in central and eastern Europe. French commanders were forced to leave large garrisons in towns for if the French moved on, a veritable uprising would follow in their wake. Routine despatches required whole troops of cavalry to ensure their safe delivery for isolated riders were an easy quarry for the marauding bands of covert, cut-throat killers – otherwise known as guerillas – that seemed to lurk silently and stealthily in every hideout the Peninsular landscape offered.

There is, however, another and more significant point – at least from the British perspective – to consider when dealing with the various repercussions Napoleon's invasions were to have and that is that the Peninsular War gave Britain an excuse to land an army on the Continent of Europe, an army that was to emerge as one of the finest of all those belonging to the nations embroiled in the long conflict that collectively has come to be called the Napoleonic Wars.

The record of the British Army since 1793 had been patchy at best; some successes had been achieved, notably in India and, in 1801, in Egypt, although the years after these dates had been littered with dismal failures and farcical tragedies, Egypt (1807) and Buenos Aires (1806–07) being amongst the more infamous examples of the period. When the British Army under Sir Arthur Wellesley landed in

Portugal in August 1808 it was still reeling from these failures and Wellesley was only too aware of the price of failure. The army was inexperienced and largely untried and with it he was about to face an army which had enjoyed years of unbroken success throughout Europe. It was an army small in number and, more significantly, being the only army the government was able to send abroad, it was a precious one of which Wellesley would have to take great care, not only for strategical but also political reasons. The government placed great pressures and constraints upon Wellesley, pressures which, in spite of his subsequent successes, would bedevil him throughout the war. Nevertheless, six years and almost thirty battles and sieges later it was an army which Wellesley – by then the Duke of Wellington – said could go anywhere and do anything, such was its superb condition.

It is probably true to say that Wellington's infantry provided the cornerstone of his success as a military commander, for despite their much publicised lapses into undisciplined behaviour, they were rarely to let him down when it came to the crunch. The army in the Peninsula was divided into divisions, although at Roliça and Vimeiro it was such a small army it was brigaded. However, by the close of the war it totalled some eight divisions, numbered 1 to 7 plus the Light Division. Each of the divisions soon gained nicknames depending on their substance or reputation. For example,

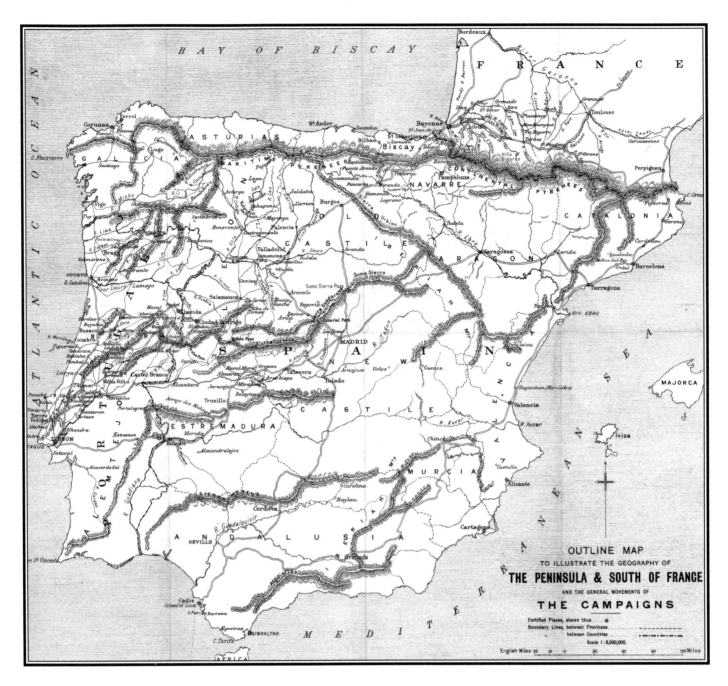

OUTLINE MAP
TO ILLUSTRATE THE GEOGRAPHY OF
THE PENINSULA & SOUTH OF FRANCE
AND THE GENERAL MOVEMENTS OF
THE CAMPAIGNS

Fortified Places, shewn thus
Boundary Lines, between Provinces
between Countries
Scale 1 : 3,000,000.

English Miles 30   15   0   30   60   90   120 Miles

the 1st Division was nicknamed 'The Gentlemen's Sons', owing to the fact that it contained the Brigades of Guards, whereas the 3rd Division was known as 'The Fighting Division', because it was usually in the thick of any action. Each of these divisions was in turn divided into brigades, usually two or three in each between 1,500 to 2,000 strong. The brigades consisted of two or three infantry battalions which could vary drastically in number. In theory, each battalion consisted of ten companies, being eight centre companies, a light company and a grenadier company. The companies were 100 strong but in practice

this was rarely the case. The average battalion strength was 550 with some battalions, the 2/38th for instance, numbering just 263 at the end of 1811. Stronger battalions such as the Guards rarely dropped below 1,000 although the 1st Foot Guards suffered so severely from sickness in 1812 that they were sent away to Oporto to recuperate, their numbers having dropped to around 600.

The training of Wellington's army, as was the case with every other army, revolved around the limitations and performances of the weapons at their disposal. In the case of his infantry this meant musket drill with the heavy, 39-inch flintlock musket known as the 'Brown Bess', a musket which was destined to sweep the French from many a dusty Spanish battlefield during the next six years. It was hardly an accurate weapon – its effective range was about 300 yards – and any infantryman fortunate enough to hit his target at anything over 100 yards could consider himself very lucky indeed. However, the combined power of hundreds of these muskets when fired into the dense masses of enemy troops was often enough to provide the deciding factor in battle.

The musket was a clumsy weapon to load, a total of twenty movements being necessary to load the ball into the barrel of the musket which was rammed down with an iron ramrod, before it was ready to fire. In the hands of trained infantrymen the 'Brown Bess' could be fired three times a minute, although in emergencies the charge of ball and cartridge could be loaded by inserting them down the barrel with a charge of powder and simply slamming the butt-end of the musket on the ground instead of using the ramrod. This did not always secure the ball, however, and when the musket was not levelled it would often roll out of the barrel. Also, young and inexperienced infantrymen, out of panic or excitement, would often forget to withdraw

their ramrods and fire them off, leaving themselves nothing with which to load their muskets. The limitations of the 'Brown Bess' were that heavy rain would render it almost impossible to fire, the flint requiring a spark to ignite the charge of powder in the firing pan. Misfires were common also, although it is reckoned that only two out of every thirteen shots did so. This was a far better ratio than the French muskets with their inferior quality flints, although try telling this to any British infantryman whose misfire occurred at the very moment that an enemy soldier closed with him. A far more accurate weapon was the Baker rifle, used by the rifle regiments of the army, the 5/60th and the 95th, as well as the light battalions of the King's German Legion. It was always a welcome relief to any hard-pressed infantrymen to hear the reassuring clanging sound of the Baker rifle coming to their assistance. It was a shorter barrelled weapon than the 'Brown Bess' and was accurate at almost three times the range. Like the 'Brown Bess' it was liable to misfire, and owing to its rifled barrel it was difficult to ram the bullet down and was slow to load, a trained rifleman being capable of just two shots a minute. Nevertheless, it was the most effective weapon of the Peninsular War and although unsuitable for use as the main

Three brothers who served in the Peninsula. General Sir Henry Wyndham KCB, ADC to the Duke of York, George Wyndham, 20th Light Dragoons, and Charles Wyndham, 10th Light Dragoons.

infantry weapon it proved mightily successful in skirmishing. When the French withdrew their own rifles as being too slow, the marksmen of the 5/60th and the 95th were left with a distinct advantage.

The advantages accrued from the use of the 'Brown Bess' and the Baker rifle were very real indeed but it was the tactics employed by the two opposing armies that provided the more marked contrast in their fortunes. It is generally accepted that the British line triumphed time and time again over the French column. French historians may have tried to disagree over the years but it is a fact. However, it is also a great generalisation that warrants further investigation, something which space precludes here in this book. Nevertheless, we must take a brief look at this scenario that occurred many times in the Peninsula as it holds the key to many of Wellington's great victories. The problem for the French, approaching in column, was, of course, that no matter how strong their column, only the front ranks and those on the flanks were able to bring their muskets to bear, whereas the British, standing in a two-deep line, could fire every single one of their 'Brown Besses', something which happened with consummate ease

on many occasions. In very simple terms, it all came down to mathematics. But it was far more complex than that, and we cannot assume that the French commanders were not unaware of this equation. It has now become apparent that on many occasions the French, although advancing in column, actually attempted to deploy into line as they closed with the British only to be set upon by the rigid red ranks of British infantry who drove them back before they had a chance to complete their manoeuvre, something which happened at Waterloo, for example, at the crucial moment of the Imperial Guard's attack.

The intimidating spectacle of solid red lines standing silent and still provided a marked contrast to the noisy, raucous approach of the French columns, whose officers ran up and down waving their swords and shakos in the air, encouraging the men who grew ever more reluctant as they neared the British lines. The French were used to seeing their columns shatter opposing armies elsewhere in Europe but here in the Peninsula they came up against a new kind of opponent who simply stood and waited, unruffled and unimpressed by their blustering, clamorous approach. As the French neared them a sense of unease would begin to

French infantry under fire from the Royal Horse Artillery during the Peninsular War.

'News from the Front.' Wellington's headquarters in the Peninsula. The Moorish architecture would have us believe that this is southern Spain. A wounded cavalryman is brought in by a peasant whilst British officers look on. Wellington's HQ was rarely the scene of such hustle and bustle as depicted here by Hillingford. Indeed, apart from a few orderlies his headquarters often appeared deserted.

spread through the dense ranks of their column as, in the words of one of their officers, "the enemy's fire, so long reserved, would be very unpleasant when it did break forth." When the French were just a few yards from them the British would bring their arms to the 'ready' position and a voice would cry out "fire!" A tremendous volley would then crash out, engulfing the leading ranks of Frenchmen in a thick white smoke while a huge weight of lead tore into them.

The effects of such a fire at close range were deadly, but if the effects in human terms were great, the effects on French morale were even greater. Those in the rear and centre ranks were unable to see what was going on up front. All they would be aware of was that something dreadful had happened and, not waiting to find out what it was, they would, more often than not, begin to melt away to the rear. Those in the front ranks who had survived the storm of lead now faced cold steel as the British line cheered, charged and chased them back to their own positions before returning in triumph. This scenario was one

psychological barrier that the French were never really to overcome.

There were other factors in Wellington's success in using this tactic, such as the careful use of a heavy screen of riflemen and light troops who would harry and hustle the French all the way along their line of approach. But perhaps the single most significant and crucial element of his strategy lay in the choice of ground. Even a cursory study of the battlefields of the Peninsular War and Waterloo show that for the most part the French found themselves attacking uphill, against an enemy which often remained hidden out of sight on the reverse slope of a ridge or hill. When the French attacked at Sorauren and Busaco, for instance, they were not only facing a tough, determined enemy, they were also embarking on an exhausting climb that would be difficult enough in peacetime for an unarmed man, let alone someone groaning beneath the weight of a 60lb pack. This choice of ground invariably involved Wellington in placing his men on the reverse slope of a hill, not only to shelter his men from enemy artillery fire, but also to

British infantry, wearing their white fatigue jackets, at drill c.1808. Sergeants put them through their paces while officers look on.

conceal them from sight. At Busaco, for instance, the French thought they were attacking the centre of the Allied line whereas, in fact, it was the left. The attacking French would reach the crest of the hill or ridge, apparently deserted, only to be met by a withering fire from the British line that would suddenly appear as if from the very earth, much to the horror of the shocked and surprised French.

The hallmark of Wellington's success, therefore, was the tactical combination of a two-deep line and skilful use of ground but perhaps the most enduring image of the British infantry of his age, and in particular at Waterloo, was the infantry square. The two-deep line was a more than effective measure against enemy infantry but against cavalry it was largely an ineffective and suicidal formation to use. There were occasions when British infantry scored successes against enemy cavalry when in line, notably at El Bodon and Sabugal in 1811 but generally speaking a square was a much safer formation to adopt. When Ney launched his massed cavalry attacks against Wellington's position on the ridge at Waterloo the hard pressed Allied infantry were immediately deployed in squares, each having ranks some four deep. Of course, this was not a formation exclusive to Wellington but was the standard infantry tactic against enemy cavalry. The legions of heavily armoured curassiers and

brightly coloured hussars swept around Wellington's squares at Waterloo like waves around rocks but when the vast tide of men and horses had receded the solid stoic squares still stood, immoveable and impassive. These squares bristled with steel and it was nigh on impossible to get a horse to charge directly at them. In fact, the breaking of an infantry square was a rare occurrence although it did happen in the Peninsula on two occasions but even here both incidents were the results of an accident and a freak of nature.

On the morning after the battle of Salamanca Bock's German Dragoons came up with the French rearguard at Garcia Hernandez and charged. The French instinctively formed square but one of Bock's leading horses was shot and carried on straight into the square, smashing a hole in its front rank. Bock's men quickly seized their chance and within a short space of time more dragoons had managed to get into the square which quickly lost its cohesion. The French were badly mauled on this occasion and the majority forced to surrender. At Albuera, in May 1811, it was a freak of nature that caused one of Colborne's infantry brigades to be decimated by enemy cavalry. It happened following a violent rain and hail storm which quickly rendered the mens' muskets useless and taking advantage of this, and the poor visibility, Soult's Polish lancers charged and set

Royal Horse Artillery at the battle of Salamanca, July 22nd 1812. Behind the artilleryman kneeling on the right stands a lancer, presumably taken prisoner during the day. His guard stands behind him.

about the helpless British before they had a chance to form into square. Caught in line, they were virtually annihilated by the Poles who used their long vicious lances to deadly effect. In the resulting disaster Colborne's brigade suffered some of the worse casualty rates of the whole war. One British cavalry officer, a Lieutenant Colonel Talbot, of the 14th Light Dragoons, had a theory that infantry squares could be broken by riding directly at them. At Barquilla, in July 1810, he had an opportunity to test this when he launched his men against a square of about 200 French infantrymen who had been detected on a foraging trip. Unfortunately for Talbot the charge went terribly wrong. His men had to negotiate a defile, their charge lacked any sort of impetus and when Talbot rode against the square he was shot and bayonetted as he rolled into its front ranks.

For infantry the square was a safe haven against cavalry provided the men held their nerve and maintained their formation. At Waterloo, the infantry welcomed the cavalry charges as they came as a relief from the terrible pounding they were receiving from Napoleon's artillery for which an infantry square was an easy target. Artillery could blow away such a formation with canister shot

with devastating ease but at Waterloo this potentially catastrophical scenario never materialised; Ney attacked without artillery support and the squares remained safe and solid.

So there we have it, the square and the line. Of course, there were many more factors that combined to provide Wellington with his victories between 1808 and 1815 but it is fair to say that in battle, where the campaigns were decided, it was these formations that yielded such a harvest of success for him. But although these tactics proved triumphant for Wellington throughout his campaigns in the Peninsula and later at Waterloo one should not imagine that he was purely a defensive general, as many of his critics would have us believe. One should consider the speed with which he moved against the fortresses of Ciudad Rodrigo and Badajoz to take them, with French armies in close proximity on both occasions. Consider too, his dynamic attack at Salamanca to seize on French mistakes and again at Vittoria when he smashed Joseph's army. His operations in crossing the Bidassoa and Adour rivers bear all the hallmarks of a great offensive general also. At Waterloo, of course, he was forced by circumstances to fight a holding battle, hanging on grimly while he waited for Blücher's Prussians to arrive. But here again he employed the tactics used to such good effect in Spain and Portugal, the crowning glory being the repulse of Napoleon's Guard by Wellington's own Foot Guards, the ultimate triumph of the British line.

Wellington's cavalry and artillery tactics were dictated by the limited numbers of each of these arms available to him. In fact, in 1811 only six cavalry regiments were present in the Peninsula, each consisting of four squadrons of about 200 men. The number of regiments increased by 1813 to 15 but this still represented just 10% of his total force. His reliance on infantry, however, was not only due to the fact that he simply had more men in that particular department of his army. When Wellington returned to Portugal in 1809 following his acquittal of charges arising from the Convention of Cintra he was deprived of Lord Henry Paget, undoubtedly his best cavalry commander who had led the cavalry with distinction during the retreat to Corunna (Paget was persona non grata after eloping with Wellington's sister-in-law). Paget was not to return to Wellington's army until the Waterloo campaign and this lack of a suitable cavalry commander in the Peninsula was to have serious consequences. General Le Marchant was perhaps the best cavalry commander after Paget but he was unfortunately killed during the latter stages of the battle of Salamanca, his first command. General William Lumley was also a fine cavalry commander but saw limited service in the Peninsula.

As we may look back with pride at the achievements of British infantry, so we may shudder when we look at some of the exploits of British cavalry between 1808 and 1815. At Benavente and Sahagun during the retreat to Corunna, Paget's hussars had achieved notable successes over their French counterparts but the barren years from 1809 onwards provided a poor crop of battle honours. This of course has much to do with their relatively small numbers but their actions during the Peninsular War were often marked by a total lack of discipline resulting in near disaster on more than one occasion. The 'steeplechase' run by the 23rd Light Dragoons at Talavera was echoed by the Union Brigade at Waterloo when on both occasions the cavalry lost control and suffered accordingly from their own reck-lessness. It was only towards the latter end of the Peninsular War, when Wellington was able to fight the French with an equal number of cavalry that they began to achieve results on the battlefield. Off the battlefield, however, it was a different story as on reconnaissance and outpost duties his cavalry did sterling work. Chief amongst these were the hussars of the King's German Legion who were by far his most accomplished exponents of outpost and reconnaissance work and on the battlefield, as we have seen, it was German cavalry that wreaked havoc amongst the French squares at Garcia Hernandez.

Small numbers and the lack of first class cavalry commanders handicapped Wellington's cavalry from the outset but one cannot blame these factors alone. Indeed, there was perhaps something lacking in their training which may have provided an important reason for their disappointing service record. This lies in the fact that many of Wellington's cavalry regiments, and in particular the Household Cavalry and some of the heavy dragoon regiments, had spent most of their time in England putting down mobs and rioters and acting as a sort of police force. Remember, these were volatile days when the memory of the French Revolution was still fresh in people's minds and an undercurrent of revolution often simmered away beneath the surface at home. As a result, many of the heavy cavalry regiments that came out towards the end of the Peninsular War were ignorant of even the basic rudiments of warfare and these had to be quickly learnt on the job, often to their cost. Other regiments, the famous Royal Scots Greys, for instance, saw no overseas service at all after 1795 and only travelled abroad in 1815 for the Waterloo campaign.

The principal weapon of the cavalry was the sabre. The light cavalry, namely the light dragoons and hussars, were armed with a curved sabre with a sharp blade measuring 33 inches which was effective when slashing at an opponent. The heavy cavalry, on the other hand, were armed with a heavy, straight bladed sabre, 35 inches long, which was no good for anything other than chopping. It was useless as a thrusting weapon, although no doubt there were many unfortunate French troops who found themselves on the wrong end of the point of one of them. It was much more effective as a slashing weapon but even here, unless the blade was sharp, a blow would usually end in a broken limb. Nevertheless, it could be a fearsome weapon to which the battered and bruised wreckage of D'Erlon's corps could testify as it staggered back to the French lines, following the charge of the Scots Greys at Waterloo. The light dragoons and hussars were also armed with carbines although they were rarely used except in skirmishes. But perhaps the most terrifying weapon used by cavalry in the Peninsula was not used by Wellington's cavalry but by Napoleon's lancers, and in particular the Poles. These highly skilled horsemen were armed with the lance, a weapon seldom encountered by the British before the war which allowed the Poles to kill and maim without too much danger to themselves. To lie on the ground was futile as a short sharp stab in the back was an easy task for a lancer. At Albuera, the carnage after the Polish lancers had set about Colborne's infantry brigade was one of the worse sights of the entire war. Three infantry battalions were virtually annihilated in a matter of minutes, the 3rd Foot losing 643 out of 755 men. The British cavalry chose not to use the lance until after the end of the Napoleonic Wars but they did come up against it on several occasions, notably at Waterloo where the lancers played havoc with the retreating Scots Greys whose horses were blown after their momentous demolition of D'Erlon's corps. Perhaps the most famous episode involving a British cavalryman was played out here when Sergeant Ewart, of the Greys, captured the eagle of the French 45th Regiment, slaying a Polish lancer as he did so.

One final, but nonetheless important, factor regarding Wellington's use of cavalry in the Peninsula was the ground. We have already seen that the choice of ground played a significant part in Wellington's battles, but for the cavalry the terrain in the Peninsula was largely unsuitable for mounted warfare. The great plains of Leon from Burgos to Ciudad Rodrigo, and in the south around Estremadura are ideally suited for cavalry. Unfortunately, when Wellington was campaigning in these areas it was at a time when his cavalry was in short supply. Numbers began steadily to increase until by 1813 he could call on the service of almost 9,000 Allied cavalry. However, by then, he found himself fighting in the north east of Spain which was difficult cavalry country. When he began his operations in the Pyrenees and the south of France it was almost impossible for his cavalry to operate satisfactorily, the area being rife with defiles, rivers and other natural obstacles that make this such a spectacular region.

The shortage of numbers and difficult terrain were two reasons which also bedeviled Wellington's artillery. He operated throughout the early years of the war with a woefully small number of guns and even in the latter stages of the war he was often outgunned (at Vittoria he had 90 guns, the French 150). However, as with all of the arms of his small but precious army, he used his artillery judiciously, choosing not to concentrate his guns but instead place small units in vital places from where he often directed them himself. The exacting terrain made it difficult to transport guns at times and this was made worse by a lack of horses with which to draw them. Fortunately, Wellington was served by a splendid corps of artillery officers, the largest body of professionally trained officers in the army.

The guns of the artillery were the death dealers during the Napoleonic Wars. Infantry often stood for hours on end in the face of a storm of shot and shell, unflinching as large iron balls came bouncing in to inflict fearful wounds on row upon row of men. Guns normally ranged from between 6- to 12-pounders, although even larger guns up to 36-pounders were used in siege warfare. The standard British gun in the Peninsula was the 9-pounder. By far the commonest form of projectile was the roundshot, a solid iron ball capable of knocking down whole files of men at a single blow. One of the advantages of Wellington's use of the reverse slope of a ridge was that his men were able to lie down out of sight of the enemy guns although even then the odd roundshot would come bouncing over the top to kill and maim. Common shell was a hollow ball filled with explosives which was ignited by a fuse. Often, common shells would come spinning and spluttering into an infantry square only to be defused by a quick thinking infantryman who, if he was lucky enough and quick enough, could pull the fuse out of the shell and render it harmless. Spherical case was in effect shrapnel, and had been invented by Henry Shrapnel. This consisted of a hollow shell with a thin case, which was filled with musket balls. It too had a fuse, and was timed to explode above enemy infantry, the musket balls spreading death in a downward direction. Case shot, or canister, was an equally nasty form of death. A thin tin case was filled with bullets which, when fired from a gun, burst, much like a shotgun spreads its pellets. Used against tightly-packed infantry or cavalry, canister was lethal and the results devastating.

Apart from Henry Shrapnel's invention, there were other innovations which saw service in Wellington's army. Probably the most famous was the rocket, invented by William Congreve. This consisted of a large rocket weighing either 9, 12 or 18 pounds which was placed on a firing tripod and launched. Wellington was never a very strong advocate of the weapon but it did, nevertheless, see service in Spain, the south of France, and at Waterloo. The Peninsular War also saw an early use of the 'creeping barrage', employed at San Sebastian in 1813. Sir Thomas Graham's troops had become bogged down whilst attacking the breaches in the walls and so he gave orders that his artillery should fire over the heads of his attacking columns even though they were still at the walls. This of course meant that the French defenders had to retire from the walls whilst the barrage was in progress and when it lifted the British stormers would be able, hopefully, to gain the breaches before the defenders could return to their positions. The plan worked perfectly and while the attacking British troops pressed

their faces into the ground, all manner of shot and shell screamed over their heads to crash into the defenders' positions. When the barrage lifted they scrambled up and stormed into the town and the place was taken.

These then were Wellington's main fighting units. What began the war as a small, relatively untried army developed into one of the finest armies Britain has produced, an army with which he later said he could go anywhere and do anything. But of course none of these units could have functioned without the assistance of the support arms, the commissariat, the engineers, intelligence, transport and medical services.

Wellington's army was essentially that, it was his army, for he was careful to keep a close watchful eye on the civil departments of the army as well as those mentioned above. The main task of the Commissariat Department was to keep the troops supplied with food and drink and to see that their rations were delivered on time and to the correct place. With the army's reliance on this form of supply, rather than the French way of living off the land, it was vital that provisions were made available on time and in good quantities. Any breakdown in the system was liable to induce the men to turn to plundering the local population, a practice strictly forbidden by Wellington. Also, everything taken by the British Army had to be paid for, as it was vital for them not to cause any trouble with the locals who were, after all, allies. Documents

'Troops bivouacked near the Village of Villa Velha, on the Evening of the 19th of May 1811.' A marvellous study by Major Thomas St Clair illustrating the various occupations in camp. A barber gives a shave, goats are milked, horses are fed and watered whilst men idle away the time.

have since shown, however, that many Spaniards and Portuguese looked upon both French and British as being as bad as one another whether they paid for their food or not. At the end of the day they were left with nothing. When the British occupied Madrid, for example, the people made a great fuss although many were afraid that when the British left the French might return and exact reprisals. The French were often given the same welcome when they entered a town after the British had departed, a signal often being given to the French meaning it was safe for them to enter. It was inevitable that the commissariat would fail at some point, usually during a retreat, for example from Burgos and to Corunna and it was on these occasions that the British troops resorted to plundering in order to feed themselves, although this was often an excuse for them to go off in search of drink which was always to be found in plenty. Nevertheless, by 1813 the commissariat was supplying over 100,000lbs of biscuit, 200,000lbs of forage and were slaughtering 300 head of cattle for meat each day. When Wellington crossed the Pyrenees and entered France the commissariat found it little problem to feed the army, by then around 80,000 strong.

As well as the commissariat, which was a civil department, there were eight other departments at headquarters; the Quartermaster General, Adjutant General, Military Secretary, Chief of Artillery, Chief Engineer, Surgeon General, Apothecary General and Paymaster General. (A masterful analysis of these departments can be found in S.G.P. Ward's Wellington's Headquarters. Oxford, 1957.) Between them, these departments saw to everything relating to the daily administration of the army, including medical and spiritual matters, the gathering and dissemination of intelligence, the army's communications and, perhaps the most important, its movements and quartering.

When Wellington spoke of his men in the Peninsula he used what has become probably the most famous sobriquet of all, 'the scum of the earth'. However, it is also the most misquoted, for he went on to say that it was wonderful that they [the army] should have made such fine fellows of such men. Furthermore, although he may well have been exasperated by the behaviour of his men at times, he was, when referring to the 'scum', not referring to his soldiers but to the men who enlisted.

These men were gleaned by the recruiting sergeants who, with their recruiting parties, would travel the countryside, stopping at small towns and villages. Here, villagers, who often knew little of the world in which they lived other than the few miles around them, were held spellbound by the recruiting sergeant who would sit each evening by the fireside of an inn spinning wild tales of the adventures of their countrymen, of the glories of war and of the threat posed by the ever-present bogeyman, Bonaparte. With a few mugs of ale inside them and with the King's Shilling gleaming brightly in their eyes, the attraction proved too great for many a man and before long they were ensnared and found themselves marching to the beat of the drum. For many men, the bounty offered by the recruiting parties, ranging from between £16 to £40, was the main temptation but for a good many others the prospect of regular food and shelter, and of pay and companionship, proved equally great. For some even, it was the naive thought that it was indeed their duty to fight the Corsican usurper, brought about by fears imbued in the minds of the British population since the beginning of the 19th century by a well-honed and efficient British press whose savage propaganda served only to fuel such fears. In 1805 the threat of invasion was a very real one indeed and although Nelson had long since dealt Napoleon's plans a severe blow at Trafalgar the threat of invasion by Bonaparte's battalions, portrayed as demonic, devilish hordes by the likes of Cruikshank and Gilray, still lingered in the British people's minds right up until his last gamble at Waterloo in 1815.

Other men were recruited as a result of conditions at home. The prospect of a violent death on the battlefield figured little in the mind of a starving man, with little or no prospects at home, when weighed against the advantages, however tenuous and slender, of life in the army. Others simply joined to escape the torments of brutal employers, of mounting debts or of unfortunate escapades with women. Such men would find a home in the army, a home which in spite of the rigours of campaign life and of a harsh system of discipline, would provide a lifestyle which was

more than preferable to the kind of life they led at home in Britain.

When Wellington referred to the recruits as the scum of the earth he said they had enlisted purely for drink, and he may well have been right, for in many cases, gin was indeed 'the spirit of their patriotism.' It is perhaps this element of the army that has often given it such a bad name over the years, an element blamed for the appalling outrages perpetrated during the aftermaths of Badajoz and San Sebastian and during the retreat from Burgos. However, this element may be said to have posed only a latent threat to the discipline of the army for it was another source of recruit that proved to be the catalyst on these occasions, a section of the army that proved to be the stimulus and motivating force behind such shocking scenes. These recruits came from an even lower level of British society and may well be termed the scum of the earth. They were the men of the underworld, the criminals, pickpockets, poachers, smugglers, bully-boys and thugs, who, if not on the run from the law, had been caught, convicted and offered the choice between jail and the army. Such men were usually to be found at the heart of any dark deed in the Peninsula and more often than not were the men who tumbled into an open grave in front of a firing squad, or were left kicking and dancing from a gallows.

They cared little about the consequences of their illegal actions and appear to have considered it an occupational hazard if they received a few hundred more lashes across their already scarred and lacerated backs. They were usually the first to desert, given the chance. Every regiment, no matter how fine a service record, could count amongst its number at least fifty or so of these blackguards and scoundrels whose influence on the weak willed – whose actions were determined by the amount of drink put away – was as evil as it was absolute. The hard core of criminals in Wellington's army was always to be found at the forefront of its misdemeanours but their drunken clowning confederates posed no less a problem, for whenever and wherever the demon drink was to be found and got it was usually consumed to excess with equally excessive consequences.

A better type of recruit was the man who joined the regular army from the militia. The men from the numerous regiments of militia that served almost as a second force at home, have drawn undeserved criticism at times, often being dismissed as being raw recruits, with little or no sense of soldiering. However, these men were not allowed to volunteer for the regular army until they had served for at least a year in the militia. This meant, of course, that they had undergone a great deal of

British riflemen skirmishing in the Peninsula. In the distant centre British infantry form square against French cavalry whilst officers observe the fight through telescopes. This painting by Dighton gives a good illustration of the type of warfare waged by the riflemen of the 5/60th and the 95th.

drilling and were not the real type of raw recruit that was to be found in the country's pothouses. Indeed, even as disciplined a unit as the Brigade of Guards accepted men from the militia and when the Coldstream Guards, for example, fought at Waterloo, their ranks were full of militiamen who had been drafted in. The militia, being a permanent force, represented a prime source of recruits for Wellington's army and it was a supply that was utilised to the full. Indeed, shortly after the capture of San Sebastian, in September 1813, Wellington's army numbered just under 55,000 which was almost the same as the total number of militiamen who had volunteered for the regular army since 1809.

These then, were the main sources of recruits for the rank and file; the miscreants, the miserable, the malcontents, and the militia. But what of the officers?

It is often stated that Wellington's army was officered almost entirely by the aristocracy and landed gentry, and that they bought their commissions. These claims, however, are wide of the mark on both accounts for in 1809 there were just 140 officers in the army who were peers or sons of peers and almost half were serving with either the cavalry or the three regiments of Foot Guards. These latter regiments were brigaded together into the 1st Division of the army and were naturally nicknamed, 'The Gentlemen's Sons'. However, the majority of Wellington's officers hailed from the professional classes which encompassed everybody from the landed gentry to doctors and lawyers. A large number of new officers, of course, were the sons of officers already serving in the army. Also, with the need to supply about 1,000 officers a year to the army during the Peninsular War it was not necessary to have to obtain a commission by purchase. In fact, only one in five first commissions were purchased and with casualty rates being much higher than during peacetime most promotions were by seniority.

Almost any literate young man was accepted into the army once he had passed his sixteenth birthday. It may seem odd that a young man could join as an officer bereft of any kind of military training at all, but this was the case with sixty-five out of every hundred officers in Wellington's army. Only those officers, one in five, who had joined via the militia had been trained in the art of war, or

who had joined as a Volunteer, gentlemen rankers who learned their trade carrying a musket in the ranks until an ensigncy became vacant. Cadets from the Royal Military College provided a small number also but on the whole Wellington's officers joined with little or no knowledge of military training. However, as gentlemen they had, in the main, the respect of their men and were consequently able to command, something which they did from the front.

The officers of the Guards, with a higher proportion of aristocratic officers, commanded even more respect. Indeed, John Kincaid, of the 95th Rifles, bemoaned the fact that there were not more aristocratic officers in the army as they were able to command more willing obedience from their men with less effort. This is borne out by the extremely low number of court martial cases involving the Guards compared with the line regiments.

Overall the system worked. As in all walks of life there were 'rotten apples', but these undesirable officers were few and far between. During the Peninsular War thirty officers were cashiered, the heaviest penalty an officer could incur, for various offences ranging from irregular business dealings with merchants, to drunkenness, disobeying senior officers and public brawling. On two occasions only were officers cashiered for cowardice. Perhaps the most astounding case involved an officer who was cashiered for 'flagrant immorality', after he had co-habited with the wife of a private soldier and fought with and beat her understandably jealous husband!

This, then, was Wellington's army. It drove him to despair on occasions and shocked him on others; it moved him to tears and astonished him with its bravery. It is fitting that we close this introduction with his own observation upon it. 'The national character of the three Kingdoms was strongly marked in our Army. I found the English regiments always in the best humour when we were well supplied with beef; the Irish when we were in the wine countries and the Scotch when the dollars for pay came in . . . I assure you it was a fact . . . and I will venture to say that in our later campaigns, and especially when we crossed the Pyrenees, there never was an army in the world in better spirits, better order, or better discipline.'

THE BATTLES
1808–1815

Roliça

August 17th 1808

The battle of Roliça, fought on August 17th 1808, was the first battle of the Peninsular War involving the British Army under Sir Arthur Wellesley. There had been a skirmish between three companies of riflemen from the 95th and some French piquets close to Obidos on August 15th but the engagement at Roliça marked the beginning of six long hard years of fighting in the Peninsula for the British Army.

Wellesley's force of some 9,500 men had landed on the Portuguese coast at Figueira, about 100 miles north of Lisbon, on August 1st 1808. Having been reinforced by Major General Sir Brent Spencer who had sailed from Cadiz with a further 5,000 men Wellesley began to march south towards Lisbon on August 10th. Wellesley had divided his army into seven infantry brigades, six British and one Portuguese, but he was hampered slightly by a shortage of horses that meant that barely two-thirds of his light dragoons were mounted and that he could only pull three of his five batteries of guns. So, while his small army marched off along the dusty road to Lisbon, the unmounted dragoons were left behind to kick their heels in frustration while the remaining batteries of guns stayed silently with them.

At Obidos, barring the road to Lisbon, lay about 4,500 French troops under General Delaborde who had been sent by Junot to act as a delaying force to hold up Wellesley until 9,000 reinforcements under General Loison, at that time resting at Abrantes further to the east, could arrive. However, before they could do so the two armies clashed.

Wellesley enjoyed an advantage of around 3 to 1 in manpower, an advantage which was pressed home quickly as Delaborde abandoned his position at Obidos on August 16th and retreated to a much more defensible position at the village of Roliça. This position consisted of a long valley, surrounded by hills on all sides save to the north facing Obidos which was open. Wellesley's plan involved dividing his force into three columns. While the centre column, consisting of the brigades under Hill, Nightingall and Catlin Craufurd, advanced against the village of Roliça, a column away on the British right flank, under Trant, and a larger one on the left flank, under Ferguson, began to steal forward around the flanks of Delaborde's position. It was a classic pincer movement but while the French troops watched and marvelled as the British troops, in their as yet unspoilt red jackets, deployed and advanced, they were unaware of the trap that was closing around them.

However, the wily Delaborde was not one to be taken in too easily and as he watched Wellesley's troops from the top of a windmill he saw the manoeuvre unfolding. Also, he had detached a unit away to his right to watch for Loison's force and this unit reported Ferguson's movement as soon as it was spotted. As the British troops came on in the centre the French guns opened up and exchanged shots with Wellesley's artillery while the cavalry of both sides postured and played on the flanks to little effect. Meanwhile, Delaborde's line of tirailleurs engaged the British light companies in the centre as well as the riflemen from Ferguson's column on the British left. Delaborde's main force in the village did not engage the British, however, for just as Wellesley's pincer operation was closing in Delaborde calmly gave orders for a withdrawal and the British movement snapped its empty jaws shut in frustration as the French pulled back.

Wellesley's frustration was compounded when he saw the strength of Delaborde's second position. It lay atop the steep hills at the bottom of the valley, about one mile south of Roliça, with four very distinct rocky gullies leading up to the top. It was up these gullies that Wellesley's men would have to attack as the hill was too steep elsewhere. Undaunted, Wellesley decided to employ the same enveloping tactics he had used earlier in the day although any serious outflanking manoeuvre was impossible owing to the excellent protection afforded the flanks of Delaborde's position by the deep gullies.

Once again, the columns of Trant and Ferguson pressed forward on the flanks, this latter column engaging the French unit anxiously awaiting the reinforcements under Loison. In the centre, meanwhile, heavy skirmishing ensued at the foot of the main French

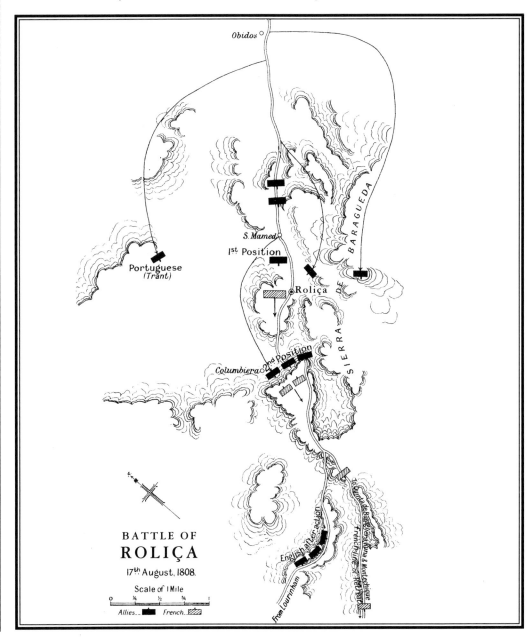

BATTLE OF
ROLIÇA
17th August, 1808.

Scale of 1 Mile

position while British artillery played upon the enemy. Wellesley intended waiting until his two flanking columns were in a forward position before launching his main attack in the centre but unfortunately, Colonel Lake, of the 1/29th, misread the situation and instead of confining himself merely to skirmishing decided to lead four companies of his battalion straight up one of the gullies leading to the top of the hill. Before he realised his mistake the naturally alarmed Lake found himself some 200 yards in the rear of the main French position. Trapped, and in an impossible position, Lake's men were swept by fire from the French troops around them but in spite of the turmoil and confusion Lake somehow managed to extricate his men out of the gully only to find the entire French centre waiting eagerly to welcome them. The men of the 29th fought like tigers but they were faced with enormous odds and the four companies were virtually annihilated. Just four officers and thirty unwounded men were taken prisoner while a handful of shocked and dazed survivors managed to find their way back to the main British line. Lake himself paid for his mistake with his life.

While Lake's attack floundered Hill, watching with some concern, ordered the 1/9th forward to help but even as the battalion hurried forward Wellesley decided to launch a general attack and all at once, with bugles blaring, the whole of the British line advanced. Soon, the rock strewn face of the hill was covered with red-coated British infantry who clambered not only up the four gullies but up the steep slopes between them while at the top the French greeted them with volleys of sustained musketry, clouds of thick smoke hiding them from their approaching adversaries. Dozens of brave men dropped as they struggled to reach the top but soon a few determined units clawed their way up to the French position and as more and more of their comrades joined them the French were pushed steadily back in fierce fighting. Only now did the British superiority in numbers begin to tell and Delaborde, realising his predicament, gave orders for a retreat, his four infantry battalions coming away two at a time, all the while covered by French cavalry in a skilfully executed operation.

An orderly withdrawal ensued with Delaborde's force moving away to the south towards Zambugeira. But here his army lost all cohesion as it entered a defile and as the British closed on them a somewhat panicky French force abandoned three of its guns and lost a number of men who were made prisoners by their pursuers. Once out of the defile, however, Delaborde's men were safe and Wellesley called a halt to the pursuit after receiving news that Loison's force was a mere five miles away.

The battle of Roliça, the first British battle of the Peninsular War, had ended in victory at a cost of 485 men lost during the day's fighting compared to 600 French killed and wounded.

WELLESLEY'S ARMY
AT ROLIÇA
Total 14,000

1st Brigade, Rowland Hill,
1/5th, 1/9th and 1/38th

2nd Brigade,
R. Ferguson
1/36th, 1/40th and 1/71st

3rd Brigade,
M. Nightingall
1/29th and 1/82nd

4th Brigade, B.F. Bowes
1/6th and 1/32nd

5th Brigade, Catlin Craufurd
1/45th and 1/91st

6th Brigade, H. Fane
1/50th, 5/60th and 4 coys. 2/95th

20th Light Dragoons (Part of), C.D. Taylor
3 Artillery Batteries, W. Robe

Vimeiro

August 21st 1808

Four days after Roliça Junot, with 13,000 men and 24 guns, marched north from Lisbon to attack the British at Vimeiro, a few miles south of Roliça. Wellesley himself had been reinforced by a further 4,000 men, belonging to the brigades of Anstruther and Acland, who had come ashore at the river of the Maceira river, about fifteen miles south of Roliça. These troops, which brought the number of men under Wellesley's command to 17,000, were welcome reinforcements. Not so welcome, however, was the 53 year-old Sir Harry Burrard who had arrived off the mouth of the Maceira on August 20th.

Burrard had arrived in Portugal to assume command of the army although this came as no great surprise to Wellesley who had been forewarned of his coming by Castlereagh. It was entirely a political move from which Wellesley could take little comfort. Furthermore, two more British officers, Sir Hew Dalrymple and Sir John Moore, both of whom were senior to him, were also on their way to Portugal. Nevertheless, Wellesley joined Burrard aboard his ship and having appraised him of the situation, Burrard

Despite being wounded Piper Clarke, of the 71st Highlanders, continues to play his pipes at the battle of Vimeiro, August 21st 1808.

decided that it would be unwise to take any further offensive action before the arrival of Moore's reinforcements which were known to be due shortly. Having been informed of this Wellesley returned to his troops, determined to do his best as long as he remained in command, while Burrard remained on his ship for the night.

When Wellesley retired for the night he did so having placed six of his infantry brigades with eight guns on the western ridge lying on the south of and running parallel to the Maceira river while a single battalion was placed on the eastern ridge as guard. The river itself flowed south through a defile between the two ridges and continued on to the rear of the village of Vimeiro which itself was situated on a flat-topped, round hill. Here, Wellesley had placed his other two infantry brigades as well as six guns. The village was separated from the two ridges not only by the Maceira but also by a tributary which flowed along the southern foot of the eastern ridge. The hush of night had hardly descended upon the British camp when reports came in that the French were advancing in force from the south. In fact, the French under Junot numbered around 13,000 men, still 4,000 fewer than Wellesley but having five more guns. Once again Delaborde's division was present along with 6,000 men under Loison.

Long before dawn showed itself on the morning of August 21st Wellesley was up on the western ridge, peering through his telescope, but as yet no French troops were to be seen so the British troops whiled away the early morning cooking their breakfasts. At about 9 o'clock, however, clouds of rising dust were spotted away to the east and soon the glint of bayonets, shako plates and other accoutrements could be seen as they sparkled in the shimmering sunlight.

From the direction of Junot's approach it was obvious that Wellesley's left flank was being threatened which prompted a hasty redeployment of his forces, mainly involving the transfer of three of his brigades from the western ridge to the eastern ridge, leaving Hill's brigade and two guns alone on the western ridge. Wellesley himself also moved to the eastern ridge from where he controlled the battle.

The village of Vimeiro itself was held by the brigades of Fane and Anstruther and it was against this position that the main French thrust appeared to be heading. The British troops here consisted of four companies of the 2/95th and the 5/60th, all deployed in a heavy skirmishing line in front of Vimeiro Hill, while on the crest itself were the 1/50th, the 2/97th and the 2/52nd. Behind them, on the reverse slope of the hill were the 2/9th and the 2/43rd, both in support. These troops were supported by twelve guns. Heading towards these 900 British infantrymen were some 2,400 French troops under General Thomieres who were formed into two columns supported by cavalry and artillery and screened by a shield of tirailleurs. The ensuing clash between the two sides marked a significant point in the Napoleonic Wars and set the pattern for a whole series of actions fought in the Peninsula between the British and French armies.

As the dusty French columns advanced against the British infantry on Vimeiro Hill they did so in the traditional, and up until this point the all too successful, style that had swept Napoleon's armies to victory after victory. Cavalry cantered along on the flanks, field artillery bounded along over the broken ground, while in front of the columns hundreds of tirailleurs engaged the British skirmish line as a prelude to the assault on the main British line. The formula had been tried and tested and it had proved successful. And yet here, on the slopes of the hill in front of Vimeiro, Wellesley's skirmishers had turned the tables for so effective was his light infantry screen that the men of the 5/60th and the 95th were only forced back following the intervention of the main French columns. The columns themselves were suffering at the hands of the British artillery which dealt out death in a new form, shrapnel, which swept the French troops with dozens of musket balls from their exploding cases. But it was the clash between the British line and the French column that was to become the standard form of conflict and perhaps the most enduring image of the war in the Peninsula.

At Vimeiro, this scenario was premiered with devastating results. The French columns, 30 ranks deep by 40 wide, advanced noisily and confidently against the 900 British troops, formed in a silent, two-deep line. As the French approached to within 100 yards the British troops, in this case the 1/50th, levelled their muskets and delivered a crashing volley into the tightly packed ranks of Frenchmen. As the column came on, so the effects of each of the succeeding volleys, fired at fifteen-second intervals, increased. The French ranks thinned at each discharge while they themselves were able to bring only 200 of their own muskets – those in front and on the flanks – to bear on the British. It was a somewhat simple mathematical equation that the French com-

manders were never quite to comprehend during the war and when they did try to deploy their men into line the effects of concentrated British musketry made it almost impossible. Thomieres did his best to get his men into line but it was hopeless. The columns melted away to the rear with Fane's riflemen close on their heels.

To the south of this first column, Thomieres' second column was making progress towards the British line. The column, also some 1,200-strong, suffered less from artillery fire owing to the nature of the terrain over which it passed but when it neared the British line it began to suffer the same fate as the column on its right. Anstruther's brigade duly dealt the decisive blows, the precise, controlled volleys of the 2/97th rolling from one end of its line to the other, ripping great gaps in the French column, and when the 2/52nd and 2/9th closed in on each side of them the French resolve disappeared and once again Fane's riflemen enjoyed a brief chase after them before being called back. In their panic, the French abandoned all seven of the guns they had brought forward with them, the horses and gunners falling victims earlier to the accurate fire of the Baker rifles.

With the initial French attacks having been repulsed Sir Harry Burrard picked his moment to appear on the battlefield. There appeared little danger to the British at this time, however, and Sir Harry allowed Wellesley to finish the battle himself.

No sooner had Burrard satisfied himself as to the progress of the battle than the French committed two more columns to the attack. Once again the village of Vimeiro was the centre of the attack, carried out by two columns, each of two battalions of grenadiers. The British line steadied itself once more and braced itself for yet another attack. Colonel Robe's gunners worked furiously at their guns as they poured shot and shell into the leading French column. Enemy artillery attempted to reply but their fire was ineffective and there was a real danger of firing into their own men who were skirmishing with Fane's riflemen. In spite of the fire being poured into the column it pushed on, moving across the ground lying between the routes of the last two French attacks. Gradually, the enveloping fire from 2,000 British muskets of the 2/9th, the 1/50th and the 2/97nd brought the column

Lieutenant Colonel Henry Francis Mellish, 10th Hussars. Mellish was aide-de-camp to General Ferguson during the battle of Vimeiro and was Assistant Adjutant General for a period during the Peninsular War.

shuddering to a halt and as Wellesley's men advanced down the hill the French column finally gave way and scattered, abandoning four guns that had been brought forward with it.

While this last attack had been in progress the second column of grenadiers had managed to move round the left flank of the 1/50th and soon had a clear run into the village of Vimeiro itself. The French incurred heavy losses as they swept into the village through a hail of lead and cannon shot. Here, in the narrow, jumbled maze of houses – a sort of prequel to the fighting at Fuentes de Oñoro – the French came face to face with the 2/43rd which Anstruther had thrown forward. The ensuing fighting was chaotic and confused and bayonets were bent and bloodied. The British troops, in spite of their inferior numbers, managed to thrust the French from the village and the British line was restored.

Wellesley had just 240 British cavalry available to him, all from the 20th Light Dragoons under Colonel Taylor, but with all of the French attacks until now having been repulsed he chose the moment to launch them in a

counter-attack. Taylor's men, having dispersed a French infantry square, quickly became intoxicated with their success and rode on at speed, outdistancing their own supporting guns and doing little damage to the French. Almost half the light dragoons were either killed, wounded or taken prisoner – including Taylor himself who was mortally wounded – when they collided with fresh, and more numerous, French cavalry. The charge was just the first in a sad series of misadventures of the British cavalry in the Peninsula, punctuated by rare but glorious triumphs.

On the eastern ridge above Ventosa, which lay at the eastern end of the ridge, the French were again attacking in strength with 3,000 French infantry under General Solignac who was supported by a small number of cavalry and three guns and a further 3,200 infantry, supported by dragoons, under General Brennier. These first of these two forces advanced on Ventosa itself while the second force passed to the north with the intention of attacking the ridge from the north-east.

The results of both of these attacks were predictably similar to the earlier French

Caton Woodville's depiction of the fighting at the cemetery in Vimeiro, August 21st 1808.

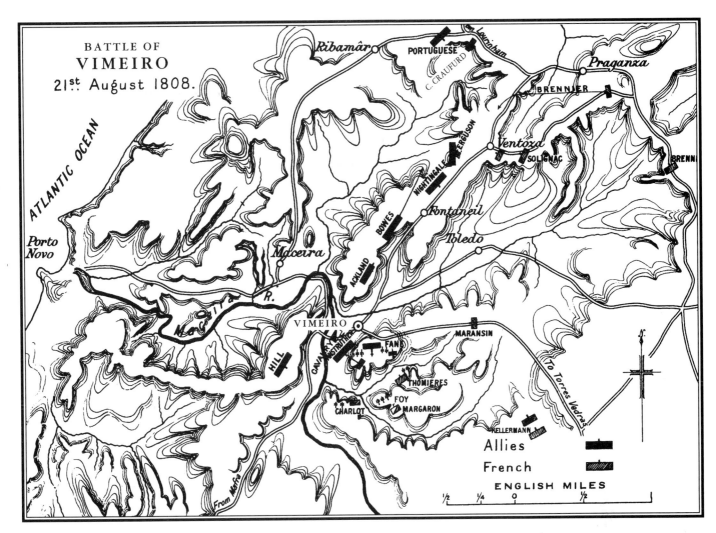

BATTLE OF
VIMEIRO
21st August 1808.

ATLANTIC OCEAN

Ribamâr   PORTUGUESE   C. Craufurd   Louriham   BRENNIER   Praganza

BRENN

FERGUSON   Ventoza   SOLIGNAC

NIGHTINGALE

Porto
Novo

BOWES   Fontaneil   Toledo

Maceira

ACKLAND

Maceira R.

VIMEIRO   MARANSIN

HILL   CAVALRY   ANSTRUTHER   FANE   To Torres Vedras

THOMIERES

CHARLOT   FOY   MARGARON

From Maños   KELLERMANN

Allies

French

ENGLISH MILES
½   ¼   0   ½

attacks elsewhere on the battlefield as both Solignac and Brennier advanced in column against their British adversaries who waited for them in line. The first force, consisting of three columns, struck that part of the line held by Ferguson's brigade. The French were met by a devastating series of volleys, fired by platoons, which blasted away the heads of the columns and prevented Solignac, desperately trying to deploy his own men into line, from making any progress at all. After a few minutes the French were in full retreat, once more abandoning their guns.

No sooner had Solignac's attack come to grief than Brennier's columns fell upon the rear and flank of three of Ferguson's battalions, the 1/71st, 1/82nd and 1/29th. By the time the first two of these battalions adjusted their positions to meet them Brennier's men closed on them and in a confused fight both the 71st and 82nd were pushed back, the French retaking the guns which had been abandoned by Solignac. However, the 1/29th

had sufficient time to alter its position and was soon setting about the right flank of the attacking French columns who were forced to halt in the face of the 29th's musketry. Ferguson's other two battalions reformed and together the three British units forced Brennier's men back. The French appeared to have little stomach for the fight and were soon fleeing in a disorderly fashion, leaving behind them their commander, Brennier, who was wounded and taken prisoner. The three guns, retaken briefly by the French, were once again in Wellesley's hands along with a further three guns which had accompanied Brennier.

It was barely noon, and every single French infantry battalion present at Vimeiro had been thrown into the attack, only to be seen off by the devastating effects of British musketry. 720 British troops had been either killed or wounded whereas the French had suffered three times that number including 450 killed. Now was the time to advance and pursue the defeated French who had been all but routed that morning. The road to Lisbon now lay open, a fact that should have spelt the end for Junot and his army, but Sir Harry Burrard decided that any further action was unnecessary and the glorious opportunity went begging despite the impassioned pleas of a very frustrated and angry Sir Arthur Wellesley. Junot's force, therefore, was allowed to retreat to Lisbon without any hindrance.

Burrard himself did not enjoy the position of commander-in-chief for too long for the very next day an even older general, Sir Hew Dalrymple, in turn superseded him. Dalrymple also decided that any further action was unnecessary and together the two elderly generals, devoid of any real military experience and totally failing to grasp the advantageous military situation facing them,

agreed to the notorious Convention of Cintra, whereby it was agreed that Junot and his army, along with their arms and accumulated plunder, would be given free passage back to France unmolested. Following this, Burrard, Dalrymple and Wellesley were recalled to England to explain before a Court of Enquiry how they had allowed the French army to escape. Wellesley himself had not even been privy to the treaty but signed it nevertheless when ordered to do so by Dalrymple.

With all three men having returned to England command of the 30,000 British troops in Portugal devolved upon the 47 year-old Sir John Moore who was about to lead the army through one of the most tragic episodes in the Peninsular War, an episode which was ultimately to cost him his life.

Sahagun

December 21st 1808

The misbehaviour of the British cavalry in the Peninsula was one of the more unsatisfactory aspects of the war, ranking alongside the inexpert siege operations which, albeit successful on three occasions, were similarly fraught with calamity. Indeed, the misadventures first displayed by Wellesley's cavalry at Vimeiro were to continue to dog the army throughout the campaign and continued even at Waterloo. The cavalry did have its moments, however, and during Sir John Moore's campaign in the winter of 1808–09 two outstanding actions were fought by the cavalry, under the command of Lord Henry Paget, at Sahagun and Benavente.

With all three signatories of the Convention of Cintra having been recalled to England the British Army in Portugal was left under the command of Sir John Moore. His force numbered around 30,000 and on October 6th 1808 he received orders from London to march north from Lisbon to join up with a further 10,000 troops who were on their way to Portugal under the command of Sir David Baird. Once united with Baird, Moore was to act in conjunction with the Spaniards who were holding positions on the Ebro river although the British government had not stipulated how this was to be done. And so in

mid-October Moore, having left 10,000 British troops behind to defend Portugal, began his march north towards Salamanca.

As his army marched north Moore was assured by the Spaniards that all Spain was ready to rise against Napoleon – who had come in person to enforce his brother's authority and drive the British into the sea – provided substantial British help was to be had. Moore, however, had no experience of dealing with the very brave but very proud Spaniards, who never did today what they could leave until tomorrow. There was no effective insurgent Spanish government and the *Juntas* that sprang up everywhere claiming to act in the name of the absent king were composed of jealous local magnates, each of which appointed his own general, while all Spanish generals considered it as beneath their dignity to accept orders from an English heretic.

The tired and weary British troops began to trundle into Salamanca on November 13th but fifteen days later came the news that Napoleon, at the head of 200,000 troops, had smashed the Spanish armies. Moore, waiting at Salamanca and still not having been joined by Baird, had to decide whether to retreat, which would leave a hopeless situation, or to advance right across Napoleon's lines of communication, his objective being to relieve the pressure on the Spanish capital Madrid which he still thought lay in Spanish hands. This might force Napoleon to move against him and thus allow the Spaniards to reorganise their revolts against the French. Moore chose this second course and so began his bold march across Napoleon's front. However, unbeknown to him, the capital had already fallen. Napoleon duly moved against the British but the promised Spanish risings either did not occur or were easily suppressed and Moore, in the depths of winter, was forced into a fighting retreat to Corunna, where transports were to assemble to bring away the British army.

After what seemed like weeks of marching and counter-marching both Baird's and Moore's forces concentrated at Mayorga on December 20th and the following morning the first of Paget's two fine cavalry actions was fought. An enemy force of light cavalry, acting as a screen for the main French army, lay at Sahagun, just a tempting nine miles beyond the British piquets. The prospect of a daring surprise attack on the French cavalry was enough to warm the blood of many a freezing British trooper and long before dawn on the

morning of December 21st Paget was in the saddle along with the 10th and 15th Hussars bound for Sahagun.

The French cavalry commander, Debelle, had neglected to post any vedettes other than a guard on the main road. The guard was quickly surrounded and taken before it realised what was happening although one French trooper did manage to escape and rode hell for leather back to Sahagun to raise the alarm. Within minutes the place was a hive of activity as trumpets stirred the shivering French troopers into life. Paget immediately ordered General Slade to charge into the town with the 10th Hussars while he himself took the 15th Hussars and dashed round to the rear of the place in order to sever the French cavalry's escape route. Without waiting for the 10th Hussars, who had yet to appear, Paget formed his own troopers and with a cheer charged straight into the town. The two French regiments, the 8th Dragoons and 1st Provisional Chasseurs, were still in the act of forming and the sudden appearance of Paget's sabre-wielding troopers totally unnerved them. Debelle had twice as many men as Paget but this counted for nothing as the 15th Hussars crashed into the chasseurs, hurling them backwards and causing the dragoons to

British hussars on the attack at Sahagun, December 21st 1808.

This old print by Andrew Weir, dated 1811, shows a British 15th Hussar in action against a French 8th Dragoon at Sahagun, on December 21st 1808.

General Sir Edward Kerrison, Bart. 7th Hussars. Kerrison served in the Peninsula and was awarded medal clasps for Sahagun, Benavente and Toulouse. He also served at Waterloo.

turn and run. The British hussars quickly warmed to their task and hacked and hewed their way through the enemy ranks to leave thirteen officers – including two lieutenant colonels – and 157 men killed, wounded or taken prisoners at a cost to themselves of just fourteen casualties.

On December 29th, eight days after Sahagun, Paget fought another splendid cavalry action which, although not being credited as an 'honour', reaffirmed Paget as the most gifted British cavalry commander of the war. The action was fought at Benavente as Lefebvre-Desnouettes, commanding the cavalry of the French Imperial Guard, pressed hard on the heels of the retreating British Army. The French cavalry were being held at bay by a small number of British cavalry at the bridge over the Esla at Castro Gonzalo prompting Lefebvre to ride downstream to look for another way across. This was done by way of a ford a few hundred yards from the bridge and soon the French commander had crossed along with four squadrons of chasseurs of the Guard, numbering about 600 men. The rest of the French cavalry, meanwhile, looked for other fords across the river.

No sooner had Lefebvre crossed the river than he found himself faced by about 130 men of the 18th Light Dragoons who had ridden down to meet them. After a brief flurry of skirmishing the British cavalry retired and were joined by a troop of the 3rd Dragoons, King's German Legion. The two units charged once more and this time cut their way through the French first line before fighting their way out of the melee in the face of overwhelming enemy numbers. The British cavalry withdrew a second time, falling back upon the town of Benavente where Lord Paget waited with the 10th Hussars who were hidden out of sight. Lefebvre's chasseurs came on with confidence towards Benavente, totally unaware of the 450 British hussars who lay in wait for them. Along with the 200-odd men of the 18th Light Dragoons and the 3rd Dragoons KGL, Paget's hussars now outnumbered the French. When Lefebvre had been lured a sufficient distance away from the bridge and his supports Paget gave the order to charge and all at once the British cavalrymen came whooping down upon their startled French adversaries. The ensuing fight went the way of Paget's cavalry who set about the chasseurs with their sharp, curved sabres, while the 3rd Dragoons chopped down with their heavier, straight-bladed swords, cutting off limbs and breaking heads and bones.

The French were soon in full retreat and were chased for a full two miles back to the bridge across the Esla, leaving behind 55 killed and wounded as well as 72 prisoners.

Lefebvre-Desnouettes was himself taken prisoner by trooper Grisdale of the 10th Hussars when the French commander's horse refused to swim across the water. British casualties numbered about fifty and most of those were amongst the 18th Light Dragoons and 3rd Dragoons KGL, the 10th Hussars coming through the fierce action virtually unscathed.

The remaining units of French cavalry had been unsuccessful in trying to find a way across the river and gave up the attempt when a few rounds from a British horse artillery battery were thrown in amongst them. This left Paget as victor upon the field, and victor of a fight witnessed by the Emperor Napoleon himself who watched, exasperated, from a distance. With the pursuing French having been dealt a bloody nose Moore's rearguard was allowed to continue its retreat, unhindered for the time being, towards Astorga, the next port of call upon the long, terrible road to Corunna. The action at Benavente was not given the status of an official battle honour although a clasp was given to the survivors when the General Service Medal was awarded in 1847.

Lord Henry Paget had proved himself beyond doubt the finest British cavalry commander but his presence in the Peninsula was only brief and ended upon his return to England in January 1809. Indeed, he returned to see active service with the army only in time for Waterloo where he commanded the cavalry with great distinction, he himself losing a leg towards the end of the great battle. His absence from Wellesley's army during the rest of the Peninsular War was due to the fact that he had eloped with Wellesley's sister-in-law and as such was hardly likely to be welcomed as a 'brother in arms'. His absence was sorely felt and it was to prove a major disadvantage to the British Army in the Peninsula.

The 10th Hussars at Benavente, December 29th 1808.

Corunna

January 16th 1809

The actions at Sahagun and Benavente, however brilliant, were the only notable successes of the otherwise disastrous Corunna campaign. The retreat was carried out in terrible conditions amidst slushy snow and ice and matters were made worse by the total breakdown of the Commissariat which in turn led to widespread indiscipline amongst the men. The roads quickly turned into quagmires beneath the tramping of thousands of feet and the

The superb painting, 'The Rearguard', by James Beadle. Robert 'Black Bob' Craufurd and his Light Brigade form up on the road to Vigo during the Corunna campaign of 1809–09.

troops suffered dreadful hardships in the bitterly cold winter weather. Hundreds of men – as well as the women and children that had accompanied the army – gave up the will to live and, unable or unwilling to go on, simply lay down to die in the bleak Galician mountains or were captured by the pursuing French. And there was little help forthcoming from the local Spanish people who were naturally reluctant to help a so-called 'friendly' army that had left behind in its wake a trail of burning, pillaged hamlets, the sprawling, bloody bodies of the occupants bearing testament to the lawlessness of some units of the army.

Quite often those in the rear, tired of running, would turn about and face their tormentors and deal them a bloody nose. More often than not, however, they would be hacked down by French sabres or trampled beneath the hooves of the enemy cavalry. Hundreds of those that survived the ordeal suffered terrible mutilations from French sabres during these attacks. Indeed, the French suffered similar privations in pursuing Moore's army. They too suffered dreadfully in the perishing cold but at least they could console themselves with the fact that it was the British who were on the

receiving end of most of the punishment along the gruelling road to Corunna.

The retreat continued with all but the most disciplined units of the army – the Guards and the rearguard – suffering a total breakdown of order. On December 31st the Light Brigade, under Robert Craufurd, which had distinguished itself during the trials of the retreat, was detached from the army supposedly to ease the burden on the commissariat. Craufurd pushed his men on to Vigo, unhindered by any French pursuit, where his brigade eventually embarked safely in ships bound for England. This move, however, deprived Moore of one of his better units and the Light Brigade was certainly missed throughout the rest of the campaign and during the battle fought on January 16th.

The retreat finally came to a climax between January 11th and 16th when Moore's tired and tattered army dragged itself into Corunna, units arriving one by one in various states of dilapidation. The tall masts of the ships waiting in the harbour at Corunna were a welcome sight for Moore's men as they limped into the town but little did they realise they would be called upon to fight one last battle in order to ensure the safe re-embarkation of the army. As each hour passed so Soult's troops got nearer and nearer to their quarry until by midday on January 15th the French had reached a position just a mile or two to the south of the town. Stores were hurriedly destroyed as was any excess ammunition but the men themselves were not yet able to begin boarding the transport ships as it became obvious that a battle would have to be fought the next day.

Moore's men occupied some rocky hills overlooking Corunna with his left flank protected by the River Mero. His right flank, however, rested upon the heights of San Christobal and was unprotected. Soult had roughly the same number of men but had forty guns to Moore's nine. On the morning of January 16th the French attacked the British position along the entire length of its front, the heaviest attack being launched against the right flank where the French assault was accompanied by heavy and destructive artillery fire. The battle swayed one way then the next, particularly in the centre where the important village of Elvina changed hands several times while on the right of the British line Edward Paget's brigade, held in reserve, was thrown into the fray to repulse the French attack there. It was at the height of the battle that Moore was struck and terribly wounded by a round shot that flung him from his horse. Baird, assuming command, was also wounded and as evening fell command devolved upon Sir John Hope although by this time all serious fighting had subsided and the battle was carried on only by the opposing artillery.

The French troops were as exhausted as the British and as night fell the battle ground to a halt leaving the British troops to hurry down to the waiting ships that were boarded without any interference from the French. Both sides had suffered around 900 casualties during the battle which had ended in a British victory and Moore died knowing he had done his duty. As his men climbed into the ships a sad and sombre ceremony was being carried out on the ramparts of the town as Sir John

Moore's Highlanders storm into the village of Elvina during the battle of Corunna.

Moore's body was lowered into the ground.

The army was saved, however, in spite of its poor condition and reduced numbers. When it disembarked at the ports along the south coast of England a week later it did so largely at night in order to spare the public the spectacle of seeing the terrible state of the men. Although 10,000 troops still remained at Lisbon the main British Army had been driven from the Peninsula. Its spirit was not broken, however, and barely three months later the army returned, this time to stay, to begin its long, hard but eventually triumphant march to victory.

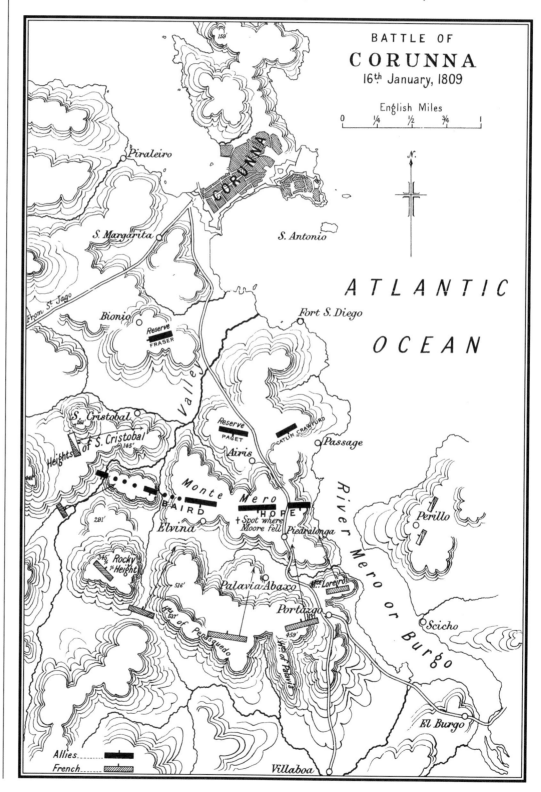

MOORE'S ARMY DURING THE RETREAT TO CORUNNA

*No reliable figures are available for Moore's army at Corunna. Tho following is
a list of those brigades and regiments who took part in the retreat.*

1st Division, Sir David Baird,
Warde's Brigade,
1/1st Guards, 2/1st Guards
Bentinck's Brigade,
1/4th, 1/42nd, 1/50th
Manningham' Brigade,
3/1st, 1/26th, 2/81st

2nd Division, Sir John Hope,
Leith's Brigade,
51st, 2/59th, 76th
Hill's Brigade,

2nd, 1/5th, 2/14th, 1/32nd
C. Craufurd's Brigade,
1/36th, 1/71st, 1/92nd

3rd Division, Fraser,
Beresford's Brigade,
1/6th, 1/9th, 2/23rd, 2/43rd
Fane's Brigade,
1/38th, 1/79th, 1/82nd

Reserve Division, Edward Paget,
Anstruther's Brigade,

20th, 1/52nd, 1/95th
Disney's Brigade,
1/28th, 1/91st

1st Flank Brigade, Robert Craufurd,
1/43rd, 2/52nd, 2/95th
2nd Flank Brigade, Charles Alten,
1st and 2nd Light Batts. KGL

Cavalry, Lord Paget,
7th, 10th and 15th Hussars, 18th Light
    Dragoons, 3rd Light Dragoons KGL

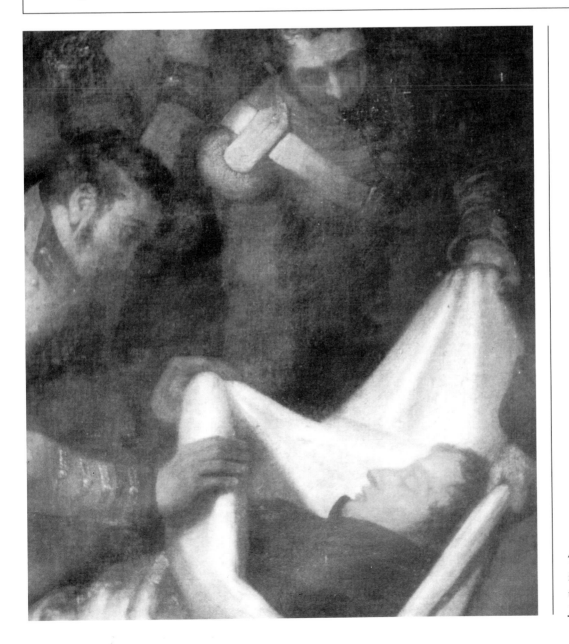

The body of Sir John Moore
is lowered into its grave after
the battle of Corunna on
January 16th 1809.

Douro

May 12th 1809

The 10,000 British troops left behind by Moore at Lisbon had been placed under the command of Sir John Craddock but on April 22nd 1809 Wellesley, having been cleared of all charges arising from the Convention of Cintra, arrived at Lisbon aboard the frigate *Surveillante* to resume command of the army. Within two weeks of his arrival Wellesley had formed his plan for the coming campaign which would see Soult driven from Portugal.

The plan involved an advance upon Oporto in order to deal with the French force under Soult before returning south to confront the forces of Victor and Lapisse, at the time concentrated around Ciudad Rodrigo and Talavera respectively. The rugged nature of the terrain meant that these latter two French commanders would not be able to unite with Soult before Wellesley came up with him and he was able to formulate an elaborate plan to deal with him.

Wellesley decided to divide his 36,400 Anglo-Portuguese troops into three forces. General Mackenzie was left at Lisbon with 12,000 while William Carr Beresford, with 6,000 men, would march to Amarante to sever Soult's line of retreat. Wellesley himself would command the remainder of the army,

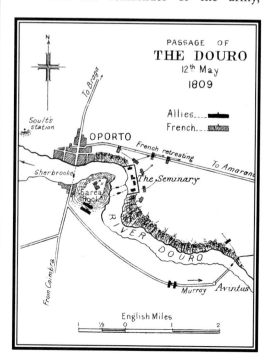

consisting of 16,000 British and 2,400 Portuguese troops and would advance directly upon Oporto.

Wellesley's force marched from Coimbra on May 8th and on May 11th the French piquets above Grijon, just south of Oporto, were cleared from the main road. When these piquets reached Oporto they hurriedly crossed the Douro and destroyed the bridge of boats across the river – the only bridge still intact – behind them. With all bridges across the Douro destroyed Soult felt fairly certain that any attack upon Oporto could only be made from the west and as such all French defences were duly fashioned to meet the threat from this direction.

On the morning of May 12th Wellesley's troops began to filter into the suburb of Villa Nova, on the south bank of the Douro and soon afterwards Wellesley himself arrived to survey the scene from the monastery of Serra do Pilar, a commanding viewpoint high above the river. Putting his telescope to his eye Wellesley scanned the north bank of the river and saw little activity. Two columns of French troops appeared to be in the process of evacuating the French sick and wounded while down below some French soldiers idled away their time at the quayside guarding some barges that were moored there. Away to his right, however, there were no signs at all of any French troops, the majority of whom were crammed into Oporto itself preparing for an Allied attack from the west. The area to his right, around a bend in the river, was out of sight of the main part of the town and was an obvious choice for a concealed crossing. Furthermore, the landing area was dominated by a strong, high-walled building, the Bishop's Seminary, which, if taken, could quickly and easily be turned into a strongpoint in order to cover other troops crossing the river. This area was unguarded and Soult's overconfidence was now to cost him dear.

While Wellesley surveyed the scene before him a Portuguese barber was hastily rowing across the river to inform the British that four wine barges lay unguarded on the northern bank of the river, a fact brought to Wellesley's immediate attention by Colonel John Waters, commanding Wellesley's scouts. Waters was immediately ordered to cross the river and bring the barges back, a feat accomplished with the aid of four local peasants and a priest. Once the barges had been secured Wellesley said simply, "Well, let the men cross," and so the crossing of the Douro began.

First across the river were the 3rd Foot who glided silently and swiftly over the water, one officer and twenty-five men in each of the small barges. As soon as the barges touched the opposite bank the men leapt out and dashed into the grounds of the Seminary whilst the barges re-crossed the river to fetch more troops across. While the ferrying continued makeshift firesteps were constructed along the inside of the walls of the Seminary and barricades thrown up. More British troops crossed the river, including General Edward Paget, and before the French realised what was happening some 600 of them were firmly

secured on the northern side of the Douro.

Shortly before midday a messenger had ridden into Soult's headquarters bearing the news of the crossing but even then Soult – who was still in bed – dismissed the reports, adding that they were probably Swiss troops bathing on account of their red jackets. However, when the crackling of musketry from the east was heard Soult sprang into life and soon afterwards General Foy, with three battalions of infantry, was attacking the Seminary in a bid to regain the building. Artillery was brought up also but British guns, firing from the convent on the southern bank of the river, silenced them and Foy's attempts at recapturing the building proved fruitless.

Further up the river, to the west, the local people had come out of their houses to bring more barges across from the quayside and soon the 1/29th was crossing the river followed by the Coldstream and 3rd Foot Guards under Sherbrooke. By the time these troops leapt from their barges the French were in full

---

ALLIED ARMY, MAY 1809

WELLESLEY'S COMMAND,   17,378

SHERBROOKE'S DIVISION,   6,706
Guards Brigade, H. Campbell,
1/Coldstream, 1/3rd Guards, 1 Coy 5/60th
4th Brigade, Sontag,9
97th, 1 Coy 5/60th, 2nd Batt. of Detach.,
     2/16th Portuguese
5th Brigade, A. Campbell,
2/7th, 2/53rd, 1 Coy 5/60th, 1/10th
     Portuguese

PAGET'S DIVISION,   5,145
6th Brigade, Stewart,
29th, 1st Batt. Detach., 1/16th Portuguese
KGL Brigade, J. Murray,5
1st, 2nd, 5th and 7th Line Batts. KGL

HILL'S DIVISION,   4,370
1st Brigade, Hill,
1/3rd, 2/66th, 2/48th, 1 Coy 5/60th
7th Brigade, Cameron,
2/9th, 2/82nd, 1 Coy 5/60th, 2/10th
     Portuguese

Cavalry, Stapleton Cotton,
14th Light Dragoons (2 squadrons), 16th
     Light Dragoons, 20th Light Dragoons

(part), 3rd Light Dragoons KGL (small part).

Artillery, 4 batteries, 24 guns.

BERESFORD'S COMMAND,   6,000

BRITISH,   1,825
3rd Brigade, Tilson,
2/87th, 1/88th, 5 Coys 5/60th, 1st
     Portuguese Grenadiers
2 Squadrons 14th Light Dragoons,

PORTUGUESE,   4,175
5 Batts. Infantry, 2 squadrons cavalry,
2 batteries, 12 guns.

MACKENZIE'S COMMAND,   12,000

BRITISH,   4,575
2nd Brigade, Mackenzie,
3/27th, 1/45th, 2/31st, 2/24th
Cavalry, Fane,
3rd Dragoon Guards, 4th Dragoons

PORTUGUESE,   7,425
10 Batts. Infantry, 5 Squadrons cavalry,
3 Batteries, 18 guns.

retreat towards Amarante. This retreat should have cost Soult even more casualties for his routed troops were in danger of being attacked by Murray who had earlier crossed the Douro to the east. Instead, only the 14th Light Dragoons engaged the French, capturing some prisoners for the loss of 36 men themselves.

Wellesley's daring crossing of the Douro had been a master stroke which had resulted in the total defeat of Soult's forces in and around Oporto. He had achieved it with the loss of just 23 killed and 98 wounded as opposed to French casualties of 300 killed and wounded as well as 1,500 prisoners. The victory was followed up a few days later at Salamonde where units of the British Army caught up with and scattered Soult's rearguard. Eventually, Soult was forced to burn his baggage and throw his 58 guns down the mountainside in order to facilitate his retreat which ended only when he had recrossed the border into Spain. Wellesley, meanwhile, called a halt to the pursuit and returned to Oporto before considering his next move which would have to be south against the French forces of General Victor.

Talavera

July 27th–28th 1809

The 48th Regiment at the battle of Talavera, July 28th 1809.

Having driven Soult from Portugal Wellesley looked to the south, towards Victor whose force was concentrated in and around the old Roman town of Merida. His Spanish allies were frustratingly difficult to get on with, as Moore had found to his cost the previous year. In spite of this, it was agreed that the British Army should co-operate with the Spaniards in a joint operation against Victor's force. In fact, so eager were the Spaniards about the plan that they agreed not only to feed Wellesley's army but also to provide much needed transport for it. This having been agreed upon Wellesley crossed the border into Spain and

marched his army to a pre-arranged area of concentration, north of the Tagus at Plasencia.

Victor's 20,000 men, meanwhile, had moved north-east from Merida to Talavera where he hoped to unite with other French forces under General Sebastiani, who had 22,000 men at Madridejos, and Joseph Bonaparte, in command of a further 12,000 men at Madrid. In theory, this would allow the French to field a combined army of more than 50,000 men, all of whom were tried and tested soldiers. Against this Wellesley and Cuesta, the Spanish commander, could field 55,000 of whom 35,000 were Spanish.

Wellesley's doubts as to the merits of the Spaniards surfaced fairly soon as did his frustrations when they failed to fulfil any of the promises regarding transport and supplies. And when he rode south to Almaraz to inspect the Spanish Army Wellesley was more than a little disillusioned when he saw the poor condition of their arms and equipment. The seventy year-old Cuesta himself gave little cause for optimism and he adopted a singularly belligerent attitude towards his British ally as a result of which many hours were lost as the two men argued over the strategy to be employed against the French. Eventually, Wellesley and Cuesta agreed to unite their armies at Oropesa, about thirty miles west of Talavera.

The two forces duly met as planned on July 20th and three days later had a perfect opportunity to attack Victor who had yet to meet either Sebastiani or Joseph and who was outnumbered by just over two to one. Cuesta refused to move, however, and the chance was lost although he did agree to attack at dawn on the 24th, although by then, of course, Victor had retired towards Madrid.

Wellesley was naturally furious and when a buoyant Cuesta decided to set off in pursuit of Victor it was Wellesley's turn to refuse to budge. This was with good reason as intelligence reports showed that the French were only days away from uniting which would give them a combined strength of 54,000 men. Nonetheless, Cuesta gave chase and was predictably mauled by Victor's veterans on July 25th.

By July 27th Wellesley had positioned his army a few miles to the west of the Alberche river which flows north from the Tagus just east of Talavera. Later that day he narrowly avoided capture whilst carrying out a reconnaissance from the top of the Casa de Salinas, a semi-fortified building on the left bank of the Alberche. As he peered out in the direction of the French army he just caught sight of a party of French light infantry, stealing around the corner of the building. He rushed down the stairs, mounted his horse and rode hell for

The great charge of the 29th (Worcestershire) Regiment against the French 24th Regiment on the Cerro de Medellin, Talavera, July 28th 1809.

leather away from the building followed by a couple of volleys from the enemy infantry. It was the first of a couple of occasions in the Peninsula where Wellesley narrowly avoided capture, the other notable occasion being at Sorauren in 1813.

There was some skirmishing throughout the rest of the day including the celebrated incident during the evening involving four battalions of Spanish infantry who, when apparently 'threatened' by some distant French cavalry, let loose a shattering volley before running away at the sound of their own muskets, stopping only to plunder the British baggage train.

That night Wellesley had drawn his army up along a front stretching north to south from the heights of Segurilla to Talavera itself. On the right were positioned Cuesta's 35,000 Spaniards, the right flank resting upon Talavera being the strongest part of the line. The left flank of the British line rested upon the Cerro de Medellin, a large, domineering hill, separated from the heights of Segurilla by a wide, flat valley nearly a mile wide. In front of the Allied position, and directly opposite the Cerro de Medellin, was the Cerro de Cascajal which was soon to become the centre of the French position and between the two hills, running along the valley between them, was a small stream called the Portina.

The sun had long since gone down when at around 10 o'clock, under the cover of darkness, an entire French division stole across the Portina and fell upon the British and German troops, on and at the foot of the Medellin, who were dozing off after a hard day in the field. The French advanced in three columns, one of which got lost and, failing to find any of its objectives, returned to the main French line. The other two columns, however, caused a great deal of panic in the British lines and at one point even occupied the summit of the Medellin after managing to completely pass by Donkin's brigade which occupied the forward slopes of the hill.

It was during this confusion that Rowland Hill almost got himself captured when, riding forward to investigate with his brigade major, he found himself confronted by a number of French voltigeurs, one of whom tried to drag Hill from his horse. The two British officers quickly turned tail and rode off but the brigade major was killed when the French opened fire. Hill then brought forward Stewart's brigade of the 2nd Division, amongst which was the 29th who drove the French from the summit amidst a blaze of spectacular musketry which lit up the night with each volley. The situation was eventually restored and the French returned to their original positions having lost about 300 men, the British losing a similar number.

A single French gun, fired in the gloom at about 5 o'clock on the morning of July 28th, signalled the beginning of the main French attack. The gun triggered off a rippling fire that rolled along the French position from about 60 of their guns. On the Medellin Wellesley's men were ordered to lie down as enemy cannonballs came bouncing in amongst them whilst on the slopes of the hill British gunners worked at their own guns in reply.

From his position high on the Medellin, which was shrouded in smoke, Wellesley could see nothing of what was going on below but the sounds — soon to become so familiar to him and his army — were unmistakable. Large numbers of French tirailleurs were pushing back his own skirmish lines although Wellesley's light companies and riflemen disputed every yard of broken ground. The French came on in three columns, each three battalions strong, altogether numbering nearly 4,500 men from Ruffin's division. The most northerly of the columns, movd around the Medellin, exchanged fire at long range with the 29th but went no further. The other two columns, however, hit that part of the British line on the Medellin which was held by Stewart's and Tilson's brigades. As at Vimeiro the French attack was hampered by its formation and the outnumbered British brigades easily outgunned the French columns, sweeping them with fire and forcing them to a standstill. French attempts to deploy into line proved futile and impossible amidst the concentrated, controlled platoon fire from the 29th and 48th Regiments. After just a few minutes those at the back and in the middle of the French columns, unable to see what was happening up front but aware that something very unpleasant was happening to their comrades, decided not to wait and see for themselves but simply melted away to the rear, very few of them having fired any shot in anger. Ruffin's attack had ended in failure and his beaten battalions were pursued for a short

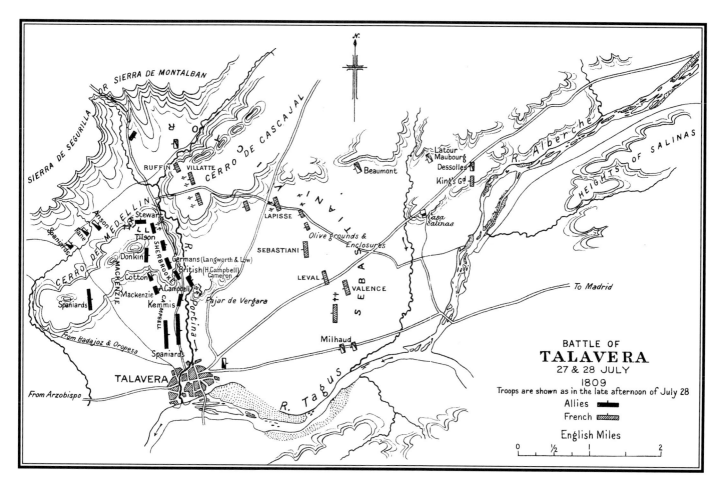

BATTLE OF
TALAVERA
27 & 28 JULY
1809
Troops are shown as in the late afternoon of July 28
Allies ▬▬▬
French ▨▨▨

English Miles

distance across the Portina having suffered over a thousand casualties.

The initial French attack having been repulsed by 7am the battle lapsed into a duel between the two sides' artillery. This lasted for just an hour and no more serious fighting occurred for another five hours, during which both sides quenched their thirst in the shimmering heat at the Portina brook and took advantage of the lull to collect their wounded.

At 1 o'clock in the afternoon the peace was shattered by another French artillery barrage that heralded a large-scale infantry assault on the right of Wellesley's line around the Pajar, a semi-fortified farmhouse that marked the junction of the British and Spanish sectors of the Allied line. Laval's division numbered 4,500 men who began to advance across the broken ground and through the olive groves to begin their attack on that part of Wellesley's line held by Campbell's 4th Division.

Again Laval's men attacked in three columns, each three battalions-strong supported by guns, but as had happened earlier in the day his men found Campbell's musketry too hot to handle and the French columns broke and fled before they did too much damage and having abandoned seventeen of their guns. Laval's attack was only the prelude to the main French attack, however, and shortly afterwards some 80 French guns were blazing away at the right centre of the British line in an attempt to soften it up before the main infantry assault which would be delivered by no less than 15,000 seasoned troops under Sebastiani and Lapisse.

It sounds rather repetitive to say that the French columnar formation gave the British line a distinct advantage but that is exactly what happened – again. The twelve French battalions could bring only 1,300 muskets to bear on their British adversaries, some 6,000 men of Sherbrooke's 1st Division, amongst whom were some of the best troops in the army, the Foot Guards and the King's German Legion. The irresistible and pulverizing firepower of these troops was turned on the French to devastating effect and soon enough the French veterans were streaming back across the Portina. Unfortunately, three of the brigades who had seen them off, including the Guards and the Germans, were carried away with their success and, pursuing them too far, were in turn severely mauled by the French, large numbers of whom were still fresh. Sherbrooke's men returned to the British line in a sorry state, particularly the Foot Guards who had lost 611 men.

This misadventure caused a large gap in the Allied centre upon which some 15,000 French cavalry and infantry bore gleefully down with relish. There was no second Allied line and Wellesley could spare only a single battalion to plug the gap. It was a major crisis. Fortunately, the battalion, the 1/48th, was the strongest in the army but it still had to face a French attack of overwhelming numerical strength. The 48th was supported by the three battalions of Mackenzie's brigade which were moved slightly to their left to join the 1/48th. These battalions, numbering around 3,000 men, opened their ranks to let in the survivors of the Guards who formed up behind them and with a great cheer announced their intention to rejoin the battle.

The British troops waited silently in line as the French came noisily on, British 6-pounder guns tearing gaps in their columns as they did so. Lapisse's battalions had advanced to within just fifty yards when nearly 3,000 nervous British fingers twitched on the triggers of their Brown Bess muskets and whole files of Frenchmen came crashing to the ground amidst rolls of thick grey smoke. The shattered French columns shuddered to a halt in the face of the savage onslaught. A series of withering volleys ripped into them at the rate of four every minute and although they stood to trade fire with Mackenzie's men the French could not match the firepower of their enemies. In the face of such an onslaught, in which the Guards and the 14th Light Dragoons joined, Lapisse's battalions broke and fled back across the Portina leaving some 1,700 of their comrades behind them to mark their failure.

All French attacks to the south of and directly at the Medellin had resulted in bloody failure and the French troops watching from the Cascajal did not relish the thought of tasting any more of such treatment. It was decided, therefore, to test the mettle of Wellesley's left flank to the north of the Medellin, Ruffin's infantry division being the instrument of this test. The nine battalions of Ruffin's division had already been heavily engaged the night before and on the morning of the 28th itself, and the men showed little inclination to attack in any positive manner, a reluctance not unnoticed by Wellesley who decided to launch his cavalry against them.

Ruffin's columns advanced amidst heavy shelling from the Allied artillery and when Anson's cavalry brigade, consisting of the 23rd Light Dragoons and 1st Light Dragoons King's German Legion, was spotted advancing along the floor of the valley to the north of the Medellin, the French formed square which

---

WELLESLEY'S ARMY AT TALAVERA
Total 20,641

1ST DIVISION,
 J.SHERBROOKE   5,964
Campbell's Brigade
1st Coldstreamers, 1/3rd Guards, 1 coy
  5/60th
Cameron's Brigade
1/61st, 2/83rd, 1 coy 5/60th
Von Langwerth's Brigade
1st and 2nd Line Batts. and Light Coys,
  KGL
Von Lowe's Brigade7
5th and 7th Line Batts. KGL

2ND DIVISION, R.HILL,   3,905
Tilson's Brigade,

1/3rd, 2/48th, 2/66th, 1 coy 5/60th
Stewart's Brigade,
29th, 1/48th, 1st Batt. Detach.

3RD DIVISION,
 A.MACKENZIE,   3,747
Mackenzie's Brigade,
2/24th, 2/31st, 1/45th
Donkin's Brigade,
2/87th, 1/88th, 5 coys. 5/60th

4TH DIVISION,
 A.CAMPBELL,   2,960
Campbell's Brigade,
2/7th, 2/53rd, 1 coy 5/60th

Kemmis's Brigade,
1/40th, 9th, 2nd Batt. Detach. 1 coy
5/60th

CAVALRY,   2,969
Fane's Heavy Brigade,
3rd Dragoon Guards, 4th Dragoons
Stapleton Cotton's Light Brigade,
14th Light Dragoons, 16th Light
  Dragoons
Anson's Light Brigade,
23rd Light Dragoons, 1st Light
  Dragoons, KGL

Artillery, Engineers, Staff Corps,   1,096

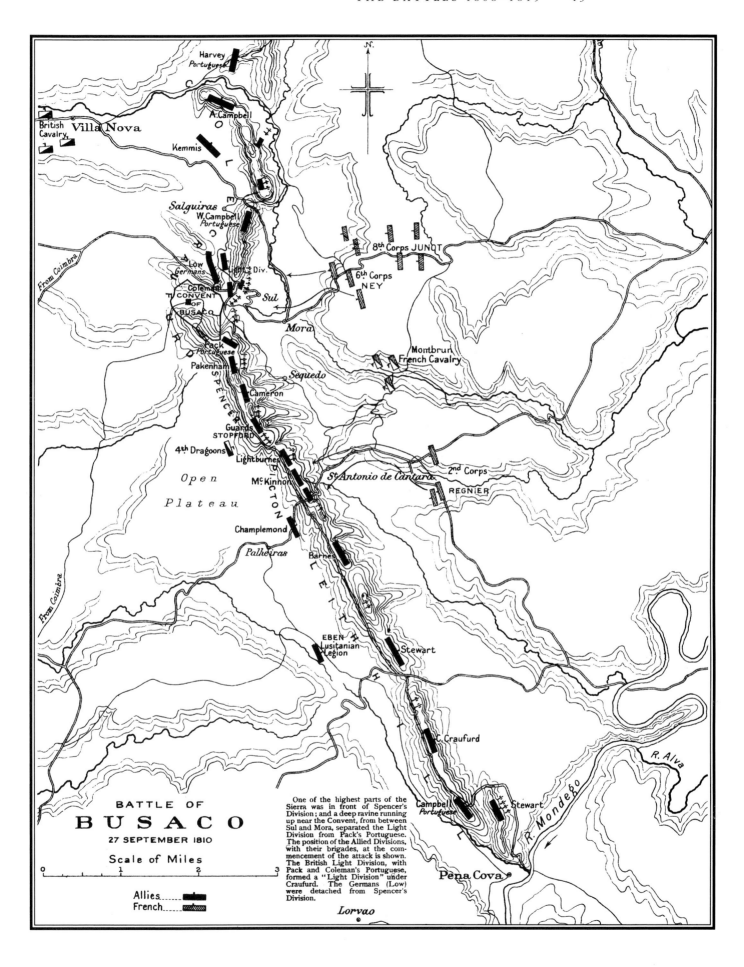

Harvey
Portuguese

A. Campbell

British
Cavalry

Villa Nova

Kemmis

Salguiras

W. Campbell
Portuguese

Low
Germans
Coleman
CONVENT
OF
BUSACO

Light Div.

Sul

8th Corps JUNOT

6th Corps
NEY

Mora

Montbrun
French Cavalry

Pack
Portuguese

Pakenham

SPENCER

Sequedo

Cameron

Guards
STOPFORD

4th Dragoons

Lightburnes

Open

McKinnon

Plateau

PICTON

St Antonio de Cantara

2nd Corps
REGNIER

Champlemond

Palheiras

LEITH

Barnes

From Coimbra

EBEN
Lusitanian
Legion

Stewart

From Coimbra

HILL

C. Craufurd

R. Alva

Campbell
Portuguese

Stewart

R. Mondego

BATTLE OF
BUSACO
27 SEPTEMBER 1810

Scale of Miles
0   1   2   3

Allies
French

One of the highest parts of the
Sierra was in front of Spencer's
Division; and a deep ravine running
up near the Convent, from between
Sul and Mora, separated the Light
Division from Pack's Portuguese.
The position of the Allied Divisions,
with their brigades, at the com-
mencement of the attack is shown.
The British Light Division, with
Pack and Coleman's Portuguese,
formed a "Light Division" under
Craufurd. The Germans (Low)
were detached from Spencer's
Division.

Pena Cova

Lorvao

most of which were sustained during the fighting in Sula. The 43rd and 52nd between them lost just three men killed and two officers and eighteen men wounded, an astonishingly low figure. Of the 6,500 men used by Loison 1,200 had become casualties including 21 officers who were killed and 47 wounded including an enraged General Simon who was taken prisoner by privates Hopkins and Harris of the 52nd.

Just to the south of this attack eleven more battalions, under Marchand, had attacked but these too met with a similar fate. They were roughly handled by Pack's Portuguese brigade and thrown back down the hillside along with the rest of the attacking French columns. Indeed, the battle of Busaco marked the 'coming of age' of the Portuguese troops during the war and from hereafter, Wellington's British troops were more than happy to fight alongside their Portuguese allies who had previously been looked upon with some misgivings.

All French attacks had been bloodily repulsed before noon and although there was some skirmishing throughout the afternoon the battle of Busaco was as good as over. Wellington had again triumphed at the cost of 1,252 casualties. Massena, on the other hand, had seen 4,600 of his men killed, wounded or taken prisoners including 300 officers which, according to Jac Weller, 'was the highest proportion of officers to men that the French suffered in the whole war.'

Busaco was a great victory for Wellington although Massena's worshippers have tried dispute this on the grounds that Wellington was forced to abandon his position the next day after Massena's cavalry found a way round his left flank. This is an unlikely and weak claim, however, for the British commander had already decided upon his next course of action which involved a withdrawal to the pre-prepared Lines of Torres Vedras, a nasty little surprise still waiting to be discovered by Massena.

WELLINGTON'S ARMY AT BUSACO

1ST DIVISION, BRENT SPENCER, 7,053
Stopford's Brigade
1/Coldstream, 1/3rd Guards, 1 Coy 5/60th
Blantyre's Brigade
2/24th, 42nd, 1/61st, 1 Coy. 5/60th
Von Lowe's Brigade
1st, 2nd, 5th and 7th Line Batts. KGL, Det. Light Batt. KGL.
Pakenham's Brigade
1/7th, 1/79th

2ND DIVISION, ROWLAND HILL, 10,777
Stewart's Brigade
1/3rd, 2/31st, 2/48th, 2/66th, 1 Coy. 5/60th
Inglis's Brigade
29th, 1/48th, 1/57th, 1 Coy. 5/60th
C. Craufurd's Brigade
2/28th, 2/34th, 2/39th, 1 Coy. 5/60th

PORTUGUESE DIVISION, HAMILTON. 5,040
Campbell's Brigade
4th Line (2 Batts), 10th Line (2 Batts)
Fonseca's Brigade

2nd Line (2 Batts), 14th Line (2 Batts)

3RD DIVISION, THOMAS PICTON, 4,143
Mackinnon's Brigade
1/45th, 1/74th, 1/88th
Lightburne's Brigade
2/5th, 2/83rd, 3 Coys. 5/60th
Champlemond's Portuguese Brigade
9th Line (2 Batts), 21st Line (1 Batt),

4TH DIVISION, LOWRY COLE, 7,400
Campbell's Brigade
2/7th, 1/11th, 2/53rd, 1 Coy. 5/60th
Kemmis's Brigade
3/27th, 1/40th, 97th, 1 Coy. 5/60th
Collins's Portuguese Brigade
11th Line (2 Batts), 23rd Line (2 Batts)

5TH DIVISION, JAMES LEITH, 7,322
Barnes's Brigade
3/1st, 1/9th, 2/38th
Spry's Portuguese Brigade
3rd Line (2 Batts), 15th Line (2 Batts), Tomar Militia Batt.

Baron Enden's Brigade7
Lusitanian Legion (3 Batts), 8th Line (2 Batts).

LIGHT DIVISION, ROBERT CRAUFURD, 3,787
Beckwith's Brigade,
1/43rd, 4 Coys 1/95th, 3rd Caçadores
Barclay's Brigade,1
1/52nd, 4 Coys 1/95th, 1st Caçadores

THREE INDEPENDENT PORTUGUESE BRIGADES, 8,363
Pack's Brigade
1st Line (2 Batts), 16th Line (2 Batts), 4th Caçadores
Campbell's Brigade,
6th Line (2 Batts), 18th Line (2 Batts), 6th Caçadores
Coleman's Brigade,
7th Line (2 Batts), 19th Line (2 Batts), 2nd Caçadores

Cavalry 2,500
2 Squadrons 4th Dragoons

Artillery 60 guns

A trooper of the 16th Light Dragoons on patrol in the Peninsula, 1811.

Wellington wrote, 'I must request that you do all in your power to stop and discountenance as much as possible the single combats which, as I understand, are of almost daily occurrence between cavalrymen of the opposing armies; we are not prizefighters.' He no doubt had in mind episodes such as that depicted here in this imaginary but marvellous painting where both French and British armies line up opposite each other in order to witness two officers engage in single combat.

'Boots and Saddle.' A 7th Hussar, c.1813.

Lord Henry William Paget, Earl of Uxbridge and 1st Marquess of Anglesey, in the uniform of the 7th Hussars.

'The Flag of Truce.' Men of the 14th Light Dragoons exchange pleasantries with French cavalry at a bridge, somewhere in Spain. Such exchanges were frequent between British and French troops in the Peninsula.

The 9th (East Norfolk) Regiment in Portugal, just prior to the battle of Roliça, August 1808.

The 1st Foot Guards embark at Ramsgate for the Peninsula, September 1808.

Private L. Grisdall, 10th Hussars, captures the French general, Lefebvre-Desnouetes, at Benevente, December 29th 1808.

An officer of the 28th (North Gloucester) Regiment, c.1810.

Colonel Peter Hawker, 14th Light Dragoons, 1812. Hawker fought at Talavera and was wounded at Oporto in 1809. He later wrote *Instructions to Young Sportsmen*.

The storming of Badajoz, 1812. Leith's 5th Division escalading the San Vincente bastion. Note the spiked planks and the barrels of gunpowder thrown down on the stormers.

The 88th (Connaught Rangers) in the Peninsula, 1810.

The 26th (Cameronians) Regiment at the battle of Corunna, January 16th 1809.

The 48th (Northamptonshire) Regiment at Talavera, July 28th 1809. Colonel Donellan, seriously wounded, takes off his hat and gives command of the regiment to Major Middlemore saying, 'You will have the honour of leading the 48th to the charge.'

British and French troops clash at the battle of Barrosa, March 5th 1811. Cadiz is visible in the distance.

The 3rd Foot Guards at the battle of Talavera, July 28th 1808. The bareheaded officer in the centre is Robert Dalrymple who was killed during the battle.

The battle of Busaco, September 27th 1810. Robert Craufurd, centre background, launches the 43rd and 52nd Light Infantry against Loison's division with devastating results.

Barrosa

March 5th 1811

Two weeks after the battle at Busaco Wellington's army began to enter the Lines of Torres Vedras, a series of natural and man-made barriers which stretched across the Lisbon peninsula between the Tagus and the Atlantic. The system comprised mainly of three separate lines; the first, to the north, ran inland from the Atlantic to the town of Torres vedras and then on to the Tagus. The second line ran almost parallel to the first but was five miles farther south. The third lay west of Lisbon and enclosed an area from which a re-embarkation could be carried out should it become necessary. The system included the damming of streams and rivers to make inundations, castles in towns were protected by earthworks and every hill along the first two lines was crowned with a defensive work or redoubt. Coupled with the naturally rugged terrain the Lines of Torres Vedras formed an almost impregnable system of fortifications behind which Wellington placed his army along with as much food as could be gathered in from the outlying countryside.

Massena and his army were shocked when they came face to face with the lines. They were stunned by their extent and strength and it did not take long for Massena, who had absolutely no idea of their existence, to realise that it would be hopeless to attack them, particularly with the recent unpleasant experience at Busaco still fresh in his mind. He was left, therefore, with little choice but to sit down in front of the lines and wait in the hope that Wellington would come out and attack him. Wellington had no such intention, however, and while his own army grew stronger and was supplied through Lisbon by the Royal Navy, he was only too pleased to sit and wait as starvation took a hold on Massena's army.

In mid-November 1810, Massena's starving army, having made no impression at all on Wellington's lines, began to pull back and by April 1811 had recrossed the border into Spain having lost almost 25,000 men.

Whilst Massena's army was dragging itself back into Spain another 25,000 French troops, under Marshal Victor, were laying siege to the important Allied port of Cadiz which was garrisoned by an equal number of British and Spanish troops. The Allied troops were well protected by strong fortifications and their situation improved when French troops began to be withdrawn from in front of Cadiz in response to Massena's appeals for reinforcements. These requests had resulted in Soult having to pull out of Andalucia in order to besiege Badajoz, Soult in turn drawing upon Victor's force to assist him. This move reduced Victor's force to around 15,000 men.

The reduction in enemy troop numbers around Cadiz, coupled with the news of Massena's retreat towards Spain, prompted the much-encouraged defenders into launching an attack on the French besiegers. The attack involved shipping 10,000 Spanish and 4,000 British troops some 50 miles to the south to Tarifa, from where they would march north to attack the French from the rear while at the same time some 4,000 Spaniards would make a sortie from Cadiz.

Commanding the British troops was the 62 year-old Major General Sir Thomas Graham, one of the oldest but most spirited generals in the British Army. Graham had received orders from Wellington that on no account was he to serve under any Spanish general but for the sake of Anglo-Spanish relations Graham relented and agreed to serve under the inept and very haughty General Manuel La Peña, the choice of the Spanish *junta*.

Graham's force set sail on February 21st 1811 although bad weather prevented the force from landing at Tarifa and forced it on instead to Algeciras where it disembarked on February 23rd. The Spanish contingent did not arrive until February 28th but soon afterwards the whole Allied force was on the march north towards Cadiz. The march was fraught with disagreements between Graham and La Peña, who insisted on making night marches which usually resulted in the troops losing their way. Nevertheless, early on the morning of March 5th the force found itself marching along the beach near the tower of Barrosa, the waves of the Atlantic crashing in on their left.

Later on that morning, La Peña's advanced guard clashed with elements of Villatte's

Dighton's drawing of the capture of the first French eagle of the war by British troops. This eagle was taken by Sergeant Patrick Masterman of the 87th Regiment.

French force although the fighting was cut short when the garrison in Cadiz launched its sortie which forced the French to withdraw. Graham, meanwhile, had positioned his British troops on the ridge of Barrosa which stretches for about a mile and a half from the coast on the left to the thick pine forest of Chiclana on the right. No sooner had Graham's men settled down than a messenger arrived with orders from La Peña who, flushed with his earlier success, wanted Graham to leave the ridge and join him. It was obvious to the British commander that the ridge would be an important strategic position in the forth-coming battle which now seemed inevitable. Nevertheless, he ordered his men to march off but only after having first left behind a com-

posite battalion under Colonel Browne, con-sisting of two companies each of the 1/9th, 1/28th and the 2/82nd, as well as five Spanish battalions.

Graham and his men had not long set off along the dusty road leading from the ridge when two animated Spanish guerrillas came riding up with the news that a French division was moving through the forest towards the ridge, just as Graham had feared, and that another division was advancing from the south. The French troops advancing through the forest belonged to Leval's division whilst the other division was Ruffins's and between them they managed to panic the five Spanish battalions into abandoning the ridge without hardly having to fire a shot, thus leaving

Browne's composite battalion all alone.

Graham was unaware of the flight of the Spaniards but was certainly made aware of the close proximity of the French when a couple of round shots came bouncing in between the trees, killing an officer of the Guards. First to turn about was General Dilkes' Brigade of Guards who pushed their way through the ranks of the 2/87th in order to get forward. When the 1st Foot Guards advanced they did so in the face of heavy French musketry from the top of the ridge, the overwhelming French numerical superiority having forced Browne's men to retire earlier.

With the British situation deteriorating rapidly Graham decided that the only solu-

tion was to drive the French from the ridge using the Brigade of Guards supported by Wheatley's brigade. Browne's six companies, meanwhile, would attack first in order to give the Guards time to deploy, news of which was delivered by Browne himself to his men with the words, "Gentlemen, I am happy to be the bearer of good news. General Graham has done you the honour of being the first to attack these fellows. Now follow me, you rascals." Browne's men advanced up the ridge with determination and courage but took heavy casualties from the French artillery and musketry. There was little cover for his men and after a few salvoes and volleys had swept away over half his men Browne ordered them

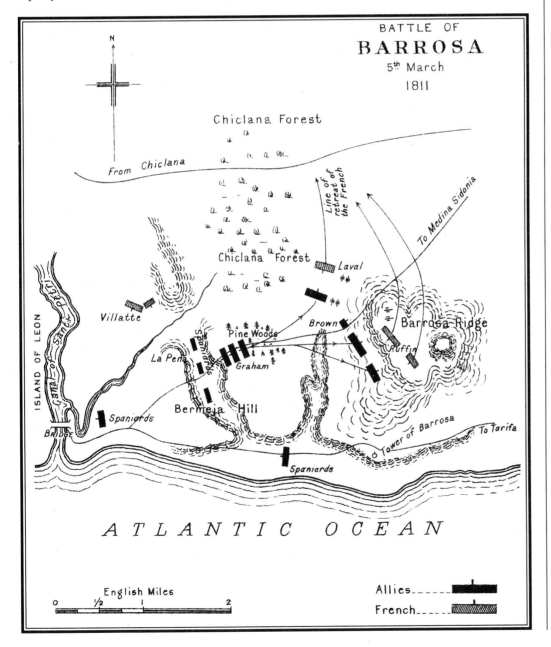

to fall back and lie down, taking advantage of what little cover there was available to them. A French counter-attack would have meant the end for Browne and his small unit but just as Ruffin began to deploy, Dilkes' Brigade of Guards appeared from the forest.

The Foot Guards advance took them along a route which afforded them rather more cover than had Browne's route and they were supported by the ten guns under Major Duncan. Nonetheless, the advance proved a difficult one as the Guards had been on the march all morning and had not had time to cook any breakfast. Four battalions of Ruffin's infantry stood atop the ridge, ready to greet them, but the Guards would not give way but fought like tigers and continued their advance. The 1st Foot Guards, in the first line, were supported by the 3rd Foot Guards with Graham himself at their head, waving his hat in the air, cheering his men forward. Browne's men too, having recovered from their earlier ordeal, now rejoined the fight and together the British troops forced the French back until they were finally on top of the ridge. Then, Graham shouted, "Now my lads, there they are. Spare your powder, but give them steel enough," and with that his men charged forward and drove the French from the ridge but only after a bitter fight.

Elsewhere, the British troops had been equally successful. On the left, Wheatley's brigade had thrown back and defeated Laval's division. During this struggle Sergeant Patrick Masterman, of the 87th, captured a French eagle after a savage little fight in which no less than seven French soldiers were killed defending it and one lieutenant severely wounded.

Soon afterwards, the battered and bruised French withdrew from the field leaving Graham's equally exhausted soldiers in possession of the ridge. Of 5,000 British troops engaged some 1,238 had become casualties against 2,062 French. Ruffin himself was wounded and one of his brigadiers, Rousseau, later died of his wounds. Five French guns were taken also.

Graham had achieved a remarkable victory without the aid of a single Spanish soldier, La Peña refusing to march to his assistance. His men had also taken the first Imperial eagle of the war which was brought home to England and laid up at Whitehall amidst great pomp and ceremony.

Fuentes de Oñoro

May 3rd–5th 1811

After a series of clashes with Wellington's advanced troops, notably at Pombal, Redinha, Cazal Nova and Foz de Arouce, Massena's starving army limped back across the Portuguese border and into Spain which it did in March 1811. Nevertheless, the French still held the vital frontier fortresses of Ciudad Rodrigo, Badajoz and Almeida and as long as they remained in French hands Wellington could never rest easy in the Peninsula. It was vital that he took these fortresses and in April 1811 he set in motion his plan to do so.

The strongest of the fortresses was Badajoz which lay to the south in Estremadura. This town was to be the object of a siege conducted by 20,000 troops under William Beresford. Wellington, meanwhile, turned his attention to the two fortresses in the north, Almeida and Ciudad Rodrigo which lay on opposite sides to each other on the border.

Wellington had some 38,000 troops close to Almeida and by the end of April was able to begin its blockade. On May 2nd, however, he received news that Massena, having revictualled his army, was on his way forward from Ciudad Rodrigo with 48,000 troops with the intention of relieving Almeida. The French line of approach lay through the village of Fuentes de Oñoro and it was to this sprawling, jumbled maze of a village that Wellington and his army marched to take up positions on May 2nd–3rd.

Wellington's position at Fuentes de Oñoro certainly lacked the impregnability of that of Busaco, for instance, but it did afford him the usual desired defensive features that became so characteristic of his battles in the Peninsula. His position stretched for well over five miles

on the left bank of the Dos Casas river that flows through the village itself. On the extreme right of the Allied position was the small village of Nave de Haver whilst Wellington's left flank rested upon the strong Fort Conception. The position centred on Fuentes de Oñoro with the right bank of the river leading down to the village being heavily wooded. The village itself was situated on the left bank of the Dos Casas, the maze of old, single-storeyed houses nestling about the river.

Wellington detached his 5th and 6th Divisions to a position in front of Fort Conception whilst the main part of his force was centred in and around the village of Fuentes de Oñoro, the majority of the troops being hidden out of sight behind a ridge that lay to the west of the village. The Light Division was posted in reserve on the right flank.

The battle began on the afternoon of May 3rd when Loison – in Massena's absence – launched five infantry divisions against the Allied position. The French columns loomed out of the woods on the right bank and plunged across the Dos Casas to attack the village which changed hands several times during some heavy and at times savage fighting. Indeed, at one point Wellington himself rode forward and personally ordered the 71st and 79th Regiments into the attack. But by nightfall all French attacks had been repulsed and Fuentes remained in Allied hands.

There was little or no fighting on May 4th and both sides took the opportunity to gather and tend their wounded. The only real movement in the French lines came when they held a grand parade during the early evening.

On the morning of the 5th Massena resumed his attack, throwing several heavy infantry columns against the Allied right flank. By doing this Massena hoped that Wellington would be drawn into weakening his left flank in order to meet the threat and by so doing would allow the French to relieve the beleaguered garrison of Almeida. Wellington held his nerve, however, and refused to fall for the ruse. Instead, he ordered Craufurd's Light Division to replace the hard-pressed 7th Division which it did in a magnificently controlled withdrawal, all the time surrounded by enemy cavalry. Craufurd's division retired across a plain for more than three miles before reaching the safety of the

The 16th Light Dragoons at the battle of Fuentes de Oñoro.

The battle of Fuentes de Oñoro, May 3rd-5th 1811. Wounded troops and prisoners are escorted from the field, at left, while in the distant centre, Norman Ramsey's Horse Artillery makes its daring dash to escape being taken by French cavalry.

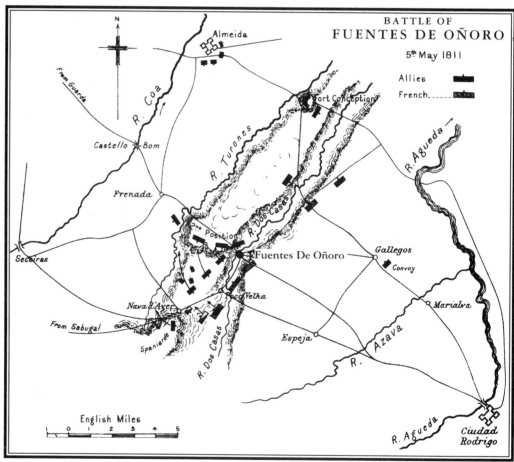

main Allied position. With this move the threat to Wellington's right flank was removed although he was forced to pull back and realign this part of the line, the 1st Division taking up a position at right angles to the main Allied line.

The fight for the village itself now flared up once more with renewed and increased violence in fighting which perhaps typifies the battle of Fuentes de Oñoro, the cruel tide of battle flowing one way then the next as the opposing armies were in turn thrust from the village. Ten French infantry battalions thrust Wellington's men from the village and pushed

them back as far as the old church on the front slope of the ridge behind but again the 1/71st and the 1/79th, supported by the 2/24th, threw them out. Massena's patience thinned faster than the ranks of his own infantry until at around midday he threw in a full eighteen fresh battalions who succeeded – as much by sheer numbers as of courage – in clearing the village of the British and Portuguese defenders. Their triumph was short-lived though, for Wellington ordered the 74th and the 1/88th to counter-attack.

The 88th were the fighting furies of Picton's 3rd Division and with a bloodcurdling cheer sent the French reeling from the streets into the alleyways and passages in the village. Here there was no escape for hundreds of Massena's men who died at the hands of the fearsome, wild-eyed Irishmen who launched into them with a frenzied and frantic bayonet charge. The 88th and 74th threw the French back and, supported by the 1/71st and 1/79th, finally ended any French thoughts of victory. A final French attack was launched at about 2pm but this was not pressed home with any real conviction and with it ended the last serious fighting on May 5th. The battle petered

out in an artillery duel and with another reckless British cavalry charge, this time by the 14th Light Dragoons.

There was no fighting on May 6th although Massena's cavalry prodded and poked away at the Allied line to the north and west in a vain attempt to find a way through Wellington's line. To the north fresh troops, who had not been involved in any of the fighting between May 3rd and 5th, sat quietly confident of being able to fend off any French attack while to the west the rocky chasm of the Coa proved unpassable and Massena was forced to call back his men.

Massena had failed in his attempt to relieve Almeida and while the battle had not been an entirely satisfactory one for Wellington it had, nevertheless, resulted in another victory at a cost of 1,545 men killed and wounded, Massena's army suffering 2,192 casualties.

When darkness descended over the battlefield of Fuentes de Oñoro on the evening of May 5th Wellington reflected upon what might have happened had Napoleon himself been present. He later said, "If Boney had been there, we should have been beaten," such was the close nature of the hard-fought contest.

British infantry in square formation against French cavalry at Fuentes de Oñoro.

WELLINGTON'S ARMY AT FUENTES DE OÑORO
Total 37,614

1st Division, Brent Spencer,   7,565
Stopford's Brigade,
1/Coldstream, 1/3rd Guards,
   1 Coy 5/60th
Von Lowe's Brigade,
1st, 2nd, 5th and 7th Line Batts KGL,
   2 Coys Light Infantry KGL
Nightingall's Brigade,
2/24th, 2/42nd, 1/79th, 1 Coy 5/60th
Howard's Brigade,
1/50th, 1/71st, 1/92nd, 1 Coy 3/95th

3rd Division, Thomas Picton,   5,480
Mackinnon's Brigade,
1/45th, 74th, 1/88th, 3 Coys 5/60th
Colville's Brigade,
2/5th, 2/83rd, 2/88th, 94th
Power's Portuguese Brigade,
9th Line (2 Batts), 21st Line (2 Batts)

5th Division, William Erskine,
   5,158
Hay's Brigade,
3/1st, 1/9th, 2/38th,
   1 Coy Brunswick Oels

Dunlop's Brigade,
1/4th, 2/30th, 3/44th,
   1 Coy Brunswick Oels,
Spry's Portuguese Brigade,
3rd Line (2 Batts), 15th Line (2 Batts),
   8th Caçadores

6th Division, Alexander Campbell,
   5,250
Hulse's Brigade,
1/11th, 2/53rd, 1/61st, 1 Coy 5/60th
Burne's Brigade,
2nd, 1/36th
Madden's Portuguese Brigade,
8th Line (2 Batts), 12th Line (2 Batts)

7th Division, William Houston,
   4,590
Sontag's Brigade,
2/51st, 85th, Chasseurs Brittaniques,
   8 Coys Brunswick Oels
Doyle's Portuguese Brigade,
7th Line (2 Batts), 19th Line (2 Batts),
   2nd Caçadores

Light Division, Robert Craufurd,
   3,915
Beckwith's Brigade,
1/43rd, 4 Coys 1/95th, 1 Coy 2/95th,
   3rd Caçadores
Drummond's Brigade,
1/52nd, 2/52nd, 4 Coys, 1/95th,
   1st Caçadores

Ashworth's Independent
   Porrtuguese Brigade,
6th Line (2 Batts), 18th Line (2 Batts),
   6th Caçadores

Cavalry   1,864

Slade's Brigade,
1st Dragoons, 14th Light Dragoons
Arentschildt's Brigade, 16th Light
   Dragoons, 1st Hussars KGL
Barbacena's Portuguese Brigade,
4th Line, 10th Line

Artillery, 8 batteries, 48 guns

Albuera

May 16th 1811

Wellington had brought the battle of Fuentes de Oñoro to a successful, if not an entirely satisfactory, conclusion on the evening of May 5th 1811. Earlier that same day, some 130 miles to the south, Beresford had begun to lay siege to the fortress of Badajoz in what was to be the first of three sieges of the place. No sooner had the preliminary operations got underway than Beresford received news that Soult was on his way from Seville to relieve the place with around 25,000 troops.

On May 13th Beresford marched south with 32,000 British, Portuguese and Spanish troops, the British contingent numbering about 7,000, and on May 15th reached the small town of Albuera. Here he was destined to fight one of the bloodiest and most desperate battles of the war.

The Allied troops were positioned along a series of gentle heights that run north to south, parallel with the river Albuera that lays just to the east. In the front centre of the Allied line lay the town of Albuera itself. Soult's army approached from the south-east and on the morning of May 16th drew up facing west. Initial French attacks were directed upon the town of Albuera itself which was held by Alten's Germans although these attacks were never really pressed home with any real conviction. Neither were the subsequent probes by the 5,600 men of Werle's infantry brigade just to the south of the bridge over the Albuera river that lay just outside the town.

However, away to the right of the Allied line, which was held by Blake's Spaniards, a real and very dangerous threat was developing. The river Albuera was easily fordable in several places, even by guns, and Soult had managed to get nineteen battalions of infantry across as well as a large number of cavalry, all of whom had managed to approach the Allied right flank without being seen on account of the area being heavily wooded. These troops debouched from the woods, much to the alarm of Beresford who immediately ordered Blake to face south to meet them, the British 2nd Division being sent as support. Beresford then rode off in blissful ignorance for Blake, still convinced that the main French attack would be delivered from the east, ignored the order and instead deployed just four of his battalions to meet the French attack from the south.

These flimsy four battalions were hardly sufficient to face even a similar number of French battalions let alone the overwhelming and overpowering force now bearing down upon them. In fact, Soult had launched an infantry attack the like of which had yet to be seen in the Peninsular War, nor would it be seen again, for no less than 8,400 French infantry, two full divisions, were advancing on the Allied right flank which, if it disintegrated, would allow Soult to roll up the Allied line.

Contrary to their usual behaviour, the Spaniards held firm and even brought the leading French division to a halt. This was achieved purely by the weight of lead fired into the French columns. Once again their formation, although numerically stronger, prevented them from bringing anything like the number of muskets to bear that the Spaniards, standing in a three-deep line, could. The Spaniards were also supported by Sir John Colborne's brigade of Stewart's 2nd Division which opened fire on the left flank of the French column. This unauthorised move – Beresford had originally ordered Stewart to form his brigades behind the Spaniards – was successful at first but soon afterwards a terrible tragedy occurred which was one of the bloodiest and notorious disasters of the war suffered by any of Wellington's troops.

The 3rd Foot (The Buffs) at Albuera. Soult's Polish lancers make a devastating attack on Colborne's brigade under cover of a hailstorm. Caught in line the British infantry suffered horrific losses in the attack. Ensign Latham, of the 3rd, defied the enemy cavalry, who were desperately trying to snatch the King's Colour from him, a remarkable feat of bravery which cost him an arm and a whole series of terrible wounds.

The 7th Fusiliers advance at Albuera. 'Nothing could stop that astonishing infantry', wrote Napier, the historian of the war, and he was right. The occasion is still celebrated by the Royal Fusiliers today.

At about 10.30am Colborne's brigade, consisting of the 1/3rd, 2/31st, 2/48th and 2/66th Regiments, stood in the firing line, pouring out a withering fire into the left flank of the attacking French columns. Five minutes later most of them lay dead, dying or wounded following an attack of deadly efficiency by some of the most feared cavalry in Europe. As Colborne's men stood blazing away a thunderstorm that had threatened all morning finally broke, the inky-black skies opening up with sheets of rain that swept over the battlefield. The British infantrymen's muskets were quickly rendered useless and as the rain lashed down into their faces the soaked redcoats failed to see two regiments of enemy cavalry that were bearing down on them, using the sudden downpour as a screen. Caught in line and unable to form square the infantry were an easy target for the cavalry who happened to be Polish Lancers, armed with a fearsome weapon hardly ever seen by the British and a superb killing instrument that enabled the bearer to kill with little fear to himself. It was also a weapon from which there was little escape, it being just as easy to thrust down and kill someone on the ground as it was to kill a man standing. The Polish Lancers dealt death all around them, violently and quickly,

and when they withdrew just a few minutes later 1,300 out of Colborne's 1,600 men had been either killed or wounded in the carnage.

Even Beresford himself was not spared during this savage attack, the Allied commander being forced to defend himself with his bare hands when a Polish lancer thrust at him. Beresford, a strong man, parried the lance and threw his would-be assailant to the ground. Six guns were also lost during the attack although all but one were later recovered.

With Colborne's brigade all but gone Beresford turned to the two other brigades of the 2nd Division, those of Abercrombie and Hoghton, to replace them as well as Zayas' Spaniards who themselves had suffered thirty per cent casualties during the morning's fighting. The two fresh brigades numbered about 3,700 men who now bore the brunt of the attack by the two French divisions, some 7,800 strong. The two sides closed with each other and engaged in a ferocious fire fight at almost point-blank range, both sides firing blind through the smoke as they unloaded huge quantities of lead into each other's ranks. The deficiency in British numbers was more than made up for by their formation. The fire from their two-deep line enveloped the heads of the French columns although this in turn was countered by French artillery that was served with deadly efficiency.

Few writers have been able to surpass the magnificent accounts of Fortescue and Napier who described the ensuing butchery as if they had been present themselves. The former wrote, 'Survivors who took part in this fight on the British side seem to have passed through it as if in a dream, conscious of nothing but dense smoke, constant closing towards the centre, a slight tendency to advance, and an invincible resolution not to retire.' The slaughter lasted for over an hour, the two sides blasting away at each other like two prize fighters, neither refusing to admit defeat. British stubbornness could not win the battle on its own, however, and French numbers began to tell.

It was just after midday and the crisis point of the battle had arrived. Carlos de Espana's Spanish Brigade refused to be brought forward into the firing line whilst the two British brigades began to thin alarmingly. At this point, Lowry Cole, without orders from Beresford, brought forward his 4th Division, consisting of some 4,000 British and Portuguese troops, and in so doing turned the tide of the battle. Cole advanced in a long line almost a mile in length with the flanks protected by a square of light companies on the right and the Lusitanian Legion on the left. After repulsing several French cavalry charges his men closed with the enemy and when the 4th Division linked up with the battered survivors of Stewart's 2nd Division they formed a

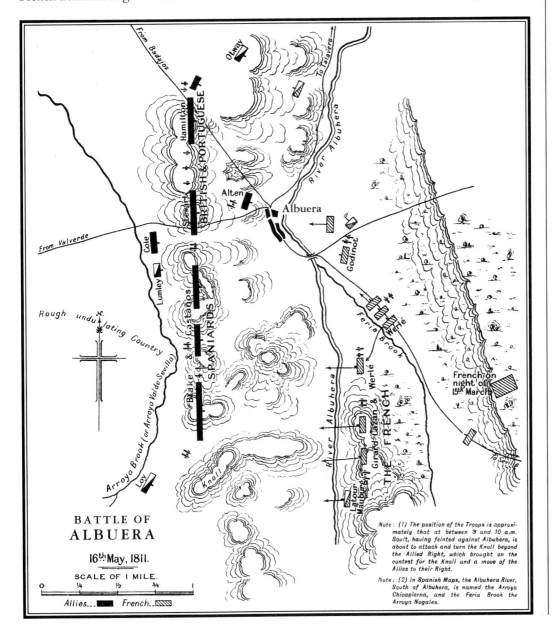

BATTLE OF ALBUERA

16ᵗʰ May, 1811.

SCALE OF I MILE.

Allies...■■■ French...▨▨

Note : (1) The position of the Troops is approximately that at between 9 and 10 a.m. Soult, having feinted against Albuhera, is about to attack and turn the Knoll beyond the Allied Right, which brought on the contest for the Knoll and a move of the Allies to their Right.

Note : (2) In Spanish Maps, the Albuhera River, South of Albuhera, is named the Arroya Chicapierna, and the Feria Brook the Arroya Nogales.

Following pages:
Caton Woodville's spirited painting of how the 57th Regiment won its nickname, 'The Die Hards', at Albuera. Colonel Inglis, severely wounded, remained where he had fallen, cheering on his men, calling on them to keep firing and 'Die Hard'. There was, however, no actual fighting in the town itself, most of the slaughter being confined to the area to the south of the town.

line which wrapped around the flanks of the French columns. Another ferocious fire fight followed during which both sides stood and traded volleys with each other until finally the French columns began to stagger backwards, the men reeling under the weight of the terrific British musketry. William Myers, commanding the three battalions of fusiliers, was quick to detect this wavering and ordered the fusiliers, the 1/7th, 2/7th and 1/23rd, to charge.

The fusiliers obeyed the order with some relief as it freed them from the hell that was erupting all around them. Their relief was short-lived though, for just as they took their first steps forward they were hit by a storm of grape shot that scythed down scores of them. William Napier, the master of Peninsular prose, wrote, 'the fusilier battalions, struck by the iron tempest, reeled and staggered like sinking ships; but suddenly and sternly recovering they closed on their terrible enemies, and then was seen with what a strength and majesty the British soldier fights.' The fusiliers advanced with a grim determination which was too much for the already decimated ranks of exhausted Frenchmen. They had seen an apparent victory snatched from them and were unwilling to endure any more punishment. Gradually, the columns began to dissolve as the French streamed to the rear leaving the equally battered and bloodied British troops 'triumphant on that fatal hill!'

There was no more fighting during the afternoon and heavy rain brought the curtain down on four hours of terrible and bloody fighting. The battle of Albuera had resulted in a British victory mainly due to the stubborn British infantry who refused to recognise defeat even when it was staring them in the face. 'No-one could stop that astonishing infantry', wrote Napier, and he was right. They had stood trading lead with their brave French counterparts until the latter could take no more. As Soult later observed of the victors, 'the day was mine, and they did not know it, and would not run.' Nearly 6,000 Allied dead and wounded was the price paid for this glory, a fact that brought Beresford in for much criticism, not only for his handling of the battle but also his choice of positions to begin with. The French themselves suffered around 7,000 in what was one of the bloodiest battles of the war.

The end result of all this butchery was that Soult, like Massena at Fuentes de Oñoro, had failed to achieve the object of his plan, namely to relieve a beleaguered French garrison, in this case Badajoz to which Wellington was about to turn his attention. The subsequent siege in June 1811 was a dismal failure, however, and it would be almost another year before the town fell, spectacularly and infamously, into Wellington's hands.

BERESFORD'S ARMY AT ALBUERA
Total 20,310

2nd Division, William Stewart,   5,460
Colborne's Brigade,
1/3rd, 2/31st, 2/48th, 2/66th
Hoghton's Brigade,
29th, 1/48th, 1/57th
Abercrombie's Brigade,
2/28th, 2/34th, 2/39th,
Divisional Light Troops
3 Coys 5/60th

4th Division, Lowry Cole,   5,017
Myers's Brigade,
1/7th, 2/7th, 1/23rd
Kemmis's Brigade,
1 Coy each of 2/27th, 1/40th, 97th
Harvey's Portuguese Brigade,
11th Line (2 Batts), 23rd Line (2 Batts),
   1st Batt. Lusitanian Legion

Hamilton's Portuguese Division,   4,819
Fonseca's Brigade,
2nd Line (2 Batts), 14th Line (2 Batts)
Campbell's Brigade,
4th Line (2 Batts), 10th Line (2 Batts)

Alten's Independent German Brigade,
1st Light and 2nd Light Batt. KGL
**Collins's Independent Portuguese
   Brigade,**
5th Line (2 Batts), 5th Caçadores

Cavalry,   1,995
British: 3rd Dragoon Guards, 4th Dragoons,
   13th Light Dragoons
Portuguese: 1st, 5th, 8th, 7th Line

Artillery, 24 British guns, 12 Portuguese guns

Arroyo dos Molinos

October 28th 1811

During the middle of October 1811 a French division under General Girard crossed the River Guadiana near Merida and began to make a nuisance of itself in the northern districts of Estremadura. It was thus proposed that Hill should put a stop to Girard's operations by making a direct attack upon him, acting in conjunction with the Spaniards. Hill discovered that the French were billeted in and around the village of Arroyo dos Molinos, just west of Trujillo and decided to launch a surprise attack on him.

Arroyo dos Molinos is tucked away beneath the rugged Sierra de Montanches with just three roads leading from it which, if blocked, would effectively prevent any troops in the village from escaping, other than by climbing the mountains themselves. The first of the three roads, leading south to Trujillo would be blocked by Wilson's brigade supported by three Portuguese battalions whilst the other two roads leading to Medellin and Merida would be blocked by British and Spanish cavalry. Hill, meanwhile, would make a frontal attack on the village with his infantry. If all went according to plan Hill should be able capture Girard together with his 5,500 infantry and cavalry.

By the evening of October 27th 1811 Hill's force, numbering around 10,000, had got to within four miles of the French when a storm got up, causing his men to take shelter from the heavy rain. To ensure total surprise Hill had seen to it that the villages nearby were surrounded to prevent any warning being given to the enemy whilst his own troops spent the storm night in the open, his men having to endure a violent hailstorm. Early on the morning of October 28th Hill covered the last few miles to Arroyo dos Molinos and encountered not a single French piquet until he was just half a mile away, the tempestuous weather having provided his force with suitable cover. The small French piquet was quickly overcome although some of them escaped and dashed off in the darkness to warn Girard and the rest of the French force.

Fortunately for the French, two regiments, the 64th and 88th, had marched an hour earlier escorted by one cavalry regiment and thus avoided capture. The remaining 4,000 French hastily prepared to make good their escape, the infantry hurriedly packing their baggage while the cavalry prepared to mount up. Girard himself was still having his breakfast in the house of the Alcalde. All was hustle and bustle when suddenly Hill's leading troops, the 71st and 92nd, burst into the village with a crash of musketry, their pipes skirling above the din. The charging cheering Scots swept aside the French battalion trying to hold the village, capturing scores of prisoners and taking Girard's baggage, while a startled General Bron, commanding the cavalry, emerged from his house only to be pulled rudely from his horse by a happy, exuberant Scot who then paraded his 'trophy' before his comrades.

After clearing the village of French troops the 71st came upon the rear of a French brigade still trying to form up for the march. The French were quickly thrown into disarray by the 71st who opened up into the rear of the French column, as did three Allied guns that had come forward. The column hurried on along the road leading to Merida but soon found its way barred by the Allied cavalry, forcing Girard to launch his own chasseurs and dragoons against them in order to buy time for the escaping infantry. The French cavalry fought gallantly against the Allied cavalry, consisting of the 9th Light Dragoons and the 2nd Hussars KGL, but they were outnumbered and forced to retire leaving many of their number to be taken prisoners.

Girard's infantry, meanwhile, set off along the Trujillo road at the foot of the mountains with the Allied infantry of Howard's brigade hot on their heels. As they peered through the early morning mist they saw to their horror Wilson's brigade rushing to cut them off. The three leading companies, the light companies of the 28th, 34th and 39th, attacked the column without hesitating, hoping to check the French and allow Howard's brigade to come up. Surprisingly, Girard, despite having a vastly superior number of troops at his disposal, ordered his men to disregard the three British companies and instead try to escape by

---

HILL'S FORCE AT ARROYO DOS MOLINOS

Howard's Brigade,
1/50th, 1/71st, 1/92nd

Wilson's Brigade,
1/28th, 1/34th, 1/39th
Portuguese,
4th, 6th, 10th, 18th
  Line, 6th Caçadores

**Cavalry, Long's
  Brigade,**
9th Light Dragoons,
  13th Light Dragoons,
  2nd Hussars KGL

heading for the mountains on their left. This decision precipitated a remarkable scene with officers hastily abandoning their horses and infantry scrambling up the steep slopes to escape. Girard was one of the lucky ones for he, along with about 500 of his men, managed to reach the top of the mountain to evade the clutches of Hill's men. Even here, however, he was not entirely safe for the enthusiastic Spaniards of Morillo's brigade came after them and bayoneted all those they came up with.

Girard's force was all but destroyed and no less than 1,300 French troops were taken prisoner, most of whom surrendered at the foot of the mountains. As well as General Bron the prisoners included the colonel of the 27th Chasseurs, the Prince of Aremberg, and thirty other officers. Hill's force suffered just seven men killed and seven officers and 57 men wounded, the Spaniards suffering thirty casualties.

Tarifa

December 1811 – January 1812

The defence of Tarifa in December 1811 was a relatively small sideshow when compared with the greater exploits of Wellington's army during the Peninsular War. It was sufficient, however, for the battle honour 'Tarifa' to be awarded to the regiments involved.

The French forces in Estremadura under Soult had been constantly annoyed by Ballesteros' Spaniards who, whenever threatened by Soult, retired to their bases at Gibraltar and Tarifa. Ballesteros, not unwisely, had long decided against risking his men against Soult's French veterans in open battle which left the frustrated French commander with little option but to deprive him of these bases. Gibraltar was, of course, virtually impregnable, as the Spaniards themselves had long since discovered but Tarifa was considered an easier target for a strike, not only against Ballesteros but also against the Allied cause as a whole, for Tarifa provided the Allies with a powerful base from which its ships could operate along the south coast of Spain.

In October 1811 the Anglo-Spanish garrison numbered around 4,000 men but it was not until December of that year that they were called upon to defend the place in earnest against the French. This threat came from 12,500 French troops under Marshal Victor who set off from Cadiz on December 8th but did not reach Tarifa, just thirty miles away, until some twelve days later, mainly due to bad roads and to the marauding bands of guerrillas that hampered and hindered them along every step of their march. Victor began his

siege on December 22nd, his siege train having come up the same day.

The small town of Tarifa had a population of about three thousand and lies at the point of a promontory which juts out into the sea. A causeway about 500 yards long joins the town with a small island which was virtually impossible to scale owing to its almost perpendicular sides. In fact, the only way to gain access to the island was via this causeway which was protected by a retrenchment and a battery at the island end. The land between the causeway and the town was commanded by the castle and tower of Guzmans and the Santa Catalina battery which had one heavy gun. Tarifa had once been a stronghold but its defences were woefully out of date. Its walls were designed to protect it from arrows rather than from artillery. There was no ditch and it was commanded by some heights which were easily within range of the French guns. It was the northern and eastern sides of the town that were particularly vulnerable to attack and it was upon the eastern heights that Victor's men broke ground on the 23rd.

The British troops inside Tarifa consisted of the 2/47th, 2/87th, a detachment of the 82nd, the light company of the 11th, a detachment of the 2nd Hussars KGL and a detachment of the Royal Artillery, altogether numbering 67 officers and 1,707 men. The whole was commanded by Colonel Skerrett of the 47th.

Throughout the next few days the weather was so bad that the French were unable to get any of their siege guns into position. The trenches filled up with water and turned large tracts of them into liquid mud. The weather broke, however, and on the morning of December 29th ten of Victor's guns opened up against the eastern walls of Tarifa, the guns having been dragged into position the night before.

After just a few hours' bombardment the frail walls began to crumble and soon a fairly large breach had been made. At this point Skerrett's nerve went and he began to make arrangements for abandoning the place. However, Captain Smith, of the engineers, to whom much of the credit for the defence of the place is due, and Major King, of the 82nd, disagreed as did General Campbell, Governor of Gibraltar, who recalled all the transports from Tarifa to Gibraltar without a single man on board and in so doing ensured that the defence was prolonged.

The breach in the eastern wall left Tarifa open to assault but while Leval, now in charge of the siege operations, pondered his next move, Smith was organising the defence of the place. He noticed that the level of the streets was about thirteen feet below the breach and, knowing that the French would have to jump down here, covered the ground with iron railings torn from the windows, turning every second bar upwards to form a sort of chevaux-de-frise. His men worked furiously to keep the breach, by now thirty feet wide, clear of rubbish and debris in spite of the storm of grape that flew amongst them from time to time.

On December 30th Leval sent in a summons for the town to surrender which was rejected and so the French guns continued firing until by evening the breach was no less than sixty feet wide. Later that night Leval decided that the place would be stormed the following morning. No sooner had Leval's officers begun to issue orders for the assault than torrential rain began to fall, washing down from the French camp a mass of gabions, fascines, planks of wood and even corpses, all of which crashed into the palisades before the walls, breaking them down and damaging other parts of the defences. Indeed, the wreckage from the French camp was great enough to cause a fresh opening in the walls when the portcullis protecting the tower close to the breach was bent back. This new passage was repaired by morning however.

At eight o'clock the next morning Leval's grenadiers appeared opposite the walls, moving forward through a heavy shower of rain. However, instead of making for the breach, which was defended by the 87th, the grenadiers lost their way and headed for the portcullis, as a consequence of which they were hit by a terrific enfilading fire from the defenders in the breach. The officer leading the French storming party was struck down along with a small drummer boy who fell dead at his side. The rest of the grenadiers slipped and slithered in the mud and spread out to open up an ineffective fire on the defenders along the ramparts. Some of the French even managed to find their way to the breach but they were beaten back by the fire from the defenders and by grape shot from the gun in the tower. Having made no headway at all the French were left with no other choice but to return to their mud-filled trenches leaving behind 207 men including 48 dead. The Allies on the other hand had sustained losses of just 36.

With the repulse of the assault French morale fell even further. The trenches were filled with sticky, liquid mud, the batteries were all but washed away, sickness and desertion were rife and the majority of the ammunition was ruined by the rain. The men themselves were clothed in rags and had had no decent food for days. What food they did have could not be cooked properly because of the rain. The French had, in Fortescue's words, 'reached the limit of human endurance.'

The assault on December 30th turned out to be the only one to be launched by the French and after a few days more rain Victor decided to raise the siege. His men began to retire on January 5th 1812 having first burned all stores, waggons and ammunition and having abandoned a large number of guns. The siege had been a disaster and had cost the French over five hundred men, nine guns and a vast quantity of stores and ammunition. The British defenders of Tarifa lost just seventy killed and wounded during the entire siege.

BRITISH GARRISON AT TARIFA
1,758 all ranks

Colonel Skerrett (commander),
Infantry: 2/47th, 2/87th, 1 Coy 2/95th, 82nd (detach.),
Light Coys 11th
Cavalry: 1 Troop 2nd Hussars KGL
Artillery: Hughes's Company RA

Ciudad Rodrigo

January 8th–19th 1812

Although the siege of Tarifa had gone on through the winter of 1811-12 the action at Arroyo dos Molinos had effectively brought the campaign of 1811 to a close. The French Army in Spain was now commanded by Marshal Auguste Marmont, Massena having been recalled to France by Napoleon in May of 1811. But if Marmont thought that Wellington's men were to spend the winter months in cantonments he was to be much mistaken.

Wellington, in fact, had already begun a 'campaign' of disinformation which was intended to deceive Marmont into believing that there would be no further Allied operations until the spring. Whilst Wellington's various 'correspondents' throughout Spain disseminated false information regarding the Allies so-called inactivity Wellington himself purposely leaked exaggerated reports of the numbers of Allied sick and wounded in the hospitals, senior officers were allowed to go home on leave and the army itself was kept purposely scattered. All this led Marmont into

believing that he was secure until the spring whereas in fact Wellington was busy making arrangements for a lightning thrust against the two French-held fortresses of Ciudad Rodrigo and Badajoz.

Wellington's siege train was brought up in secrecy to Almeida and having satisfied himself that all was ready for the siege he began his advance forward on January 4th amidst heavy snow and cold, biting rain. On January 8th 1812 Wellington arrived before the walls of Ciudad Rodrigo and so began the first of the year's two bloody but successful sieges.

Ciudad Rodrigo stands on a low hill close to the right bank of the Agueda and is enclosed by ramparts and a wall about thirty-two feet high. On the southern side of the town the ground falls sharply away to the riverbank whilst about two thousand yards to the north of the town there runs a low ridge which runs parallel to the town's walls called the Lesser Teson. About 400 yards north of this ridge lies another larger and higher ridge called the Greater Teson. This particular ridge is about

Robert Craufurd directs his Light Division at the storming of the Lesser Breach at Ciudad Rodrigo. He was mortally wounded soon afterwards.

thirteen feet higher than the walls of the town and was, therefore, the obvious place on which to position the siege guns. A small redoubt was built on the Greater Teson to prevent this but on the night of January 8th it was stormed by two companies each from the 43rd, 52nd and 95th Rifles, supported by two companies of Portuguese Caçadores.

Siege warfare was loathed by Wellington's infantry for it was they who had to carry out the laborious and tiresome task of digging the parallels, or trenches, and of constructing batteries for the guns. Wellington possessed no sappers or miners and had to rely solely on the brawn of the infantry who disliked the work intensely. It was an unpleasant and at times dangerous occupation as the digging was carried out all the while under fire and at both Ciudad Rodrigo and Badajoz was accompanied by atrocious weather conditions that made life more than unpleasant for the men. Each division took turns digging, each spending twenty-four hours in the trenches before being relieved by the next division. Even the two Guards battalions were not spared the rigours of this work.

The works progressed so well that on January 14th General Barrie, commander of the garrison, ordered a sortie to be made which was duly delivered at 11 o'clock that morning. It was driven back by the working parties but not before great lengths of trenches had been filled in and valuable entrenching tools carried off. That same night three companies of the 40th Regiment stormed the convent of San Francisco which was being used as a outpost by the garrison.

By the morning of January 19th the Allied siege guns had blasted two breaches in the walls of the town which prompted Wellington to issue orders that the town be stormed that very night. Throughout the rest of the day the Allied guns turned their sights upon the defences and on the areas behind the breaches in order to prevent the French from retrenching there. Many of the town's guns were silenced also during the day.

Wellington drew up his plans for the assault whilst sitting in one of the forward trenches. The orders meant that Picton's 3rd Division would storm the larger of the two breaches whilst Craufurd's Light Division would storm the Lesser Breach. These two assaults were to be preceded by two diversion-

ary attacks, one by Lieutenant Colonel O'Toole who, with the light company of the 83rd and the 2nd Caçadores, was to cross the Agueda by the old Roman bridge and make an attack on the outwork in front of the castle. Campbell's brigade would make the second diversionary attack, assisting the 3rd Division by entering the main ditch and clearing away the outer French defences as far as the Great Breach.

When news of the impending storm spread through the British camp there was a flood of volunteers for the 'forlorn hope', the almost-suicidal unit that preceded the main assault columns. For any subaltern who led and survived the 'hope' there was the chance of

The 88th (Connaught Rangers) at the storming of Ciudad Rodrigo, January 19th 1812.

promotion but more often than not it meant a quick death, either by musket ball or by cannon shot. Quite often, the 'forlorn hopes' were swept away in an instant at the first deadly blast of the enemy guns but despite this there was a clamour to join the 'hope' and many were left disappointed.

The Light Division, which was to storm the Lesser Breach, formed up beneath the walls of the convent of San Francisco and as his men stood and listened Robert Craufurd, 'Black Bob' to his men, addressed them, saying, "Soldiers, the eyes of your country are upon you. Be steady, be cool, be firm in the assault. The town must be yours this night . . . Now lads, for the breach!" It was to be the last time that Craufurd spoke to his men for he was mortally wounded shortly afterwards, leading his men into the attack.

The storming of Ciudad Rodrigo got underway with the two diversionary attacks which were executed with precision and shortly afterwards the main assault began. The Great Breach was a mass of debris up which the British troops began to scramble in the face of a withering fire from within. The head of the British column was smashed into a bloody mess by the French guns whilst a storm of shot and shell, musketry and

grenades whistled through their ranks. The breach was difficult to get to on account of two ditches which the French had cut, ten feet wide and ten feet deep, and all manner of crows' feet, spikes and chevaux-de-frises were laid in the breach to make it even more impassable. Two guns were mounted above these cuts to sweep the ditch below and with each blast thinned the ranks of the 3rd Division. In spite of this stiff and stubborn opposition the breach was mounted by the men of the 88th who surged forward, throwing down their muskets and using their bare hands to climb up. They attacked the gunners using only their bayonets and before the guns could fire a third time they had been silenced. Picton's men stormed forward and began to crowd the ramparts when suddenly, beneath them, a huge mine exploded sending hundreds of them spinning backwards whilst scores were tossed into the air, their burned and blackened bodies falling back onto their comrades below.

At the Lesser Breach, meanwhile, the Light Division had been pressing on with their attack. Craufurd's men swept forward and fought their way to the top of the breach but at a cost. Craufurd himself was hit and thrown backwards by a musket ball that passed

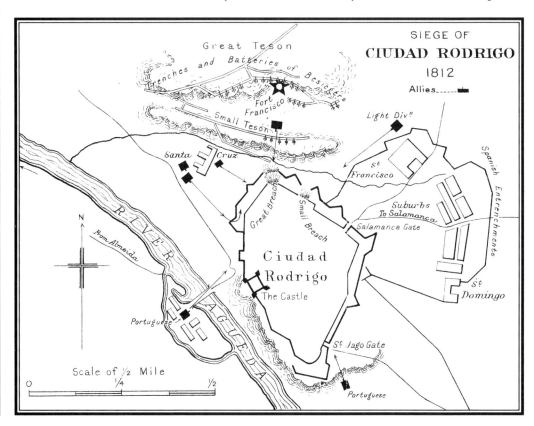

through his arm, broke his ribs, passed through his lungs and lodged close to his spine. Craufurd lingered in some agony before dying on January 24th. His death was perhaps the greatest loss suffered by Wellington during the war. His division, meanwhile, had entered the town, so quickly in fact that many of them were either killed or wounded by the same great mine that had accounted for hundreds of the 3rd Division at the Great Breach.

A few hours after the storming had begun the town was in Wellington's hands. There was some disorder in the town afterwards but this was nothing compared to that which was to occur three months later at Badajoz and the trouble was quickly brought under control by Wellington's officers.

The siege and storming of Ciudad Rodrigo had cost the army some nine officers killed and 70 wounded whilst 186 men were killed and 846 wounded. Of these, 59 officers and 503 men became casualties during the actual storming. The French garrison numbered 2,000 at the beginning of the siege of which 60 officers and 1,300 men were taken prisoner. 8 officers were killed and 21 wounded and about 500 men were either killed or wounded.

Badajoz

March 16th–April 6th 1812

With Ciudad Rodrigo in his hands Wellington moved south to lay siege once more to Badajoz, by far the strongest French-held fortress on the Portuguese border. Once again Wellington deceived the French by leaving a thin screen of cavalry behind which his main army was able to march south without being detected.

Badajoz, capital of Estremadura, was a much more formidable proposition than Rodrigo and had been besieged twice before by the British, in May and June 1811. This time Wellington hoped it would be a case of 'third time lucky.' Its fortifications formed an enclosure of nine bastions connected by walls of between 20 to 46 feet high with a castle that acted as citadel. The town was also covered by several outworks; the Fort San Christobal, the lunette Werle and the Tete du Pont, all on the right bank of the Guadiana and linked to the town by a Roman bridge. On the left bank were the lunettes Picurina, Pardaleras and San Roque, all strong outworks covering the southern approaches to the town. Inside the town the French garrison consisted of around 5,000 men of all ranks, including a detachment of the crack German Hesse d'Armstadt Regiment. Commanding these troops was the governor of the town, Armand Phillipon, who was to prove a brave and resourceful adversary.

Wellington decided to attack Badajoz by breaching its walls on the southern side at the Santa Maria and Trinidad bastions and on March 16th 1812 3,000 British troops broke ground about a thousand yards from Fort Picurina. The weather was atrocious with high winds and cold, heavy rain and for the first week or so the weather was as bad as any of the men digging could remember. In spite of this the digging, loathed by the ordinary soldier as 'navvy's work', pushed on briskly. So quick was the progress that a sortie was made on March 19th by the French who captured many valuable entrenching tools as well as doing much damage to the works.

Each day saw the unmasking of a new battery but the French themselves were not idle, constructing all manner of defensive works to make the forthcoming assault all the more dangerous. One of the most effective works constructed by the French was a dam constructed at the lunette San Roque. This dam across the Rivellas had created a false lake or inundation in front of the British trenches and meant that their attack would have to be made across the front of the French guns. This would cramp them in their approach and was something which was to cause the stormers many problems. Attempts were made to blow it up but none was successful. On the night of March 25th, 500 men of the 3rd and Light Divisions stormed the Fort Picurina and next morning work got under way constructing batteries inside it.

With two French armies marching to

The 88th (Connaught Rangers) at the storming of Badajoz. By coincidence, the troops opposed to them were the French 88th Regiment. Surely one of the best depictions of the Peninsular War, by Caton Woodville.

relieve Badajoz the taking of the place became a time problem for Wellington. He knew that it would take a while for satisfactory breaches to be made but was aware that to wait too long might force him into fighting a covering action similar to that fought by Beresford the year before at Albuera.

Throughout the rest of March and until April 5th the British guns blasted away to breach the Santa Maria and Trinidad bastions. They were reported practicable at sunset on the 5th but even as he inspected them through his telescope Wellington was informed that approaching French armies were just a few days away. He knew that to take the fortress by storm would cost him hundreds of casualties but as time was running out he gave orders that Badajoz was to be stormed that night.

The British troops duly prepared for the assault they believed would be made that night but shortly before the appointed hour a group of officers arrived in camp with a report that Wellington had postponed the assault until after dark the next night, the 6th. In the meantime a third breach would be made in the curtain wall between the two existing breaches. This delay has often been cited as one of the reasons behind the high casualty figure sustained by the British during the assault because Phillipon took the opportunity to shore up the defences and turn the breaches into death traps. The French had dug a ditch in which Wellington had hoped to form up his men but the defenders, unseen, now filled it with water and this was to cause the stormers a great deal of trouble. Also, all the accessible places had been blocked with savage chevaux-de-frise, made from razor sharp sword blades. Fascines, woolpacks and sandbags replaced fallen ramparts and the slopes of the breaches were covered with planks of wood, studded with twelve-inch spikes and chained to the ground. Barrels of gunpowder were placed ready to be rolled down into the ditch to explode amongst the British and all sorts of shells and explosives were laid along the ramparts ready for use.

Wellington timed the assault to begin shortly before 10 o'clock at night. Picton's 3rd

Division was to cross the Rivellas and take the castle by escalade; the 4th Division, under Colville, was to storm the breach in the Trinidad bastion; the Light Division was to storm the Santa Maria bastion and finally, Leith's 5th Division was to take Fort Pardaleras and continue on to storm the San Vincente bastion by escalade. A detachment under Major Wilson of the 48th, meanwhile, was to take the lunette San Roque. It will be noted that the attacks by the 3rd and 5th Divisions were intended to be just diversionary attacks, the breaches being the main points of attack. Yet, as we shall see, these two escalades were to prove the decisive factors in the storming of Badajoz.

By late afternoon on April 6th everything was ready. The hour had been set and the troops waited in darkness as the clock in Badajoz toiled away each hour until finally, at twenty minutes to ten, the attack finally got under way.

First into action was the detachment under Major Wilson that attacked the San Roque. After a brief fight the fort was taken with little resistance from the French. Shortly afterwards, the main attack began. The 'Forlorn Hope' went first followed by the storming parties who dashed forward to the edge of the ditch, placed their ladders in position and descended. More British troops stormed forward and soon the ditch was filled with men crowding together. Suddenly, a bright flame shot up exposing the British to the French who had been watching and waiting for the ditch to fill up before lighting the fuses that would explode the mines beneath it.

Some British troops who survived the first rush forward said afterwards that it was like a volcano. The columns were blown to pieces by the mines and by the incredible fire of grape and musketry that was poured into the ditch from the ramparts. Hundreds of men were swept away in an instant. The Light Division let out a deafening cheer and leapt into the chasm too, only to be flung back by the furious French fire from behind the breaches. The 4th Division joined in to attack the Trinidad bastion but in the confusion it met with disaster when the leading columns jumped into the ditch filled with water, scores drowning before the mistake was realised.

By now both the 4th and Light Divisions were mixed together and both made for the same point, an unfinished ravelin that, in the darkness, they believed to be one of the breaches. They swarmed over it but again they were met by a blaze of musketry and grape and were swept from it like sand in the wind. They were confused and blinded by the fiery explosions that erupted around them and when a Portuguese brigade joined in the attack it only added to the confusion. Blows were exchanged as the men struggled to free themselves and many were simply carried forward on the points of the bayonets of those behind. The cheering, the shouts and the sounds of the explosions and gunfire were now added to by the roar of the British guns in the trenches.

But in spite of the incredibly brave attempts by the British to mount the breaches no impression could be made and the French, gaining in confidence, came forward, jeering and inviting the British to 'come into Badajoz'. Not a single British soldier had

The fortress of Badajoz, as viewed from Fort Picurina. After a watercolour by Captain Elliscombe, Royal Engineers.

The storming of Badajoz,
April 6th 1812.

entered the town even though over forty rushes were made at the breaches. The situation was critical. The dead lay in ever increasing heaps, many of them burning, while the wounded crawled and staggered around in the darkness seeking shelter. As the frustrated and despairing troops were driven back the desperate British attacks began to fade, leaving behind nearly 2,000 of Wellington's best men smashed upon the defences.

The attack on the castle by Picton's 3rd Division had been raging with equal ferocity. Picton, in fact, had been wounded early in the attack and command passed to General Kempt. The British troops had first to cross the Rivellas which was done by either wading through the water or by crossing the dam. The dam, however, was very narrow and could only be passed in single file. Soon, it was a seething mass of impatient soldiers and when the French guns opened on it many slipped over the edge and drowned in the inundation.

When the enraged British troops finally got to the castle walls the ladders were placed against them and were quickly mounted by the men. At the top they were met by French defenders armed with bayonets, muskets and pikes and they simply pushed the ladders from the walls to send them crashing down amongst the crowds of soldiers waiting below. Time after time the British troops mounted the ladders only to be tossed back by the French who hurled logs, rocks and barrels of gunpowder down on them. An hour had passed but, as at the breaches, no impression could be made. However, just as the French began to sense victory Colonel Ridge, of the 5th Regiment, seized one of the ladders and placed it against the castle where the wall was lower and an embrasure afforded the men some protection. Ridge called out to his men to follow him and soon the ladder was crowded from top to bottom, so quickly in fact that before the French could push it away the weight had become too great and the ladder stayed firmly in place against the wall. Ridge pressed on with his sword guarding his head and with the bayonets of those behind him thrust upwards to protect him. Then, incredibly, he was standing on the castle ramparts.

The British troops rushed furiously up the ladders to support him and at last the tide seemed to turn in their favour. More British troops came up to consolidate the position and soon the castle was in British hands. Tragically, Ridge, the first man to enter the town, was shot dead soon afterwards as he led his men through the gloom of the castle which Phillipon had hoped would provide a last place of refuge in the event of the British attacks on the breaches being successful. Now, that hope had gone and with it went all hope of holding the town.

As the 3rd Division cleared the castle news of its fall gradually filtered back to Phillipon and then to the French troops defending the breaches. The news came as a great shock to them and panic and disorder quickly set in.

Away at the San Vincente bastion the 5th Division had also escaladed the high walls, the men performing a remarkably brave feat in climbing the walls in the face of stiff opposition. Once inside, they made for the breaches with bugles sounding the advance and when they were answered by those of the 3rd Division all French resistance at the breaches collapsed.

All this time Wellington had been watching intently with some dismay as his men were smashed against the defences but just as he was about to sound the recall an officer rode up with the news that Picton's men had taken the castle. Upon hearing this news Wellington ordered the 4th and Light Divisions into the breaches once more but this time they met with only limited resistance. Even so, the breaches were incredibly difficult to negotiate and the men still had trouble getting through.

It was now about two o'clock in the morning of April 7th and Badajoz was finally in British hands, Governor Phillipon managing to escape across the Guadiana to the Fort San Christobal where he and his staff surrendered a few hours later.

Inside the town all hell was let loose as the victorious British troops embarked on the now infamous orgy of debauchery and destruction, fuelled not only by the fury of the assault but also by the large amounts of liquor found inside the town. They had endured a miserable last 21 days in the trenches and had suffered terribly getting inside the town. Once there, however, their anger found vent and they dissolved into a dangerous mob of drunken disorderly soldiers.

BRITISH TROOPS INVOLVED IN THE STORMING OF BADAJOZ

3rd Division, Picton
Kempt's Brigade,
1/45th, 3/60th, 74th,
1/88th
J. Campbell's Brigade,
2/5th, 77th, 2/83rd,
94th

4th Division,
Kemmis's Brigade,
3/27th, 1/40th
Bowes's Brigade,
1/7th, 1/23rd, 1/48th

5th Division, Leith
Hay's Brigade,
3/1st, 1/9th, 2/38th
Walker's Brigade,
1/4th, 2/30th, 2/44th

Light Division,
1/43rd, 1/52nd, 1/95th,
3/95th

SIEGE OF
BADAJOZ
1812

English Miles

Allies

In all, the capture of Badajoz cost Wellington some 5,000 men of whom 3,000 had become casualties during the assault, including five generals, Picton, Kempt, Bowes, Harvey and Colville who were all wounded. The 4th and Light Divisions suffered 1,000 casualties, all of whom were struck down in a small area just one hundred yards long in front of the breaches. It was little wonder, therefore, that Wellington was moved to say afterwards, "The capture of Badajoz affords as strong an instance of the gallantry of our troops as has ever been displayed. But I anxiously hope that I shall never again be the instrument of putting them to such a test as that to which they were put last night."

Almaraz

May 19th 1812

The fall of the fortresses gave Wellington command of the two major routes between Spain and Portugal. But while his army recovered its breath after the storming of Badajoz, news arrived of a renewed threat to Ciudad Rodrigo by Marmont, prompting a move north to the area between the Agueda and Coa rivers where Wellington concentrated his army. The threat was removed and Marmont was forced to withdraw back across the Agueda.

While Wellington prepared for the advance into Spain, Hill was again detached with a small force, this time to attack the pontoon bridge over the Tagus at Almaraz which constituted the main French crossing point over the river west of Toledo. Also, by capturing the bridge at Almaraz communications between Marmont and Soult, north and south of the Tagus, would be severed. Hill's force, numbering around 6,000 men with nine guns, was virtually that which had surprised Girard at Arroyo dos Molinos and on May 12th 1812 he began his march south-east.

The task facing Hill was not an inconsiderable one as the bridge of boats – the old stone Roman bridge having been partially destroyed – was protected on both banks of the Tagus by strong works. The southern end of the bridge was guarded by a bridge-head which was revetted with masonry whilst overlooking this was the strong Fort Napoleon. This fort, capable of holding 450 men, was situated on top of a hill with its front looking out over a steep bank that dropped away sharply. It was not a difficult climb for any attacking troops to negotiate, however, and entry into the fort was made slightly easier by two large scarps, rather like steps, which would bring the troops on to the ramparts of the fort. The rear of the fort sloped down to the bridge-head and was protected by a palisaded ditch and loop-holed tower which would act as the last place of refuge should Hill's men gain entry into the fort. On the northern bank stood Fort Ragusa in which was stored all the garrison's supplies and ammunition. This five-sided fort also had a twenty-five feet high loop-holed tower which, like that inside Fort Napoleon, was to be the last place of defence. The fort was also covered by a field work close to the bridge.

The French had further strengthened the position at the bridge by way of securing the main road from Trujillo at a point about six miles south of the bridge. Here, where the road climbs the craggy range of mountains called the Sierra de Mirabete, the pass was commanded by an old castle around which the French had built a rampart some twelve feet high which housed eight guns. This connected to a fortified house close to the road by two small works, Forts Colbert and Senarmont, which together with the castle formed a very strong line of defence. The mountains were impassable to any wheeled vehicles such as guns and waggons which would, therefore, have to brave the fire of the French guns in order to pass through. The only other way across the mountains was two miles to the east of Mirabete via the pass of La Cueva. The road on the southern side of the mountains was passable to vehicles but once through the pass the road deteriorated into little more than a second-rate footpath.

Hill's plan involved dividing his force into three columns. The first, consisting of the 28th, 34th and the 6th Caçadores, under General Chowne, was to storm the castle of

Mirabete. The second, or centre column, consisting of the 6th and 18th Portuguese infantry, along with all the artillery, was to proceed along the main road and attack the works by the road defending the pass. The third column, Howard's brigade, consisting of the 50th, 71st, 92nd and a single company of the 5/60th, and commanded by Hill himself, was to climb the road leading through the pass of La Cueva and approach Almaraz via the path. The three columns duly set off at nightfall on May 16th but when dawn broke all three were still some way off from their objectives, so difficult was the rough nature of the terrain.

It was clear to Hill that there was little chance of being able to surprise the garrison at the bridge and instead looked for another way by which he could get his guns through the mountains. The element of surprise was not lost yet though the French garrison was still unaware of the presence of Hill's force and it suddenly occurred to Hill that he might be successful if he left behind his guns and attacked Fort Napoleon and the bridge using his infantry only.

On the evening of May 18th Howard's brigade set off as before through the pass of La Cueva, this time reinforced by the Portuguese Caçadores. By dawn on May 19th Hill's men had reached a point just half a mile from Fort Napoleon but they had been spotted during the morning as they clambered across the mountains. The garrison inside Fort Napoleon, commanded by Major Aubert, was thus alerted and was duly strengthened, the two centre boats of the bridge being taken away as a precaution.

The attack on the bridge at Almaraz got underway at daylight when Major Chowne's guns opened up against the castle at Mirabete, the garrison of Fort Napoleon climbing onto the ramparts to watch. The defenders, having been warned of the presence of Hill's troops, were well prepared for the assault but they were still taken somewhat by surprise when the 50th and part of the 71st burst from their cover and charged up towards the fort in the teeth of a withering fire from the defenders and from the guns in Fort Ragusa. Scores of British troops struck down as the dashed forward in the open – and in daylight – but they would not be denied and when they reached the top of the hill they flung their ladders against the scarp, the men pulling themselves on to the first of the two steps. Once accomplished, the ladders were heaved up and placed on the step in order for the men to reach the top of the ramparts. Then, panting through exhaustion and all the time under heavy fire from within, the men scaled the ladders and were soon engaged in hand-to-hand fighting with the defenders along the ramparts.

First up was Captain Candler of the 50th who leapt over the parapet but was dead before he reached the ground, several French musket balls thudding into his body. His men followed him and after firing off a last volley the defenders gave way and began streaming down towards the bridge-head. The commander of the fort, General Aubert, refused to run, however, and put up a gallant fight, even refusing the offer of surrender, until a disgruntled sergeant of the 50th eventually ran him through with his pike. Other French troops had tried to get inside the tower but the British troops were so close that this was impossible and scores were forced to surrender. A large number of French were also struck down during the pursuit to the river afterwards, the guns of Fort Ragusa unable to fire for fear of hitting their own men.

The defenders of the bridge-head did not wait to meet the British but joined in the retreat across the pontoon bridge. The guns inside Fort Ragusa opened up a brief fire against Fort Napoleon but when this was answered by the captured guns in that fort they quickly stopped and soon afterwards the garrison of Fort Ragusa was making its way, along with the rest of the fugitives, in a panic-stricken retreat towards Naval Moral. The action had lasted forty minutes and when it was over four grenadiers of the 92nd swam across to Fort Ragusa and brought back some boats which enabled the bridge of boats to be repaired.

Shortly afterwards the rest of Hill's force arrived to find the action had ended in success with the French abandoning all of their works on either side of the river. These works were blown up by Hill and the bridge itself was then dragged across to the south bank and burned.

The castle at Mirabete remained in French hands, however, owing to a misunderstanding on the part of William Erskine who spread false news that Soult's entire force was coming

---

HILL'S FORCE AT ALMARAZ

Howard's Brigade,
50th, 71st, 92nd,
1 Coy 5/60th

Wilson's Brigade,
28th, 34th,
1 Coy 5/60th

Ashworth's Portuguese Brigade,
6th and 18th Line,
6th Caçadores

Cavalry, 13th Light Dragoons
Artillery, 9 British and Portugues guns

forward. This caused Hill, who had intended to reduce the castle, to retire to Trujillo and the chance to achieve complete success was lost.

Hill's raid on the bridge at Almaraz had cost him 33 killed and 148 wounded, of which 28 killed and 110 of the wounded belonged to the 50th Regiment. French losses were estimated at about 400, 259 of whom were prisoners.

Salamanca

July 22nd 1812

The year of 1812 had begun in a blaze of glory for Wellington's army and Hill's attack on the forts at Almaraz set the seal on a remarkably successful five-month period. The triumphant roll was not finished yet though, for in July Wellington achieved one of his and the British Army's greatest victories.

The spectacular gains achieved by Wellington during the first half of the year became all the more significant when news began to filter through to him of the steady withdrawal from Spain of a large number of French troops, including the Imperial Guard, who were destined to take part in the fateful invasion of Russia that year. From now on, the already hard-pressed and harassed French armies would fight with an increased disadvantage, one which the Spanish guerrillas in particular were quick to seize upon.

The French armies in Spain were placed under the command of Napoleon's brother, Joseph, and it was Marmont's Army of Portugal, some 52,000-strong, that posed the more immediate problem for Wellington, whose own troops numbered just over 60,000. During the first days of June Wellington began to concentrate his army for a thrust into central Spain against Marmont, a move that would threaten the main French communications and a move that would almost certainly bring French reinforcements rushing to Marmont's assistance. Wellington hoped to prevent this latter eventuality by planning a series of concerted moves and concentrations elsewhere in Spain to keep the French forces occupied. Having satisfied himself that all these arrangements had been made Wellington, on June 13th, began his advance from Ciudad Rodrigo with 48,000 men and 54 guns.

Four days later the Allied army entered Salamanca unopposed although Marmont had left garrisons in three small forts in the western suburbs of the town. These were besieged and fell on June 27th. For the next three weeks the two armies were in close proximity to each other and on July 18th marched parallel with each other on opposite sides of the Guarena river, the bands of the two armies playing as they marched. This close marching continued for the next two days and by the night of the 21st both armies had crossed the river Tormes and camped within a few hundred yards of each other.

That night Mother Nature provided her own spectacular backdrop to the campaigning when a violent storm broke overhead and when the moon disappeared behind the inky black clouds it was left to the silver streaks of lightning to illuminate the surrounding countryside. Several troopers of the 5th Dragoon Guards were killed by lightning while dozens of horses bolted, charging over their riders as they lay on the ground. To their confusion was added a torrential downpour from which there was little shelter. These types of weather conditions were to be repeated at Sorauren and, more famously, at Waterloo, by which time Wellington's men had come to look upon such storms before battle as an omen of victory.

On the morning of July 22nd both armies resumed their march south, still parallel with each other, the rays of the sun warming the troops on both sides after their soaking the night before. The two armies marched across flat, rolling countryside with no remarkable features other than two very distinctive-shaped hills, the first, a rounded ridge to the northeast of the village of Los Arapiles called the Lesser Arapil, and the second, called the Greater Arapil, a box-shaped hill some 100 feet high about half a mile to the south of the Lesser Arapil. These two hills lay in the middle of an undulating plain, about nine miles long, stretching from the small village of Calvarasa de Arriba in the east, to Miranda de Azan in the west. The village of Los Arapiles lay just to the left of centre of the plain.

Marmont's intention was to sever the road leading to Ciudad Rodrigo, along which Wellington had begun to send his baggage and supplies. To accomplish this Marmont needed to outstrip his opponents and turn west across the head of the leading British columns. At around 8 o'clock on the morning of the 22nd Marmont's troops became involved in a race with a Portuguese brigade to occupy the Greater Arapil. Some brief but heavy fighting occurred here but the Portuguese were driven back and Marmont was left in possession of the Greater Arapil while Wellington occupied the Lesser Arapil.

There was little fighting throughout the rest of the morning as both armies continued their march south-west. Marmont, meanwhile, watched from his lofty position on the Greater Arapil and spotted a cloud of dust rising from behind the Lesser Arapil in the direction of Ciudad Rodrigo which seemed to confirm his belief that Wellington was retreating. The column was, in fact, Pakenham's 3rd Division which Wellington had brought forward to Aldea Tejada either to protect his right flank or to act as an independent force. The French columns were moving faster than Wellington's own men who had halted around the village of Los Arapiles and by early afternoon the divisions of Thomieres, Maucune and Clausel were well on their way heading west to the Rodrigo road and were strung out in a long line some four miles long.

It soon became apparent that the leading French division, that of Thomieres', was outstripping Maucune's division which was following behind, and a considerable gap opened up between them, something that did not go unnoticed by Wellington who was having lunch in the village of Los Arapiles. Wellington peered through his telescope and could hardly believe what he was seeing. Sending his lunch flying through the air, he exclaimed, "By God! That will do!" and galloped off to Aldea Tejada to order Pakenham to attack immediately.

It was about 3.30pm and the long, dusty columns of French troops were hurrying across the Ciudad Rodrigo road to cut off Wellington's escape route. Thomieres himself

must have felt fairly safe and secure, and he was certainly unaware of the storm that was about to break around him. That storm arrived in the shape of Pakenham's 3rd Division which suddenly appeared on Thomieres' right flank supported by 1,100 cavalry who scattered the leading French companies like sheep. The shock of seeing Pakenham's battalions just a few hundred yards away must have been immense. One moment the French were grasping the initiative, the next they had it wrenched violently from them by nearly 6,000 British and Portuguese infantry who smashed into them, unleashing volley after volley into their packed and panicking ranks. Thomieres' leading column was ripped apart by the ferocity of the attack which saw hundreds killed and wounded in minutes. Thomieres himself was killed and the casualty figures for the two leading battalions are comparable with those sustained by Colborne's brigade at Albuera the previous year; the leading regiment lost 1,031

'Ned, do you see those fellows over there? Throw your division into column and drive them to the devil.' Wellington issues orders to Pakenham to begin the Allied attack at Salamanca.

Pakenham's 3rd Division smashes into Thomieres' division to begin the rout of Marmont's army at Salamanca.

of its 1,449 men, while the second regiment lost 868 out of 1,123 men. With Thomieres gone and the leading regiments destroyed the rest of Thomieres' division disintegrated and fled in panic to the south-east.

Leith's 5th Division, supported by Bradford's Portuguese, had been launched into the attack about forty minutes after Pakenham. Advancing directly south from Los Arapiles the 8,500 Allied troops struck at Maucune's division which had been following Thomieres at a distance. The French, numbering about 5,000 men, were outnumbered but expected help shortly from Brennier's division which was hurrying to its support. Maucune had seen the damage that the Allied cavalry had done to Thomieres' division and accordingly formed his nine battalions into squares. Unfortunately, on this occasion it was the wrong formation and when Greville's and Pringle's brigades came up, after having advanced through a heavy French artillery barrage, they simply levelled their muskets and unloaded them into the dense French ranks, sweeping away the French squares with three devastating volleys.

The French troops who survived this onslaught broke and fled in the same direction as the survivors of Thomieres' division. It was now, more than ever, that they needed to be in square formation for as they looked back they saw, to their horror, Le Marchant's brigade of heavy dragoons thundering after them, their long, heavy sabres glinting in the bright sunlight. The fugitives tried to defend themselves as best they could but they were easy meat for the dragoons who swept over them with ease, chopping and hacking all around them. Five French battalions were left totally destroyed in the wake of Le Marchant's men who now saw before them, running to aid Maucune's men, the 4,300 men of Brennier's division.

Brennier's men were exhausted by their hurried, mile-long dash to aid Maucune and even though they had time to form square they were not steady enough to resist the power of the dragoons. A ragged volley brought a few horses and riders crashing to the ground, horses which smashed into the squares causing great confusion and panic. Other dragoons came charging in and in a few minutes Brennier's division, too, was streaming away towards the woods to the south-east.

Le Marchant's dragoons soon became drunk on success and got completely out of control. Even Le Marchant could not hold them in check. The French ran around like frightened sheep as the dragoons flayed in every direction. Unlike other cavalry 'misadventures' during the Peninsular War there was no effective enemy cavalry force to take advantage of the disorder and Le Marchant's men went about their business unopposed. Le Marchant himself did manage to keep one squadron in check, however, which engaged some French infantry close to the woods to the south-east of the battlefield. Here, tragically, Le Marchant met his death when he was hit by a single musket ball that broke his spine. It was a bitter blow to Wellington who had seen one of the few capable cavalry commanders taken from him. He died knowing his men had done their job and when they returned, breathless and excited to their own lines, they could look back over a trail of devastation which had contributed to the destruction of no less than three whole French divisions. And it had taken just forty minutes.

Further to the east of Los Arapiles Wellington's men were not so successful for when Cole's 4th Division advanced to the east of the Greater Arapil it was flung back in bloody disorder by two fresh French divisions, but not before having engaged a numerically superior enemy in a furious fire-fight. On the

Greater Arapil itself Pack's Portuguese brigade met with a similar fate. These French success combined to provide Clausel – now in command following serious wounds to first Marmont and then Bonnet, who was killed – with the prospect of being able to stem the tide of the battle and possibly even retrieve the situation for the French.

His counter-attack was intelligently planned and executed with flawless precision by 12,000 men of the French 2nd and 8th Divisions who strode doggedly across the plain between the two Arapiles while Sarrut's division held Pakenham's victorious 3rd Division in check on their left flank.

The bold French manoeuvre was strangled at birth however for Wellington had anticipated the move with almost clairvoyant-like accuracy. He had deployed the two British brigades of Clinton's 6th Division in the by now standard two-deep line, with Rezende's Portuguese in line behind them. On Clinton's right were Spry's Portuguese while Anson's brigade, from Cole's 4th Division, was brought up alongside on Clinton's left.

Clausel's men advanced under heavy fire from the Allied artillery on and behind the Lesser Arapil which mowed down whole files of men. When their columns had got halfway across the plain between the two hills they came face to face with Clinton's lines which opened up a rolling volley that engulfed the heads of the columns, sending them staggering

Le Marchant's heavy cavalry in action at the battle of Salamanca, July 22nd 1812.

backwards. For a few brief minutes the French returned the fire but their formation was against them. Although numerically superior to Clinton's men their columns could not match the firepower of the British lines and they were driven back in disorder.

Of Marmont's eight infantry divisions, all but three had been swept away and Wellington's men pressed forward on all sides to complete their victory. The sun had begun to set when Wellington ordered Clinton forward in pursuit of the fleeing French fugitives but when they had passed the Greater Arapil Clinton's men came up against Ferrey's division, some 5,500 men who had yet to see any serious action during the day. Ferrey formed his seven battalions into a three-deep line and, for a change, it was the turn of the red-jack-

eted British to experience the firepower of such a formation. The French checked the British advance and even forced them back. In fact, Ferrey was only forced to retreat when threatened on his flank. Unfortunately, Ferrey was not amongst those who fled the battle-field as he was cut in two by a roundshot from an Allied gun.

The battle was as good as over and thousands of defeated French troops streamed away to the woods to the south-east and to the bridge at Alba de Tormes. After several days of hard marching and due to the rigours of the battle itself Wellington's men were too exhausted to affect a serious pursuit. However, since the bridge over the Tormes at Alba de Tormes was held by Spanish troops under Carlos de Espana, Wellington was quietly

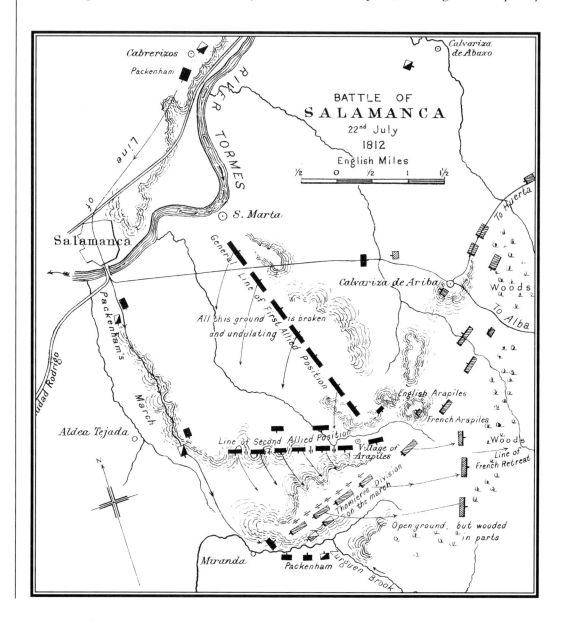

WELLINGTON'S ARMY AT SALAMANCA
Total 48,569

1ST DIVISION, H.CAMPBELL 6,423

Fermor's Brigade
1/Coldstreamers, 1/3rd Guards,
    1 Coy 5/60th
Von Lowe's Brigade
1st, 2nd and 5th Line Batts. KGL.
Wheatley's Brigade
2/24th, 1/42nd, 2/58th, 1/79th and
    1 Coy 5/60th

3RD DIVISION, PAKENHAM 5,877

Wallace's Brigade
1/45th, 74th, 1/88th, 3 Coys 5/60th
Campbell's Brigade
1/5th, 2/5th, 2/83rd and 94th
Power's Portuguese Brigade
9th Line (2 Batts.), 21st Line (2 Batts.)
    and 12th Caçadores

4TH DIVISION, L.COLE 5,236

Anson's Brigade
3/27th, 1/40th and 1 Coy 5/60th
Ellis's Brigade
1/7th, 1/23rd, 1/48th and
    1 Coy Brunswick Oels
Stubb's Portuguese Brigade
11th Line (2 Batts.), 23rd Line (2 Batts.)
    and 7th Caçadores

5TH DIVISION, J.LEITH 6,691

Greville's Brigade
3/1st, 1/9th, 1/38th, 2/38th and
    1 Coy Brunswick Oels
Pringle's Brigade
1/4th, 2/4th, 2/30th, 2/44th
    1 Coy Brunswick Oels
Spry's Portuguese Brigade
3rd Line (2 Batts.), 15th Line (2 Batts.)
    8th Caçadores

6TH DIVISION, H.CLINTON 5,541

Hulse's Brigade
1/11th, 2/53rd, 1/61st and 1 Coy 5/60th
Hinde's Brigade
2nd, 1/32nd and 1/36th
Rezende's Portuguese Brigade
8th Line (2 Batts.), 12th Line (2 Batts.)
    9th Caçadores

7TH DIVISION, J.HOPE 5,183

Halkett's Brigade
1st Light, 2nd Light, KGL. and
    remainder Brunswick Oels
De Bernewitz's Brigade
51st, 68th, and Chasseurs Britanniques
Collins's Portuguese Brigade
7th Line (2 Batts.), 19th Line (2 Batts.)
    2nd Caçadores

LIGHT DIVISION, C.ALTEN 3,548

Barnard's Brigade
1/43rd coys. of 2/95th, 3/95th and
    1st Caçadores
Vandeleur's Brigade
1/52nd, 1/95th and 3rd Caçadores

INDEPENDENT PORTUGUESE BRIGADES 4,499

Pack's Brigade
1st Line (2 Batts.), 16th Line (2 Batts.),
    4th Caçadores
Bradford's Brigade
13th Line (2 Batts.), 14th Line
    (2 Batts.), 5th Caçadores

CAVALRY 4,025

Le Marchant's Brigade
3rd Dragoons, 4th Dragoons,
    5th Dragoon Guards
Anson's Brigade
11th Light Dragoons, 12th Light
    Dragoons, 16th Light Dragoons
V. Alten's Brigade
14th Light Dragoons, 1st Hussars KGL
Bock's Brigade
1st and 2nd Dragoons KGL
D'Urban's Brigade
1st and 11th Portuguese Dragoons

ARTILLERY 1,186
British (54 guns)
114 Portuguese (6 guns)

---

confident of being able to capture the whole. Unfortunately, de Espana had withdrawn his troops, much to the annoyance of an exasperated Wellington, and the French were able to make good their escape although hundreds of isolated and scattered fugitives were taken by Allied cavalry during the next few days.

The victory at Salamanca had cost Wellington 5,214 casualties of which 3,176 were British. The exact French casualty figure is hard to determine although it is fairly certain to have been around 14,000. Twenty guns were also taken. The battle of Salamanca nailed the belief that Wellington was just an over-cautious and defensive-minded commander and when news of the victory spread throughout Europe his reputation as one of the great commanders was assured.

On August 12th Wellington's army entered Madrid amidst much rejoicing by the people who could experience the feeling of freedom from French occupation for the first time since December 1808. The following month Wellington headed north-east to lay siege to Burgos but here the magic was to desert him during an operation which he himself was to call the worst scrape he was ever in.

Vittoria

June 21st 1813

The year of 1812 had positively glowed with success but it was to end inauspiciously with the failure to take the castle of Burgos, besieged by Wellington in September and October 1812. The Allied siege operations provided one of the unhappier sides to the campaign in the Peninsula but at least the army was successful on three occasions, albeit after some tremendous bludgeoning which cost the lives of hundreds of British soldiers. At Burgos, however, the operation was flawed from the start and a combination of bad weather, inadequate siege train and plain bad mismanagement caused a despondent Wellington to abandon the dreary place on October 19th.

The outcome of the whole sad episode was a retreat which, to those who had survived it, bore too many shades of the retreat to Corunna almost four years earlier. Once again the discipline of the army broke down, drunkenness was rife and hundreds of Wellington's men were left floundering in the mud to die or be taken prisoner by the French. It was little consolation to Wellington that while his army limped back to Portugal Napoleon too was about to see his own army disintegrate in the Russian snows. The retreat to Portugal finally ended in late November when the Allied army concentrated on the border, close to Ciudad Rodrigo. The year had thus ended in bitter disappointment for Wellington but nothing could hide the fact that taken as a whole 1812, the year of Ciudad Rodrigo, Badajoz and Salamanca, had seen the army achieve some of its greatest successes and once it had recovered it would embark on the road to even greater glory.

During the winter of 1812–13 Wellington contemplated his strategy for the forthcoming campaign. He received reinforcements which brought it up to a strength of around 80,000 men of whom 52,000 were British. The French believed that any Allied thrust

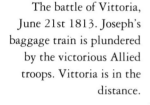

The battle of Vittoria, June 21st 1813. Joseph's baggage train is plundered by the victorious Allied troops. Vittoria is in the distance.

would have to be made through central Spain, an assumption Wellington fostered by sending Hill, with 30,000 men and six brigades of cavalry, in the direction of Salamanca. Wellington, in fact, accompanied Hill as far as Salamanca to help deceive the French further. The main Allied advance, however, would be made to the north, by the left wing of the army, some 66,000-strong, under Sir Thomas Graham, who would cross the Douro, march through northern Portugal and the Tras-o-Montes before swinging down behind the French defensive lines. The advance would be aimed at Burgos before moving on to the Pyrenees and finally into southern France. If all went well Wellington would be able to shift his supply bases from Lisbon to the northern coast of Spain and in so doing avoid over-extending his lines of communication.

The advance began on May 22nd 1813 and as the Allied army crossed the Portuguese border into Spain Wellington is reputed to have turned and waved his hat in the air, exclaiming, "Farewell, Portugal, for I shall never see you again." He was right.

Wellington left Hill's force on May 28th and joined Graham the following day. By June 3rd his entire force, numbering around 80,000 men, was on the northern side of the Douro, much to the surprise of the French who began to hurry north to meet them. Such was the speed of Wellington's advance that the French were forced to abandon Burgos, this time without any resistance, and the place was blown up by the departing garrison on June 13th. Wellington passed the town and on June 19th was just a short distance to the west of Vittoria which lay astride the great road to France.

The battlefield of Vittoria lay along the floor of the valley of the Zadorra, some six miles wide and ten miles in length. The eastern end of this valley was open and led to Vittoria itself while the other three sides of the valley consisted of mountains although those to the west were heights rather than mountains. The Zadorra itself wound its way from the south-west corner of the valley to the north where it ran along the foot of the mountains overlooking the northern side of the valley. The river was unpassable to artillery but was crossed by four bridges to the west of the valley and four more to the north.

The Passage of the River Esla, May 31st 1813. British infantry and cavalrymen help each other to gain the river bank after negotiating the rushing waters of the river, during which crossing a great deal of equipment was lost.

Wellington devised an elaborate plan of attack which involved dividing his army into four columns. On the right, Hill, with 20,000 men consisting of the 2nd Division and Morillo's Spaniards, was to gain the heights of Puebla on the south of the valley and force the Puebla pass. The two centre columns were both under Wellington's personal command. The right centre column consisted of the Light and 4th Divisions together with four brigades of cavalry, who were to advance through the village of Nanclares. The left centre column consisted of the 3rd and 7th Divisions which were to advance through the valley of the Bayas at the north-west corner of the battlefield and attack the northern flank and rear of the French position. The fourth column, under Graham, consisted of the 1st and 5th Divisions, Longa's Spaniards and two Portuguese brigades. Graham was to march around the mountains to the north and by entering the valley at its north-eastern corner was to severe the main road to Bayonne.

Joseph's French army numbered 66,000 men with 138 guns but although another French force under Clausel was hurrying up from Pamplona they would not arrive in time

and Joseph was to fight the battle with about 14,000 fewer men than Wellington.

On the morning of June 21st Wellington peered through his telescope and saw Joseph, Marshal Jourdan and General Gazan and their staffs gathered together on top of the hill of Arinez, a round hill that dominated the centre of the French line. It was a moist, misty morning and through the drizzle he saw, away to his right, Hill's troops as they made their way through the Heights of Puebla. It was here that the battle opened at about 8.30am when Hill's troops drove the French from their positions and took the heights.

Two hours later, away to the north-east, the crisp crackle of musketry signalled Graham's emergence from the mountains as his men swept down over the road to Bayonne, thus cutting off the main French escape route. Hereafter, Graham's troops probed warily westward and met with stiff resistance, particularly at the village of Gamara Mayor. Moreover, Wellington's instructions bade him to proceed with caution, orders which Graham obeyed faithfully. Although his column engaged the French in several hours of bloody fighting on the north bank of the Zadorra, it

The village of Gamara Mayor is carried by Robinson's brigade during the battle of Vittoria in this superb painting by James Beadle.

was not until the collapse of the French army late in the day that he unleashed the full power of his force upon the French.

There was little fighting on the west of the battlefield until at about noon when, acting upon information from a Spanish peasant, Wellington ordered Kempt's brigade of the Light Division to take the undefended bridge over the Zadorra at Tres Puentes. This was duly accomplished and brought Kempt to a position just below the hill of Arinez and while the rest of the Light Division crossed the bridge of Villodas Picton's 'Fighting' 3rd Division stormed across the bridge of Mendoza on their right. Picton was faced by two French divisions supported by artillery but these guns were taken in flank by Kempt's riflemen and were forced to retire having fired just a few salvoes. Picton's men rushed on and, supported by the Light Division and by Cole's 4th Division, which had also crossed at Villodas, the 3rd Division rolled over the French troops on this flank like a juggernaut. A brigade of Dalhousie's 7th Division joined them in their attack and together they drove the French from the hill of Arinez. Soon afterwards, what was once Joseph's vantage point was being used by Wellington to direct the battle.

It was just after 3pm and the 3rd, 7th and Light Divisions were fighting hard to force the French from the village of Margarita. This small village marked the right flank of the first French line and after heavy fighting the defenders were thrust from it in the face of overwhelming pressure from Picton's division. To the south of the hill of Arinez Gazan's divisions were still holding firm and supported by French artillery were more than holding their own against Cole's 4th Division. However, with Margarita gone the right flank of the French was left unprotected.

It was a critical time for Joseph's army. On its right, D'Erlon's division was being steadily pushed back by Picton, Dalhousie and Kempt, whose divisions seemed irresistible. Away to his left, Joseph saw Hill's corps streaming from the heights of Puebla whilst behind him Graham's corps barred the road home. Only Gazan's divisions held firm but when Cole's 4th Division struck at about 5pm the backbone of the French army snapped. Wellington thrust the 4th Division into the gap between D'Erlon and Gazan, as a wedge, and as the

British troops on the French right began to push D'Erlon back Gazan suddenly realised he was in danger of being cut off. At this point Joseph finally saw that he was left with little choice but to give the order for a general retreat.

The resulting disintegration of the French army was as sudden as it was spectacular. The collapse was astonishing as every man, from Joseph downwards, looked to his own safety. All arms and ammunition, equipment and packs were thrown away by the French in an effort to hasten their flight. It was a case of every man for himself. Only Reille's corps, which had been engaged with Graham's corps, managed to maintain some sort of order but even Reille's men could not avoid being swept along with the tide of fugitives streaming back towards Vittoria. With the collapse of all resistance Graham swept down upon what units remained in front of him but there was little more to be done but round up prisoners who were taken in their hundreds. The French

The 15th Hussars crossing the bridge at Tres Puentes, Vittoria.

British cavalry smash into the French rearguard during the closing stages of the battle of Vittoria.

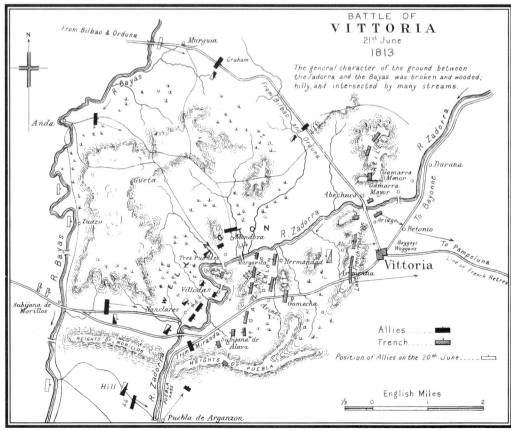

WELLINGTON'S ARMY AT VITTORIA
Total 79,000

1st Division, Kenneth Alexander Howard, 4,854
Stopford's Brigade,
1/Coldstream, 1/3rd Guards, 1 Coy 5/60th
Halkett's Brigade,
1st, 2nd, 5th Line KGL, 1st, 2nd, Light KGL

2nd Division, William Stewart, 10,834
Cadogan's Brigade,
1/50th, 1/71st, 1/92nd, 1 Coy 5/60th
Byng's or Walker's Brigade,
1/3rd, 1/57th, 1st Prov.Batt., 1 Coy 5/60th
O'Callaghan's Brigade,
1/28th, 2/34th, 1/39th, 1 Coy 5/60th
Ashworth's Portuguese Brigade,
6th Line, 18th Line, 6th Caçadores

3rd Division, Thomas Picton, 7,459
Brisbane's Brigade,
1/45th, 74th, 1/88th, 3 Coys 5/60th
Colville's Brigade,
1/5th, 2/83rd, 2/87th, 94th
Power's Portuguese Brigade,
9th Line, 21st Line, 11th Caçadores

4th Division, Lowry Cole, 7,826
Anson's Brigade,
2nd Prov.Batt., 3/27th, 1/40th, 1/48th, 1 Coy 5/60th
Skerrett's Brigade,

1/7th, 20th, 1/23rd, 1 Coy Brunswick Oels
Stubbs's Portuguese Brigade,
11th Line, 23rd Line, 7th Caçadores

5th Division, John Oswald, 6,725
Hay's Brigade,
3/1st, 1/9th, 1/38th, 1 Coy Brunswick Oels
Robinson's Brigade,
1/4th, 2/47th, 2/59th, 1 Coy Brunswick Oels
Spry's Portuguese Brigade,
3rd Line, 15th Line, 8th Caçadores

7th Division, Lord Dalhousie, 7,287
Barnes's Brigade,
1/6th, 3rd Prov. Batt. 1 Coy Brunswick Oels
Grant's Brigade,
51st, 68th, 1/82nd, Chasseurs Brittaniques
Le Cor's Portuguese Brigade,
7th Line, 19th Line, 2nd Caçadores

Light Division, Charles Alten, 5,484
Kempt's Brigade,
1/43rd, 1/95th, 3/95th, 1st Caçadores
Vandeleur's Brigade,
1/52nd, 17th Portuguese Line, 2/95th, 3rd Caçadores

Pack's Independent Portuguese Brigade,
1st Line, 16th Line, 4th Caçadores

Bradford's Independent Portuguese Brigade,
13th Line, 24th Line, 5th Caçadores
Silveira's Portuguese Division,
Da Costa's Brigade,
2nd Line, 14th Line
A. Campbell's Brigade,
4th Line, 10th Line, 10th Caçadores

Cavalry 7,424
R. Hill's Brigade,
1st and 2nd Life Guards, Horse Guards
Ponsonby's Brigade,
5th Dragoon Guards, 3rd and 4th Dragoons
G. Anson's Brigade,
12th Light Dragoons, 16th Light Dragoons
Long's Brigade,
13th Light Dragoons
V. Alten's Brigade,
14th Light Dragoons, 1st Hussars KGL
Bock's Brigade,
1st and 2nd Dragoons KGL
Fane's Brigade,
3rd Dragoon Guards, 1st Dragoons
Grant's Brigade,
10th, 15th and 18th Hussars

Artillery
3,000 British (78 guns)
300 Portuguese (12 guns)

---

abandoned the whole of their baggage train as well as 415 caissons, 151 of their 153 guns and 100 waggons. 2,000 prisoners were taken.

More incredible, however, was the fantastic amount of treasure abandoned by Joseph as he fled. The accumulated plunder acquired by him in Spain was abandoned to the eager clutches of the Allied soldiers who could not believe what they found. Almost never before nor since in the history of warfare has such an immense amount of booty been captured by an opposing force. Ironically, this treasure probably saved what was left of Joseph's army for while Wellington's men stopped to fill their pockets with gold, silver, jewels and valuable coins, the French were making good their escape towards Pamplona. Such was Wellington's anger at the behaviour of his men afterwards that he was prompted to write his famous letter to the Earl of Bathurst express-

ing his disgust and referring to some of his men as the 'scum of the earth'.

The Allies suffered 5,100 casualties during the battle while the French losses were put at around 8,000. The destruction of Joseph's army is hardly reflected in this figure, however, and the repercussions of the defeat were far reaching. News of Wellington's victory galvanised the Allies in northern Europe – still smarting after defeats at Lutzen and Bautzen – into renewed action and even induced Austria to enter the war on the side of the Allies. In England, meanwhile, there were wild celebrations the length of the country while Wellington himself was created Field Marshal. In Spain, Napoleon's grip on the country was severely loosened and there was now little but a few French-held fortresses between Wellington's triumphant army and France.

Pyrenees

July 25th to August 2nd 1813

With the French Army having been brushed aside at Vittoria there was nothing now standing between Wellington and the 'sacred soil' of France other than the rugged mountains of the Pyrenees. The French themselves were left in total disarray and a furious Napoleon ordered Joseph to relinquish his command of the army. This passed to Marshal Soult who was to provide Wellington with yet another stiff test before he could cross the border into France.

Before Wellington could continue his inexorable advance there were still two pockets of French resistance occupying the strongly-fortified towns of Pamplona and San Sebastian. These towns lay on the right and left flanks respectively of Wellington's army and would have to be taken before Wellington could turn his attention to crossing the Pyrenees themselves. Therefore, while Pamplona was blockaded the Allied siege train moved north to lay siege to San Sebastian.

The siege of San Sebastian was begun in early July 1813 but even as British troops began to pound away at the earth to dig the first parallels Soult, having restored some of the lost confidence to his shaken soldiers, was planning a counter-offensive through the Pyrenees. His suspicions that Wellington had over-extended himself were well founded for while 10,000 Allied troops under Graham lay siege to San Sebastian the rest of the 60,000 Allied troops between there and Pamplona were expected to hold a front some fifty miles long.

The battle of the Pyrenees is the collective name given to the actions that took place between July 25th and August 2nd 1813. The western Pyrenees were passable in numerous different places although it was only possible to feed artillery and waggons through the main passes at Roncesvalles, Maya and along the coast at Irun. Wellington had concentrated the bulk of his force around this latter crossing point, expecting Soult to make an attempt to relieve San Sebastian. Soult, however, had other plans and intended forcing the passes at Roncesvalles and Maya and from there advance upon Pamplona. Once having revictualled the

place and having made contact with Suchet to the south-east, he would then move north to march upon San Sebastian. In theory this would force Wellington to raise the siege and pull back to the west. Otherwise he risked seeing his army cut off and stranded along the north-eastern coast of Spain.

The right flank of Wellington's line, from Roncesvalles to Maya, was held by Hill. Echellar, to the west, was held by the 7th Division, the Light Division was at Vera whilst the left flank at Irun was held by Spanish troops. Cole's division was in reserve just behind Roncesvalles, the 6th Division was at Estevan on Hill's left, and Wellington's headquarters itself was established at Lesaca.

Soult planned his attack with meticulous detail and at dawn on July 25th 1813 his troops began to move forward from their various stations to begin simultaneous attacks on the passes at Maya and Roncesvalles.

The pass at Roncesvalles was held by about 13,000 men of Lowry Cole's 4th Division. The pass was dominated by two ridges on either side, the ridge on the west being held by Campbell's Portuguese brigade, and that to the east, upon which ran the only passable road, by Byng's brigade. The pass between the ridges, through which ran a small track, was held by Morillo's 3,500 Spaniards and the 1/57th.

The Allied troops barely had time to cook their breakfasts before they were attacked by six French divisions which Soult, who commanded the whole in person, divided into two columns, each of three divisions, one under Reille and the other under Clausel. Each of the columns numbered about 20,000 men.

Clausel's divisions attacked soon after 6am, advancing along the eastern ridge held by Byng's brigade. The French came on in overwhelming strength against the British piquets who numbered just five hundred men. However, each man in this frail piquet line was well protected by rocks which provided great cover, particularly for the company of the 5/60th which did great damage with its Baker rifles. Indeed, such was the opposition provided by these men that Clausel's divisions were held up for a full four hours. The attack here having stalled Clausel called back his men but shortly after noon it resumed and after three hours after intense pressure Byng's men were finally pushed back, ironically to a stronger position on the Altobiscar mountain. The problem with this new position was that it allowed Clausel to pass to the south-east and Orbaiceta from where he could outflank the right of the Allied position.

Reille's divisions attacked along the western ridge at about 2pm but once again the Allied piquet line held up a numerically stronger French force, another company of the 5/60th distinguishing themselves. Ross's troops were forced to use their bayonets in some close fighting until at about 4pm a dense fog descended on the battlefield to bring the fighting to an end.

Cole had been told by Wellington to hold his position at all costs but he imagined the entire French force to be creeping though the mist to encircle him. This was not the case but Cole was not prepared to stand and risk facing a night of confused fighting and instead withdrew his force back along the road to Pamplona.

While the battle for the pass of Roncesvalles was raging D'Erlon corps, numbering 21,000, advanced against the British troops holding the equally important pass at Maya. The main road from France via Urdax ran through this pass before continuing on to Pamplona. The pass itself was dominated to two mountains, the Gorospil to the east and the Alcorrunz to the west. Hill had entrusted the defence of the pass to two brigades of Stewart's 2nd Division, Cameron's and Pringle's, the former of these brigades being positioned to the west of the main road and the latter to the east.

At about 6am a strong enemy force was seen moving towards the Gorospil peak on which was positioned a single company of British infantry. Four more companies were rushed forward to join them and about four hours later the 350-odd unit was attacked in overwhelming strength by as many as 7,000 French infantry. The British manned a strong position amongst the rocks and crevices on the

Wellington, right, directs his troops during the battle of Sorauren, one of the battles of the Pyrenees.

peak but they could not be expected to hold out for long and after forty minutes of hard fighting the unit was all but wiped out and only a few dazed survivors managed to rejoin their comrades below. Three British battalions, the 2/34th, 1/28th and the 1/39th, were also thrown against the French but could not stop their advance and the ground to the east of the main road remained in French hands.

Cameron's three battalions witnessed the fighting from their positions to the west of the main road and one of them, the 1/50th, was sent to their assistance. It succeeded at first in stemming the immense blue tide that was sweeping down from the Gorospil peak and on to the Maya plateau but the French could not be stopped and the Kentish regiment was thrown back across the main road once more.

At this point Pringle sent forward half a battalion of the 1/92nd to try and halt the enemy advance. The 400 Scotsmen performed heroically amidst the heather and gorse-covered crest that must have reminded more than a few of them of the Highlands of their homeland. One historian called their display, 'one of the most magnificent exhibitions of courage and weapons efficiency in military history.' The Scots traded volleys with and held at bay an entire French division, the two sides pummelling away at each other amidst clouds of dense grey smoke from their muskets. The 92nd suffered heavy losses during their gallant effort but after twenty minutes they too were gradually forced back.

As the survivors of the 92nd fell back another French division appeared advancing up the Urdax road and by 4.30pm had overrun Cameron's camp to the west of the road giving them complete control of the pass. With French troops streaming down into the valley below the pass there was a very real threat that D'Erlon's corps would be able to push on in the direction of Pamplona. However, the French advance was checked at around 6pm with the arrival of Barnes's with the 1/6th and the 3rd Provisional Battalion which came bustling along from the west to attack the right flank of Maransin's division. The French were far more numerous but had covered several miles already that day and been involved in some of the fighting. Barnes's men were relatively fresh and together with the survivors of the 92nd halted the French columns with

their steady, controlled volleys of musketry. They were not able to clear the pass of French troops, however, which remained in enemy hands but the road to Pamplona was blocked and any further French progress thus thwarted. The day's fighting had cost Stewart's brigades 1,500 casualties, the French losing 2,000 men.

Following his withdrawal from Roncesvalles on July 25th Cole continued along the road to Pamplona and it was not until 8pm the following day that Wellington himself received news of the fight and of his unauthorised withdrawal. Wellington was not too dismayed, however, for the French could still be halted north-east of Zubiri. On the morning of July 27th, however, Wellington received news that Cole had retreated even further than this which certainly was annoying for both Cole and Picton, who had joined him on the 26th, were surrendering much territory which Wellington considered easily defensible.

Having learned that Cole was at Sorauren Wellington, accompanied only by Fitzroy Somerset, rode south to assume personal command. The hour immediately before the subsequent battle of Sorauren has provided us with two memorable incidents involving Wellington. The first came whilst he sat upon the small stone bridge in the village, writing a despatch to Murray, the Quartermaster General, who was to direct Pack's 6th Division, at the time marching to join him, forward by a new route so as to avoid Soult. Wellington was just finishing the note when a cry went up that French dragoons had entered the other end of the village. The Allied commander-in-chief quickly finished the note before leaping into the saddle and riding off out of the village with a ragged volley ringing out behind him. The second incident came when he rode up the ridge above the village, on which Cole's force was positioned. In riding forward Wellington had to pass his Portuguese troops who quickly recognised the lone rider dressed in civilian clothing. Immediately the shout went up, "Douro! Douro!" which was the name by which he was known to the Portuguese. The cry was taken up by the British troops and soon the whole British ridge was ringing out with the chant, much to the consternation of the watching French who suddenly realised who they were now dealing

The Pass of Maya, an old watercolour showing the pass from the French side. The camps of the 71st and 92nd are shown by the two lines on the right. The ridge in the centre is the Chemin des Anglais where half a battalion of the 92nd held up an entire French division.

with. In fact, Wellington purposely placed himself in a conspicuous position so that both armies knew exactly what the cheering was all about. As Napier put it, "The shrill clamour was taken up by the next regiments, swelling as it ran along the line into that stern and appalling shout which the British soldier is wont to give upon the edge of battle, and which no enemy ever heard unmoved." After two days of retreating British confidence was restored in contrast to the morale of Soult's men which plunged.

The Allied army, about 20,000-strong, was drawn up on a steep ridge – 'Cole's Ridge' it would be called later – to the south-east of Sorauren running east to west along a length of about one and a half miles. It was about 2,000 feet high. Soult's 35,000 troops were drawn up on the opposite ridge to the north. A couple of miles behind the ridge there was a second, sitting almost astride the Roncesvalles-Pamplona road, just to the south-east of the village of Huarte. This was held by Picton's 3rd Division, as well as O'Donnell's and Morillo's Spaniards.

As the afternoon of July 27th wore on Wellington felt more secure in the knowledge that a French attack was very unlikely now. Also, as each hour passed Pack's 6th Division drew closer and closer and by dawn on the 28th was expected to be on the ridge above Sorauren with the rest of the Allied force. Unfortunately, a tremendous storm broke which delayed Pack's arrival and it was not to be until just after noon that his men arrived. The storm did provide Wellington's men with some comfort, however, as they remembered the similar storm that broke on the eve of their great victory at Salamanca and in spite of the dreadful conditions upon the ridge the storm was considered a good omen for them.

The morning of July 28th was spent by Wellington watching for Pack's division which was finally spotted at around 10am. Pack's troops were, in fact, the first to be engaged at Sorauren when a French division advanced south from the village to attack them. These troops were flung back when Pack's men closed with them, Cole's skirmishers on the left flank assisting them in doing so. At around midday Soult launched five more divisions against Cole's main position on the ridge. The broken ground assisted the Allies in places and gave the attacking columns some problems. Nonetheless, Soult's columns came on in strength all the way along the ridge, pushing back the thin Allied skirmish line before them. As they approached the crest of the ridge the 3/27th and 1/48th suddenly appeared before them, silhouetted against the skyline. The resulting clash was reminiscent of Busaco as the British line emptied their muskets into the dense blue ranks of Frenchmen who were beaten back in disorder. On the left of the Allied line the French attacked with more vigour and succeeded in driving back the 7th Caçadores from around the small

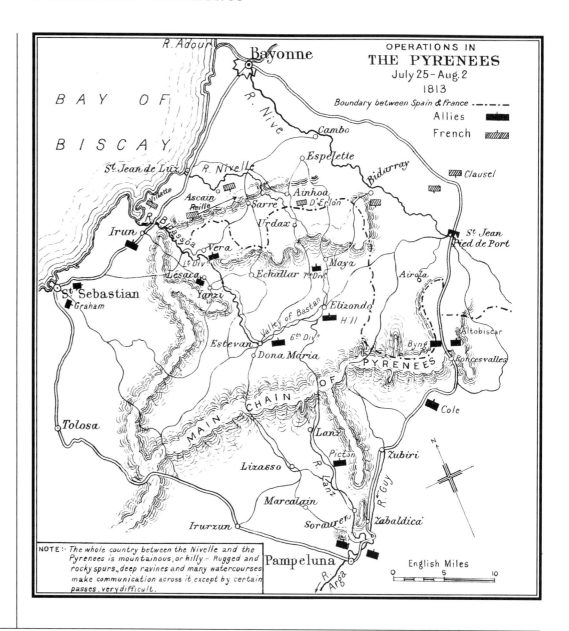

OPERATIONS IN THE PYRENEES
July 25 – Aug. 2
1813

Boundary between Spain & France ·—·—·—
Allies
French

NOTE :- *The whole country between the Nivelle and the Pyrenees is mountainous, or hilly.- Rugged and rocky spurs, deep ravines and many watercourses make communication across it, except by certain passes, very difficult.*

MAYA
Cameron's Brigade
1/50th, 1/71st, 1/92nd
Pringle's Brigade
1/28th, 2/34th, 1/39th, 2 Coys 5/60th

7th Division,
1/6th, 1/82nd, Brunswick Oels

RONCESVALLES
Byng's Brigade,
1/3rd, 1/57th, 1st Prov. Batt. (2/31st &
2/66th)
Ross's Brigade,
1/7th, 1/20th, 1/23rd, 1 Coy Brunswick
Oels
Campbell's Portuguese Brigade,

11th Line, 23rd Line, 7th Caçadores

SORAUREN (1st and 2nd Battles)
2nd Division,
Byng's Brigade,
1/3rd, 1/57th, 1st Prov. Batt. (2/31st &
2/66th)

3rd Division,
Brisbane's Brigade,
1/45th, 5/60th (4 Coys), 74th, 1/88th
Colville's Brigade,
1/5th, 2/83rd, 2/87th, 94th

4th Division,
Anson's Brigade,
3/27th, 1/40th, 1/48th 2nd Prov. Batt.
(2nd & 2/53rd)

Ross's Brigade,
1/7th, 1/20th, 1/23rd, 1 Coy Brunswick
Oels

6th Division,
Stirling's Brigade,
1/42nd, 1/79th, 1/91st, 1 Coy 5/60th
Lambert's Brigade,
1/11th, 1/32nd, 1/36th, 1/61st

7th Division,
Barnes's Brigade,
1/6th, 3rd Prov. Batt. (2/24th & 2/58th),
Brunswick Oels (9 Coys)
Inglis's Brigade,
51st, 68th, 1/82nd, Chasseurs
Brittaniques

chapel situated there. But once again the 3/27th and 1/48th advanced to break up and destroy each of the French battalions as they appeared by unleashing volley after volley followed by a swift bayonet charge.

To the east of the ridge the French had met with some success when Morillo's Spaniards were driven from the hill to the south-west of Zabaldica but when they reached the top of the hill they were confronted by the 1/40th in line. This single battalion was faced with an entire French brigade but as usual their formation gave them the advantage in firepower and after several minutes of sustained firing the French were sent reeling back down the hill in disarray.

This attack by Gauthier's brigade brought the day's fighting to a close for at 4.30pm Soult called a halt to the attack having lost around 4,000 men. The Allies themselves lost 2,652 of which 1,358 were British.

The two opposing armies remained on their respective ridges throughout July 29th, during which day both Hill's and Dalhousie's divisions marched towards Wellington at Sorauren. Soult, on the other hand, expected assistance from D'Erlon's three divisions which were marching south from Maya.

The first streaks of daylight on the morning of July 30th revealed Soult's men streaming northwards in retreat at which Wellington's guns opened up against the French troops still occupying the ridge opposite and in the village below. While Soult's men huddled for shelter from this brief bombardment British troops swept along the valley on the French left flank and up the ridge in front of them. The French were soundly thrashed here and driven back with heavy loss while those holding out in Sorauren itself were slaughtered trying to defend it from behind barricades. The fighting was virtually over by midday and Soult's troops were in full retreat everywhere and did not stop until they reached France. The 'second' battle of Sorauren had ended in bloody disaster for Soult who had failed in his objective to relieve Pamplona which was left to its fate.

Wellington, on the other hand, could again turn his attention to San Sebastian and to the invasion of France itself which would follow soon afterwards.

San Sebastian

July 25th to August 31st 1813

August 31st 1813 saw the third of the three great successful stormings carried out by Wellington's army during the Peninsular War. The siege operations on this occasion were conducted by Graham while Wellington was based at his headquarters in the Pyrenees at Lesaca.

With Soult having been thrown back across the French border there was no real reason to hurry the siege. There was little hope of there being any interference from any relieving enemy force and Graham was able to carry on the operations at a more leisurely pace than at Ciudad Rodrigo and Badajoz. On these latter two occasions, the close proximity of French relieving armies had forced Wellington to commit his troops to the assault before he was entirely satisfied with the condition of the breaches and as a result heavy casualties were sustained.

San Sebastian was rather a small town, situated on a low, sandy peninsula, dominated by a rocky mountain called Monte Orgullo, upon which was built a castle. The town was bordered on three sides by the waters of the Bay of Biscay and could only be approached by land from the south. To the east of the town flowed the river Urumea which at high water formed a sort of wide estuary. The town itself lay at the southern foot of Monte Orgullo and was separated from the castle by a line of defensive works. This meant that even in the event of the town falling to the Allies the castle was still defensible.

Graham chose the eastern wall of the town, standing about 27 feet high, as the target for his siege guns which were positioned upon the Chofre Sand Hills away to the east. Having blasted suitable breaches Graham's men would have to storm the place by crossing the Urumea at low tide.

Graham's 10,000-strong force began its

Into the breach. British troops at the storming of San Sebastian, August 31st 1813.

After four days of accurate, sustained fire the eastern wall of San Sebastian was reduced to a crumbling wreck and a practicable breach made with another, smaller breach being effected further to the north. Rey's artillery also suffered and was practically silenced although both the garrison and the Spanish population were kept busy all day and night clearing the rubbish from the walls and repairing defences in the breaches.

On August 30th Graham was satisfied with the state of the two breaches and gave orders that the place was to be stormed at noon the following day. The timing of the attack was, therefore, quite a departure from the normal practice of storming a town after dark. On this occasion, of course, the timing was purely dependent on the tide but what it did mean was that Graham's stormers would attack in full view of the defenders in broad daylight. It was not a pleasing prospect but the storming of a town afforded the British troops the chance of plunder and drink and of release from army discipline. They had acquired a taste for such things at Ciudad Rodrigo and Badajoz and no matter what obstacles were placed in their way they were not to be put off, nor would there would be any shortage of volunteers for the 'forlorn hope'.

Graham's plan involved an attack on the main breach by the 5th Division and Bradford's Portuguese, who were supported by 750 volunteers from the 1st, 4th and Light Divisions. Further to the north some 800 Portuguese volunteers would wade through the shallow waters of the Urumea and attack the smaller breach.

The morning of August 31st dawned bright and fresh after a night of heavy rain and thunderstorms and as the columns of British and Portuguese stormers formed up ready to begin the assault crowds of local people wearing their holiday clothes began to congregate in order to watch. When the signal for the assault was fired the Allied troops began to pick their way across the beach through shallow rocky pools to make their way towards the breaches which yawned silent, intimidating and invitingly before them. When the 'forlorn hope' approached the walls the watching French gunners opened up with a devastating blast of grapeshot that swept away half of 'the hope' in an instant.

For the next hour or so Graham watched

siege operations on June 28th but it was not until July 25th that the first assault was made by Oswald's 5th Division and Bradford's Portuguese brigade, neither of which was able to get inside the town which was defended by a brave and determined garrison of about 3,000 French troops under the command of General Rey.

During the next few days Soult launched his attack across the passes in the Pyrenees, an episode chronicled in the previous chapter, but with the attack having been repulsed, the Allies were able to turn their attention to San Sebastian once more.

On August 26th more siege guns arrived from England, Wellington now being able to supply his army through the ports along the coast of northern Spain, Passages in particular.

helplessly as his men were smashed against the defences while the spectators elsewhere watched in awe. The garrison proved as tenacious as those at Ciudad Rodrigo and Badajoz and all manner of shells, grenades and other combustibles were thrown down to explode amidst the columns of Allied infantry. The defenders lined the ramparts and opened up a withering fire into the attacking columns, bringing them grinding to a halt.

At this point Graham issued an order to Colonel Alexander Dickson, commanding the Allied artillery, an order based partly on inspiration and partly on desperation. Graham asked Dickson to open fire over the heads of the stormers and onto the French guns in the

Lieutenant Macguire, of the 4th (King's Own), leads the forlorn hope into the breach at San Sebastian. In order to make himself more conspicuous Macguire wore a white feather in his cap. It evidently made him too conspicuous, however, as he was shot dead soon afterwards. Another version of this painting by Beadle shows him wearing a cocked hat.

The storming of San Sebastian, August 31st 1813, the third of Wellington's successful sieges in the Peninsula.

BRITISH TROOPS AT THE STORMING OF SAN SEBASTIAN

Hay's Brigade,
3/1st, 1/9th, 1/38th
Robinson's Brigade,
1/4th, 2/47th, 2/59th,
  2 Coys Brunswick
  Oels
Spry's Portuguese Brigade,
3rd Line, 15th Line, 8th
  Caçadores

Volunteers:
1st Division volunteers,
From the Guards
  Brigades,
  KGL Brigade
4th Division volunteers,
From Ross's Brigade,
  Anson's Brigade,
  Stubbs's Portuguese
Light Division
  volunteers,
From Kempt's Brigade,
  Skerrett's Brigade,
  Portuguese Caçadores

Bradford's Portuguese,
13th Line, 24th Line,
  5th Caçadores

town. It was perhaps one of the earliest examples of a creeping barrage and was certainly a gamble, but it worked. The astonished British stormers pushed their faces to the ground as shot and shell screamed just a few feet overhead to crash into the French guns and defenders behind the ramparts. The stormers lay listening to this terrifying but pleasing symphony for about twenty minutes and when the guns lifted they stormed forward to carry the defences which had been torn apart by the guns. The breaches had all but been abandoned by the defenders and when a magazine exploded killing and wounding a large number of Frenchmen the town was as good as taken. As Graham watched from the sandhills he saw with relief his men disappear into the smoke as they drove the remaining French troops from the breaches.

San Sebastian was taken soon afterwards although the castle of La Mota held out until September 8th. Allied casualties were 856 killed and 1,520 wounded. The aftermath of the storming of San Sebastian was much the same as that at Ciudad Rodrigo and Badajoz as the victorious troops embarked upon an orgy of destruction which was made worse by a fire that engulfed the whole town. There were fierce accusations afterwards that Wellington himself had ordered the town to be put to the torch as it had been continuing to trade with France, accusations which Wellington denied although he might well have felt justified in resorting to such a measure.

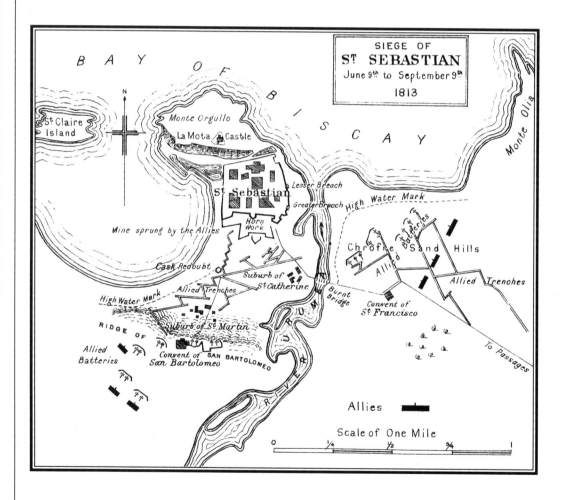

'The King, Mr President.' The two remaining unwounded officers of the 28th
Regiment toast each other after the battle of Albuera, May 16th 1811.

The 5th (Northumberland) Regiment in action, charging French cavalry at El Bodon, September 25th 1811.

British and French infantry clash at the battle of Salamanca, July 22nd 1812.

The 12th Light Dragoons at Salamanca, July 22nd 1812.

A fine portrait of an unidentified officer of the King's Dragoon Guards, c.1812.

An officer of the 6th Inniskilling Dragoons, 1811.

Lieutenant Colonel Robert Ross, 20th Regiment. Ross served in the Peninsula and after, before taking part in the North American War of 1812. He was killed at Baltimore in 1814.

Lieutenant Colonel Sir Henry Sullivan, Coldstream Guards, killed during the sortie from Bayonne on April 14th 1814.

The capture by the 14th Light Dragoons of King Joseph Bonaparte's carriage at Vittoria, June 21st 1813. While Wellington's men stopped to help themselves to the vast amount of treasure abandoned by Joseph, the French army was able to escape relatively unhindered, much to Wellington's exasperation.

The crossing of the Bidassoa, October 7th 1813. The 7th Hussars spearhead the crossing of the river with the Royal Horse Artillery and a column of infantry in close attendance .

The 85th Light Infantry in action against French redoubts during the battle of the Nivelle, November 10th 1813.

The 7th Hussars charging during the battle of Orthes, February 27th 1814.

'The Storming of San Sebastian, August 31st 1813' by Denis Dighton.

This tremendous painting shows Graham's stormers mounting the breaches at San Sebastian in the face of fierce French opposition. General Sir James Leith, whose 5th Division formed the bulk of the attacking troops, stands to the left of the painting, directing the stormers, while the waters of the Bay of Biscay lap against the walls of the town.

The road to Quatre Bras June 16th 1815. British troops hurry south to join in the fighting at Quatre Bras. The officer on the right still wears his silk stockings and dancing pumps, worn at the Duchess of Richmond's Ball the previous night.

The 42nd Highlanders at Quatre Bras. The Scottish troops are attacked by enemy lancers while carrying off the body of their commanding officer, Lieutenant Colonel Macara.

'After the Closing of the Gates at Hougoumont' by Ernest Crofts. The Foot Guards at Waterloo, June 18th 1815.

The 44th (East Essex) Regiment in square formation against French cavalry at Quatre Bras .

The 71st Highlanders in action at Waterloo.

The charge of Somerset's Household Brigade at Waterloo.

Ponsonby's Union Brigade charges at Waterloo with devastating results.

Sergeant Charles Ewart in action at Waterloo capturing the eagle of the French 45th Regiment.

Another view of the Household Brigade charging at Waterloo. Wellington watches, left, as the charge begins.

The 42nd Highlanders in action at Corunna, January 16th 1809.

The 1st King's Dragoon Guards at Waterloo, June 18th 1815.

An officer of the 95th Rifles, 1812.

Ensign John Edward Cornwallis Rous, Coldstream Guards, c.1812. Rous saw action at Salamanca, Vittoria, Nivelle, and the Nive.

'The Decisive Charge of the Life Guards at Waterloo.'

Captain Clark-Kennedy and Corporal Stiles, of the 1st Royal Dragoons, capturing the eagle of the 105th Regiment at Waterloo.

'The Battle of Waterloo, June 18th 1815.' The dead officer in the foreground is Picton. Wellington raises his hat for all to see, left.

'Drive them back, 13th!' Lord Hill gives the 13th Light Dragoons the order to charge at Waterloo, 1815.

The 7th Hussars charging French dragoons at Waterloo.

A British officer calls upon the Old Guard to surrender during the closing stages of the battle of Waterloo.

Nivelle

November 10th 1813

On the very day that San Sebastian fell to the Allies Soult made one last desperate attempt to relieve the place. The attempt ended in failure, however, and the relieving troops were ordered to withdraw. Consequently, 10,000 French troops under Vandermaesen pulled back towards Vera and the fords there across the Bidassoa river which they had crossed that morning. Unfortunately for them, the level of the river had risen dramatically and the only way across the river was via the bridge which spanned the Bidassoa at Vera.

However, as they approached it they found their way blocked by Captain Daniel Cadoux of the 95th Rifles. The French were left with little choice but to attack Cadoux and his small party of men whom the French thought would take little brushing aside. In the event, Cadoux held on for two hours, inflicting 231 casualties on the French including Vandermaesen himself, who was killed. Whilst the fighting was in progress Cadoux sent repeated requests to General Skerrett, acting commander of the Light Division and who was aware of the action, but he did nothing, otherwise the whole of the French division might have been forced to surrender. No support was given to Cadoux and finally the 95th were forced to give way. The brave Cadoux was killed along with sixteen of his men while three other officers and 43 men were wounded. With the withdrawal of the 95th the French were able to gain the safety of the opposite side of the river.

There was no let up in the Allied operations following the fall of San Sebastian. The winter rains were due and Wellington was anxious that his army get as far into France as was possible before the condition of the roads became too bad. At dawn on October 7th Wellington's army crossed the Bidassoa, the first of a series of rivers that had to be negotiated before he could push on into the heart of France. Waiting to guide the British troops across were some local shrimpers who led the men out across the river which, in spite of its wide estuary, came up only as far as the men's waists at most. The audacious crossing caught the French by surprise all the way along the river and as Wellington's men scrambled on to the opposite bank the French troops made good their escape and only in a few places did they remain to dispute the crossing. By the end of the day the operation to cross the Bidassoa had been a complete success with just 1,200 Allied casualties against 1,700 French.

Once across the Bidassoa and having established his army in France Wellington's next objective was to clear away the French from their positions in front of the River Nivelle. Soult's lines stretched from the shores of the Atlantic on the French right flank to the snow-covered pass of Roncesvalles on the left while the sixteen miles between the pass of Maya and the sea roughly followed the line of the Nivelle, thus giving us the battle's name.

The line was marked by a series of hills upon the summits of which the French had constructed strong redoubts, some containing artillery. These redoubts ran from Finodetta on the extreme left flank of the French position, to Fort Socoa, on the coast opposite St Jean de Luz. Although Soult's overall position grew in strength as he fell back on his base at Bayonne, he did not have enough men to man the lines in depth and was severely overstretched, the twenty miles of front being defended by just 63,000 men. Wellington's force, on the other hand, numbered 80,000 although 20,000 of these were Spanish troops, many of whom were as yet untried in battle.

Wellington planned to advance along the whole length of Soult's line but would concentrate his attack on the centre in particular. Any breakthrough here, or on the French left flank, would enable his men to swing north and cut off the French right flank. On the Allied left, Sir John Hope would advance with the 1st and 5th Divisions and Freire's Spaniards. Beresford would lead the main Allied attack against the French centre with the 3rd, 4th, 7th and Light Divisions, while on the Allied right Hill would attack with the 2nd and 6th Divisions, supported by Morillo's Spaniards and Hamilton's Portuguese. All preparations for the attack having been made, Wellington decided to attack on November 10th.

The French defensive line was dominated

by the Greater Rhune, a gorse-covered, craggy mountain some 2,800 feet high. The mountain is fairly accessible to anyone on foot, the rocky spurs only becoming impassable towards the top and on the eastern side. Separated from the Greater Rhune by a ravine, some 700 yards below it, is the Lesser Rhune along the precipitous crest of which the French had constructed three defensive positions. If the French defences on La Rhune could be taken, Soult's position would become very precarious as his lines would then be open to Allied attacks from different directions.

The summit of the Greater Rhune was occupied by French troops but, following the crossing of the Bidassoa and the subsequent clearing of the French from their positions along the Bayonet Ridge above Vera, they evacuated it, fearing an outflanking movement that would leave them cut off from their own forces. Before he could consider attacking the redoubts he first had to turn his attention to the French defenders along the crest of the Lesser Rhune. This position was a strong one as the southern face of it could not be assaulted owing to the precipitous slopes that led to the summit. It was possible, however, to attack the three fortified positions by moving down into the ravine before turning to the left which would enable the attacking force to take the French in their flank and sweep them from the crest. Wellington chose the Light Division for the task.

Shortly before dawn on November 10th the division carefully picked its way down from the top of the Greater Rhune and into the ravine in front of the Lesser Rhune. Once this had been done the men were ordered to lie down and wait for the order to attack. Suddenly, British guns fired from the top of the nearby Mount Atchubia as the signal for the attack to begin. The men of the 43rd, 52nd and 95th – with the 17th Portuguese Caçadores in support – swept forward up the steep slopes to assault the French positions that ran along the crest to flush the defenders from their rocky redoubts. The men were exhausted by their efforts but the surprise and boldness of their attack won the day and soon those defenders who had not been killed or taken were tumbling down the Rhune towards the redoubts atop the hills below.

Wellington and his staff atop the Rhune mountain during the battle of the Nivelle, November 10th 1813.

WELLINGTON'S ARMY AT THE NIVELLE
TOTAL 88,816 – 63,140 British + Portuguese, 25,673 Spaniards

1st Division, Kenneth Alexander Howard, 6,898
Maitland's Brigade,
1/1st Guards, 3/1st Guards
Stopford's Brigade,
1/Coldstream, 1/3rd Guards
Hinuber's German Brigade,
1st, 2nd and 5th Line, 1st and 2nd Light Batts. KGL

2nd Division, William Stewart, 8,480
Walker's or Barnes's Brigade,
1/50th, 1/71st, 1/92nd
Byng's Brigade,
1/3rd, 1/57th, 1st Prov. Batt.
Pringle's Brigade,
1/28th, 2/34th, 1/39th
Ashworth's Portuguese Brigade,
6th Line (2 Batts.), 18th Line (2 Batts.), 6th Caçadores

3rd Division, Charles Colville, 7,334
Brisbane's Brigade,
1/45th, 74th, 1/88th, 5/60th
Keane's Brigade,
1/5th, 2/83rd, 2/87th, 94th
Power's Portuguese Brigade,
9th Line (2 Batts.), 21st Line (2 Batts.), 11th Caçadores

4th Division, Lowry Cole, 6,585
Anson's Brigade,

3/27th, 1/40th, 1/48th, 2nd Prov. Batt.
Ross's Brigade,
1/7th, 20th, 1/23rd
Vasconcello's Portuguese Brigade,
11th Line (2 Batts.), 23rd Line (2 Batts.), 7th Caçadores

5th Division, James Hay, 4,553
Greville's Brigade,
3/1st, 1/9th, 1/38th
Robinson's Brigade,
1/4th, 2/47th, 2/59th
De Regoa's Portuguese Brigade,
3rd Line (2 Batts.), 15th Line (2 Batts.), 8th Caçadores

6th Division, Henry Clinton, 6,729
Pack's Brigade,
1/42nd, 1/79th, 1/91st
Lambert's Brigade,
1/32nd, 1/39th, 1/61st
Douglas's Portuguese Brigade,
8th Line (2 Batts.), 12th Line (2 Batts.), 9th Caçadores

7th Division, Carlos Le Cor, 6,068
Barnes's Brigade,
1/6th, 3rd Prov. Batt. Brunswick Oels
Inglis's Brigade,
51st, 68th, 1/82nd, Chasseurs Brittaniques
Doyle's Portuguese Brigade,
7th Line (2 Batts.), 19th Line (2 Batts.),

2nd Caçadores

Light Division, Charles Alten, 4,970
Kempt's Brigade,
1/43rd, 1/95th, 3/95th, 17th Line
Colborne's Brigade,
1/52nd, 2/95th, 1st and 3rd Caçadores,

Hamilton's Portuguese Division, 4,949
Da Costa's Brigade,
4th Line (2 Batts.), 10th Line (2 Batts.), 10th Caçadores
Buchan's Brigade,
2nd Line (2 Batts.), 14th Line (2 Batts.),

Independent Brigades
Aylmer's British Brigade,
76th, 2/48th, 85th
Wilson's Portuguese Brigade,
1st Line (2 Batts.), 16th Line (2 Batts.), 4th Caçadores
Bradford's Portuguese Brigade,
13th Line, (2 Batts.), 24th Line (2 Batts.), 5th Caçadores

Artillery 848
5 British Batteries
3 Portuguese Batteries

Spanish Troops 25,673
4 Divisions

While the 43rd and 95th were going about their business, there still remained one very strong star-shaped fort down below on the Mouiz plateau which reached out towards the coast. This was attacked by Colborne's 52nd Light Infantry, supported by riflemen from the 95th. Once again, surprise was the key to their success and as they sprang up from their positions in front of the fort the startled French defenders, in danger of being cut off, quickly fled leaving Colborne in possession of the fort and other trenches. It had been accomplished without hardly a single casualty.

Following this, Wellington's main assault began as nine Allied divisions advanced on a front of five miles, French opposition melting away before them, and when the bridge at Amotz fell to the 3rd Division – it was the only lateral communication between the left and right halves of the French army – Soult's

position fell with it. This meant that the Soult's army was effectively cut in two. By 2 o'clock in the afternoon the French were defeated and were in full retreat across the Nivelle having lost 4,351 men to Wellington's 2,450. Napier's verdict on the day was as eloquent and dramatic as usual. "The plains of France were to be the prize of battle, and the half-famished soldiers, in their fury, were breaking through the iron barrier erected by Soult as if it were a screen of reeds."

Wellington might have pursued the defeated French even further and there was a very real chance that he might cut off the French right flank. However, darkness was falling and, never one to risk the perils of a night attack, he called a halt to the day's proceeding and his men camped that night upon the ground they had won during the day.

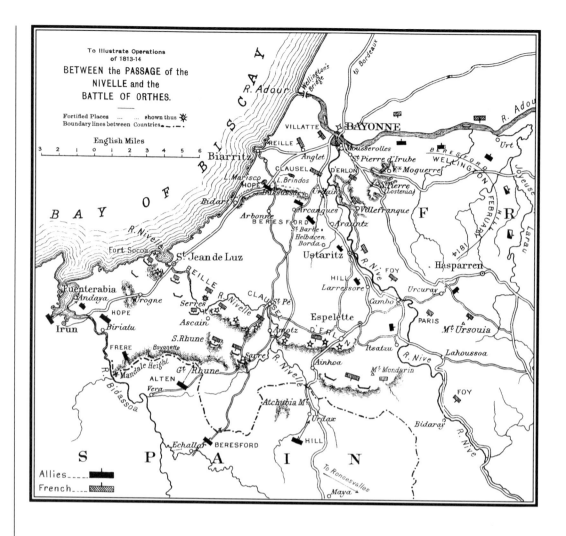

Nive

December 9th–13th 1813

At the end of the battle of the Nivelle Soult withdrew his forces to the area immediately around the strongly-defended town of Bayonne. Throughout the Peninsular War Bayonne had been the main depot for the French Army and was fiercely loyal to Napoleon. The town's defences were based on the sound principles laid down by the great French engineer, Vauban. To the west of the town lay the Atlantic and on the east the river Adour. On the northern bank of the Adour lay a strong citadel which commanded the town, while the ground to the south of Bayonne was bisected by streams, woods and enclosures, the ground itself being very muddy and soft after several days of hard rain.

Wellington planned to approach the town from both the south and east, an advance from this latter direction being intended to threaten Soult's communications with the interior of the country. In deciding upon this course of action Wellington was taking a calculated gamble as he would have to divide his army in two, part of it advancing along the Atlantic coast from the south, while the remainder would cross the river Nive – which flows south-east from Bayonne – and approach from the east.

Soult himself had established a defensive line running south-east from Bayonne along the right bank of the Nive as far as Cambo. The line was defended in strength and a flotilla of boats on the Adour enabled troops to be ferried from one bank of the Nive to the other without any trouble.

The Allied army was reduced in numbers at

this stage of the war following Wellington's decision to send all the Spanish troops, except Morillo's, back to Spain. This was as a result of numerous unsavoury incidents involving the Spaniards who sought revenge after years of French persecution. Disorder was rife amongst them, something which Wellington could ill-afford. He could not risk the possibility of a resistance movement similar to that which had dogged the occupying French in Spain and so ordered them home. Nevertheless, Wellington still had 63,500 men at his disposal, slightly less than Soult, but had a distinct numerical advantage in cavalry, 8,000 against Soult's 600. Unfortunately, there was little scope for effective use of cavalry over the ground around Bayonne.

The operations against Bayonne were hampered by bad weather and it was not to be until December 9th that the operation to cross the river Nive got under way when Hill, with the 2nd Division and Le Cor's Portuguese division, crossed at fords close to Cambo, while Beresford, with the 3rd and 6th Divisions, were to cross the Nive by pontoon bridge at Ustaritz.

Having seen Wellington divide his army

Soult was quick to seize his opportunity and on the evening of December 9th, amidst heavy rain, some 50,000 troops under D'Erlon began to move silently forward from Bayonne ready for the attack the next day. Shortly after dawn on the gloomy, misty morning of December 10th Hope's 1st and 5th Divisions, some 30,000 troops, were attacked and driven from Anglet by D'Erlon who then advanced as far as Barouillet. On Hope's right the Light Division was attacked and driven back two miles to the village of Arcangues where it held on grimly throughout the rest of the day in what was one of the most peculiar duels of the Peninsular War.

The church at Arcangues was quickly crowded with men of the 1/43rd who were soon engaged in a duel with some French artillery. The Light Division had been pushed back by four French divisions before finally drawing itself up on a position on a ridge astride the village of Arcangues. The French guns were situated on some ground about 400 yards from the church and presented an excellent target to the highly trained and experienced veterans of the 43rd. The old church was and still is lined by galleries inside which

An old watercolour, showing the centre of Hill's position during the battle of St Pierre, from the Bayonne side. The 92nd charged down the road in the centre while the coppice wood on the left was defended by the 50th and the Portuguese.

were quickly manned, the 43rd smashing in the windows to open fire while others threw themselves into firing positions in the churchyard. Although the church was hit about eight times by round shot that smacked into the walls the 43rd's marksmen wrested the initiative from the exposed French gunners, forcing them to withdraw leaving the British as victors and having left behind them 12 guns.

Throughout the next two days heavy fighting raged across the area as Soult attempted to throw back Wellington's force that remained on the left bank of the Nive. The attempt failed, however, and so Soult turned his attention to Hill's force, numbering about 14,000 men, which was still on the right bank of the river. The British force here had been severely reduced when Wellington ordered Beresford

to recross to the left bank following Soult's attack on the 10th. To meet the impending threat against Hill Wellington again ordered Beresford to return to the right bank but the pontoon bridge connecting the two halves of the Allied army was swept away on the night of the 12th after heavy rain had caused the river to swell. This left Hill isolated with a relatively small force which was now attacked by 35,000 French troops who had come forward from their positions in and around Bayonne.

The ensuing battle, although officially part of the battle of the Nive, is often called the battle of St Pierre by the British, the French choosing to call it Mouguerre after a small village above which now stands an obelisk to the memory of Marshal Soult.

The battle of St Pierre was a bloody one and

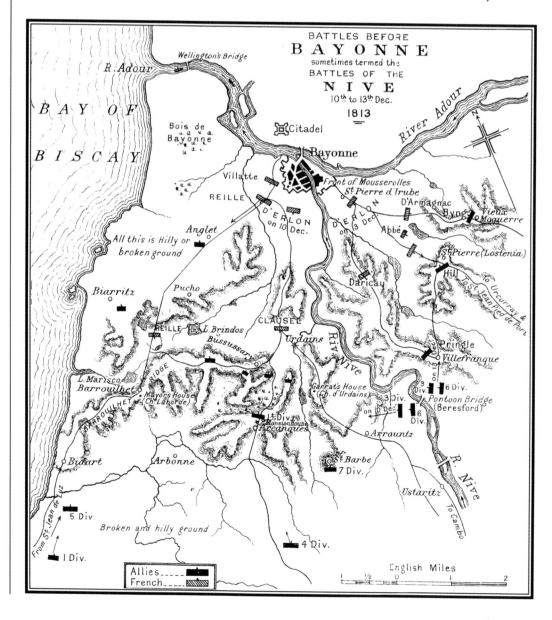

for Hill a close one which swayed one way and then the next as troops on both sides were thrown helter-skelter into the action. Ground lost by the Allies was regained at bayonet point until by noon Hill was throwing in the last of his reserves. However, with the pontoon bridge at Villefranque having been repaired, two British divisions, the 4th and 3rd, were thrown across, the 6th coming up from Ustaritz, and by the time Wellington arrived Hill was assured of victory. Wellington's arrival heralded the start of a general advance which forced Soult back into Bayonne. It was a close call – Napier, the great historian of the war, called it the most desperate of the whole campaign – and losses were high, 1,500 on the Allied side and about 3,500 on the French.

When Soult returned to Bayonne he no doubt reflected on his failure to defeat Wellington having attacked half of the Allied force with the whole of his own on two occasions. His attack had failed, however, and the morale of his troops sank even further. In order to avoid being cut off in Bayonne he withdrew the bulk of his force east along the Adour after leaving about 10,000 troops under General Thouvenot to defend Bayonne.

The battle of the Nive brought an end to the year's campaigning and the Allied troops settled into camps to the south and east of Bayonne as the cold winter weather set in. As one officer of the Coldstream Guards wrote, "Thus ended the campaign of 1813, commenced on the Douro and concluded on the Adour." It was the crossing of that river which would mark the resumption of Wellington's operations in 1814.

BRITISH TROOPS AT THE BATTLE OF THE NIVE
No accurate number is available as the battle lasted four days.

1st Division,
Howard's Brigade,
1/1st Guards, 3/1st Guards, 1 Coy 5/60th
Stopford's Brigade, 1/Coldstream,
   1/3rd Guards, 1 Coy 5/60th
Hinuber's Brigade,
1st, 2nd and 5th Line KGL
Halkett's Brigade,
1st and 2nd Light Batts. KGL

2nd Division,
Barnes's Brigade,
1/50th, 1/71st, 1/92nd
Byng's Brigade
1/3rd, 1/57th, 1st Prov. (1/31st &
   2/66th)
Pringle's Brigade,
1/28th, 2/34th, 1/39th
Ashworth's Portuguese Brigade,
6th Line, 18th Line, 8th Caçadores

5th Division
Greville's Brigade,
3/1st, 1/9th, 1/38th
Robinson's Brigade,
1/4th, 2/47th, 2/59th, 2/84th
Lord Aylmer's Brigade,
2/62nd, 76th, 85th
De Regoa's Portuguese Brigade,
3rd Line, 15th Line, 8th Caçadores

6th Division,
Pack's Brigade,
1/42nd, 1/79th, 1/91st, 1 Coy 5/60th
Lambert's Brigade,
1/11th, 1/32nd, 1/36th, 1/61st
Douglas's Portuguese Brigade,
8th Line, 12th Line, 9th Caçadores

Light Division,
Kempt's Brigade,
1/43rd, 1/95th, 3/95th

Colborne's Brigade,
1/52nd, 2/95th
Portuguese Brigade,
1st and 3rd Caçadores, 17th Line

Le Cor's Portuguese Division
Da Costa's Brigade,
2nd Line, 14th Line,

Buchan's Brigade,
4th Line, 10th Line, 4th Caçadores

Bradford's Portuguese Brigade,
13th Line, 24th Line, 5th Caçadores

Campbell's Portuguese Brigade,
1st Line, 16th Line, 4th Caçadores

Cavalry
13th Light Dragoons, 14th Light
   Dragoons, 16th Light Dragoons

Orthes

February 27th 1814

On the morning of February 23rd 1814 the left wing of the Allied army under Sir John Hope began its daring but hazardous crossing of the Adour to the west of Bayonne. The Coldstream and 3rd Foot Guards, supported by riflemen of the 5/60th, crossed the river in small groups, each party being ferried across the river in small rafts. By the end of the day a bridgehead was established and even a French counter-attack failed to stop the operation when a brace of rockets came fizzing in amongst them, sending the startled Frenchmen running for cover. By the afternoon of February 26th a bridge of boats had been constructed across the river which enabled Hope to get some 8,000 men across to the north bank. Bayonne was now completely surrounded and the blockade of the town began.

The day after Hope's blockade began Wellington, with the main Allied field army, fought a major battle at Orthes, some thirty-five miles away to the east. On February 26th Beresford had crossed the Gave de Pau with the 4th and 7th Divisions near Peyrehorade, pushing Soult back towards Orthes. The 3rd Division forded the river at Berenx while Wellington himself brought up the 6th and Light Division, plus a force of cavalry, across on a pontoon bridge which had been thrown across the Gave, also at Berenx. Hill, meanwhile, with the 2nd Division and Le Cor's Portuguese division, marched to the south of Orthes, passing to the east of the town but remaining on the south bank of the Gave.

On the morning of February 27th Wellington had with him on the northern bank of the Gave some 38,000 infantry and 3,300 cavalry as well as 54 guns. Soult's army, about 7,000 less with six fewer guns, occupied a strong position along a ridge which ran north from Orthes for about a mile before running west for three miles from the bend in the main Bayonne-Orthes road. This ran along the ridge, to the small village of St Boes upon which Soult rested his right flank. Soult's troops occupied the whole length of this ridge from which three very prominent spurs extended south towards the Gave. The spur on the extreme western edge of the ridge does not actually connect with the ridge itself, being separated by a few hundred yards. The remains of an old Roman camp were situated on the forward edge of the spur and would feature prominently in the battle.

The engagement opened shortly after 8.30am on the cold, frosty morning of February 27th when a battalion of French infantry was driven from the church and

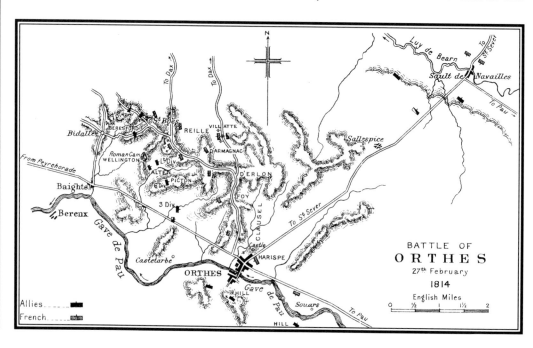

churchyard of St Boes by the 1/7th, 1/20th and 1/23rd, who made up Ross's brigade of the 4th Division. The brigade advanced further east along the ridge to clear the rest of the village but it came under fire from French artillery and could go no further. French troops under Taupin were then sent to recover the village and St Boes became the scene of severe house-to-house fighting as both sides struggled for its possession.

While the fight for St Boes flickered and flared Picton's 3rd Division entered the fray, attacking Soult's centre. His troops advanced up the two centre spurs but were held up by French artillery that swept the crests of the spurs, inflicting heavy casualties. The attack here was only intended to be a demonstration, however, and he pulled his troops back leaving just his strong skirmishing line of light troops and riflemen to prod and probe the French line, something which they continued to do for the next two hours.

Meanwhile, the fighting in St Boes intensified until at about 11.30 Wellington gave orders for an assault along the whole length of his line, leaving part of the Light Division only in reserve at the Roman Camp from where Wellington watched the progress of the fight.

On the Allied left Brisbane's brigade of the 3rd Division began to push its way up the eastern-most spur with the 6th Division following behind. At St Boes, the 4th Division was replaced by the 7th Division, while the 1/52nd advanced from the Roman camp to deliver an attack on the French brigade on the right flank of the advancing 7th Division.

These attacks were pressed home vigorously but French resistance was stiff and it was to take the advancing British columns about two hours of hard fighting to drive the French from the spurs. This was not accomplished without loss, particularly to the 1/88th, three companies of which suffered heavy losses when a squadron of French cavalry, the 21st Chasseurs, charged and overran them after catching them in line. The French cavalry suffered similarly when they received the return fire from Picton's men, half of their number being killed or wounded.

British cavalry in action at the battle of Orthes, February 27th 1814.

The French troops along the ridge were being severely pressurised by Wellington's attacking columns but it was the advance by the 1/52nd, under Colborne, that decided the day. This battalion entered the fight in support of the Walker's 7th Division just at the moment when this division, along with Anson's brigade of the 4th Division, was finally driving the French from the body-choked village of St Boes. The 52nd advanced almost knee-deep in mud but when it reached the crest of the spur, it took Taupin's division in its left flank. Taupin's men were driven back by Colborne's determined charge and fell in with those retreating from St Boes. In so doing, they precipitated a degree of panic which caused the collapse of the entire French right. It was now about 2.30 in the afternoon and with Wellington's triumphant troops pouring along the main road on top of the ridge, the day was as good as won.

At first, Soult's army began to fall back in an orderly manner with the divisions of Villatte and Harispe drawn up on his left flank to cover the withdrawal. However, Hill's corps had crossed the Gave to the east of Orthes and fell upon Harispe's division, driving it back upon Villatte. The controlled retreat soon became a panic-stricken flight which spread along the whole of the French line, Soult's men discarding great loads of equipment to facilitate their retreat to the north-east towards Toulouse.

The battle of Orthes cost Wellington 2,164 casualties while Soult's losses were put at around 4,000 including 1,350 prisoners, a number which would have been far greater had not Wellington been slightly wounded towards the end of the battle which caused him to halt and incapacitated him for the next few days. The wound was his third of the war but at least he could rest that night with the satisfaction of knowing that there was little now standing between himself and the final victory over the French.

WELLINGTON'S ARMY AT ORTHES
Total, 44,402

2nd Division, William Stewart, 7,780
Barnes's Brigade,
1/50th, 1/71st, 1/92nd, 1 Coy 5/60th
Byng's Brigade,
1/3rd, 1/57th, 2/31st, 1/66th,
   1 Coy 5/60th
O'Callaghan's Brigade,
1/28th, 2/34th, 1/39th, 1 Coy 5/60th

3rd Division, Thomas Picton, 6,626
Brisbane's Brigade,
1/45th, 5/60th, 74th, 1/88th
Keane's Brigade,
1/5th, 2/83rd, 2/87th, 94th
Power's Portuguese Brigade,
9th Line, 21st Line, 11th Caçadores

4th Division, Lowry Cole, 5,952
Anson's Brigade,
3/27th, 1/40th, 1/48th
Ross's Brigade,

1/7th, 1/20th, 1/23rd
Vasconcello's Portuguese Brigade,
11th Line, 23rd Line, 7th Caçadores

6th Division, Clinton,
Pack's Brigade,
1/42nd, 1/91st, 1/79th (absent)
Lambert's Brigade,
1/61st, 1/32nd, 1/36th, 1/11th
Douglas's Portuguese Brigade,
8th Line, 12th Line, 9th Caçadores

7th Division, Walker, 5,643
Gardiner's Brigade,
1/6th, 2/24th, 2/56th, Brunswick
   Oels
Inglis's Brigade,
68th, 1/82nd, Chasseurs Brittaniques,
   51st (absent)
Doyle's Portuguese Brigade,
7th Line, 19th Line, 2nd Caçadores

Light Division, Alten, 3,480
1/52nd, 2/95th, 3/95th,
1st and 3rd Caçadores, 17th Line,

Le Cor's Portuguese Division, 4,465
Da Costa's Brigade,
2nd Line, 14th Line
Buchan's Brigade,
4th Line, 10th Line, 10th Caçadores

Cavalry, 3,373
Fane's Brigade,
13th Light Dragoons,
   14th Light Dragoons
Vivian's Brigade,
18th Hussars, 1st Hussars KGL
Somerset's Brigade,
7th Hussars, 10th Hussars, 15th Hussars

Artillery, 6 British and 1 KGL
   battery,   1,052
1 Portuguese battery, 110

Toulouse

April 10th 1814

Wellington's victorious army was too tired to give immediate chase to the defeated French after the battle of Orthes but on March 2nd caught up with it at Aire. In the ensuing fight the Allies lost 150 men before hastening the French on their way. The pursuit stalled here, however, due to political expediency, for Beresford, with the 4th and 7th Divisions, marched north to Bordeaux which was given up to the him on March 12th. The 7th Division remained in Bordeaux while Beresford returned with the 4th Division to rejoin Wellington on March 16th.

There were further clashes between the two armies as Soult continued his retreat to Toulouse, notably at Vic Bigorre on March 19th and at Tarbes the following day, an action which Wellington later called the sharpest fight of the war.

Soult finally entered Toulouse on March 24th. His first task was to issue fresh arms and ammunition, clothes and supplies to his men.

8,000 French troops were without shoes and thousands more lacked even the most basic of equipment, much of it having been abandoned during the pursuit from Orthes. Fortunately, Toulouse was a main French army depot and stocks and supplies were plentiful. Reinforcements were also to be found here which made good some of the losses of the previous few weeks.

The city of Toulouse was surrounded by a high wall, flanked with towers, but the defences were not constructed along the lines laid down by Vauban and were nowhere near as strong as those at any of the other main towns besieged by Wellington. The wide river Garonne flows to the west of Toulouse and was a major obstacle. On the left bank of the river was the fortified suburb of St Cyprien while to the east lay the suburbs of St Etienne and Guillemerie. To the north and east of the city flowed the Languedoc Canal and even farther still to the east was the river Ers. The key to

The attack on Toulouse by the 6th Division of Wellington's Army, April 10th 1814.

The battle of Toulouse, showing the attack on the French defences along the Calvinet Ridge.

the city, however, was the Calvinet ridge which ran between the Ers and the canal to the east of the city. In fact, the feature called the Calvinet was two ridges, the second actually being Mont Rave. The ridge, standing some 600 feet high, overlooked the city and once taken Wellington's siege guns would be able to pound away at the place with ease. A series of redoubts was therefore constructed upon the ridge, notably the Augustins and the Sypiere, while other entrenchments were dug also.

On March 27th an attempt was made to bridge the Garonne but the pontoons fell some 80 feet short. On the 30th another attempt was made, about a mile further south, but this too proved unsatisfactory as the roads were not of sufficient quality to allow the passage of wheeled vehicles. The bridge was therefore taken up and laid some fifteen miles north of the city and on the evening of April 4th Beresford crossed with 19,000 men. Unfortunately, heavy rain swept the bridge away in a repeat of the episode during the crossing of the Nive, leaving Beresford stranded on the right bank of the river. On this occasion Soult chose not to attack and three days later the bridge was operational once more.

On April 8th the rest of Wellington's army crossed the Garonne leaving Hill's corps on the left bank from where it was to threaten the suburb of St Cyprien. Elsewhere, the 3rd

and Light Divisions were to attack the line of the canal along the northern front with the main attack being delivered by Beresford with the 4th and 6th Divisions who were to advance along the left bank of the Ers before wheeling to the right and moving against the French positions on the southern end of the Calvinet ridge. The northern end of the ridge was to be attacked by Freire's Spaniards who, having considerably less distance to cover, were to begin their attack only when Beresford was in position in front of the ridge.

The Allied offensive got under way at 5am with Hill's diversionary attack west of the Garonne against the defenders at St Cyprien. Several battalions worked their way around the French works here but the object of the game was to keep Soult from withdrawing his men to the area of the main Allied attack against the Calvinet ridge. Hill's attack petered out with skirmishing and artillery fire between the two sides but no attempt was made to storm the suburb. Soult soon recognised the ruse and withdrew Rouget's brigade to assist in the defence of Mont Rave.

To the north, meanwhile, Picton began his feint with an effective attack on the French positions close to the canal. However, Picton got carried away and 'seized with evil inspiration' ordered Brisbane's brigade to storm the bridge over the canal and take some French positions in and around some farm buildings and orchards. This was against Wellington's express orders and the attack was driven back with loss. Alten's Light Division, on the other hand, on Picton's left flank, acted precisely in accordance with the commander-in-chief's wishes and restricted itself to skirmishing with French piquets at the Matabiua bridge.

To the east of Toulouse Freire's Spaniards waited while these attacks progressed. Beresford's two divisions had still not arrived opposite Mont Rave owing to the boggy nature of the ground over which they marched. They were still out of range of the enemy guns and so in spite of the slow pace of their march there was little danger. However, when they had got to within a mile of the position from where they would wheel to their left they came under fire from the guns on Mont Rave. This prompted Beresford into abandoning his guns as they sank deep into the mud and slowed the columns down. The guns were left on a knoll from where they commenced firing on the guns on Mont Rave.

The impatient Freire appears to have mistaken the fire from Beresford's guns as the signal for his own infantry attack to begin and at once ordered his two brigades forward in line with two others in support. Freire's Spaniards came on bravely in the face of a heavy artillery barrage from the Calvinet ridge but when they came within musket range the defenders opened up a withering fire which brought the Spaniards to a halt just sixty yards from the French. At this point tragedy struck for the disordered Spaniards sought the shelter of a sunken road which gave them some relief from the storm of lead being turned on them. Unfortunately, they were reluctant to leave the security of the lane and when the French defenders left their trenches and came forward Freire's men were trapped like rats in a barrel. They just fired blindly into the delicious target before them and were joined by other French troops and by two heavy guns that poured out a shower of grape into the Spaniards. It was only with great difficulty that the survivors managed to extricate themselves and fled in panic back to their original positions.

Wellington acted quickly to ease the plight of the Spaniards and sent orders to Beresford telling him to wheel right and begin his attack irrespective of where he was. Beresford, however, had also seen the result of Freire's attack and decided, as he could be of little use there, to ignore the order and continued his march south. Finally, he reached his position, the 4th and 6th Divisions wheeled to their left and formed in line to begin their assault on Mont Rave. The British troops set off with a front of over a mile and a half but had gone only a short distance when two French

The 3/27th Inniskilling Regiment in action on the banks of the Languedoc Canal during the battle of Toulouse, April 10th 1814.

British troops before Paris, 1814. This atmospheric print by Dupray conjures up a rather cold, blustery morning in France at the close of the war. However, few British infantrymen saw Paris at the close of the Peninsular War, most of the regiments sailing home, or to America, from Bordeaux in June and July 1814. Only the cavalry marched north to embark for home at the Channel ports of Calais and Boulogne.

brigades, under Taupin, appeared on their west attacking in column. Six years of fighting the British had taught the French little of the disadvantage of sending column against line and in the ensuing firefight Beresford's men swept the French before them, killing Taupin himself. Soon afterwards, the two British divisions reached Mont Rave and cleared the defenders from it. Beresford then waited while he had his guns brought up.

At about 4pm the 6th Division advanced north to clear the French from the Calvinet ridge but it succeeded in driving them from the southern end of the ridge only and even that was achieved only after heavy fighting during which the Augustins redoubt changed hands five times.

While the 6th Division struggled for possession of the ridge Picton launched another attack to the north of the city. Once again he was beaten back with heavy casualties including Thomas Brisbane, commanding a brigade of the 3rd Division, who was wounded, and Colonel Forbes, of the 45th, who was killed. Altogether, Picton's division suffered 354 casualties in his vain assaults north of the canal.

At about 4.30pm Soult finally ordered the Calvinet ridge to be abandoned. The remaining defenders there had come under increasing pressure not only from the 6th Division but also from a battery of Horse Artillery that Wellington had sent forward. With the withdrawal from the ridge all French troops were now within the perimeter defined by the canal and at 5pm, with the light beginning to fade, the fighting died down. Both armies slept that night on the blood-soaked ground they had fought so hard for during the day, a day which had cost Wellington some 4,558 casualties, Soult losing 3,236 men.

The following morning Soult began to prepare to abandon Toulouse and at nightfall on the 11th his troops began to file out of the city along the road south towards Carcassone. The whole tragedy of the battle was that it need never have been fought in the first place for even as Soult's men headed south Wellington received news of Napoleon's abdication which had taken place on April 6th, four days before the battle. Toulouse, therefore, had been a tragic and needless waste of life.

Even so, there was still one last pointless postscript to the war. On April 14th, four days after Toulouse and a full eight days after Napoleon's abdication, General Thouvenot, commanding the garrison at Bayonne decided, either out of ignorance or malice, to launch a sortie against the besieging Allied troops. 843 British troops became casualties in the resulting fight including Sir John Hope, who was wounded and taken prisoner, and General Hay, who was killed. The French themselves lost 891 men in this futile action.

The Peninsular War finally ended on April 17th when Soult signed an armistice. Six years of war had come to an end and with it came the break up of Wellington's Peninsular army.

It was scattered to various parts of the world including America from where several veteran battalions hurried back to Europe in 1815 to fight once more under 'Old Nosey' at Waterloo, only to arrive too late to take part in the battle, leaving Wellington to fight with what he called, 'an infamous army', a hotch-potch mixture of British, Dutch, Belgians, Hanoverians and Nassauers. Some veteran Peninsular battalions were present at Waterloo but only around a third of Wellington's army there was British and it was a pale shadow of that which had marched, it is calculated, over 6,000 miles and had fought undefeated across the Iberian Peninsula, to help bring about the first downfall of Napoleon.

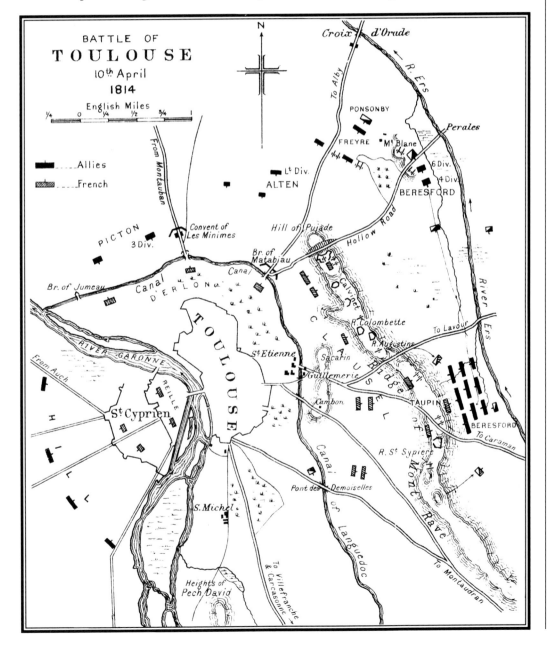

WELLINGTON'S ARMY AT TOULOUSE
Total, 40,706

2nd Division, William Stewart, 6,940
Barnes's Brigade,
1/50th, 1/71st, 1/92nd
Byng's Brigade,
1/3rd, 1/57th, 2/31st, 1/66th
O'Callaghan's Brigade,
1/28th, 2/34th, /39th
Harding's Portuguese Brigade,

3rd Division, Thomas Picton,   4,566
Brisbane's Brigade,
1/45th, 5/60th, 1/74th, 1/88th
Keane's Brigade,
1/5th, 2/83rd, 2/87th, 94th
Power's Portuguese Brigade,
9th Line, 21st Line, 11th Caçadores

4th Division, Lowry Cole,   5,363
Anson's Brigade,
3/27th, 1/40th, 1/48th
Ross's Brigade,
1/7th, 1/20th, 1/23rd
Vasconcellos's Portuguese Brigade,
11th Line, 23rd Line, 7th Caçadores

6th Division, Clinton,   5,693
Pack's Brigade,
1/42nd, 1/79th, 1/91st
Lambert's Brigade,
1/11th, 1/36th, 1/61st
Douglas's Portuguese Brigade,
8th Line, 12th Line, 9th Caçadores

Light Division, Alten,   4,275
1/52nd, 2/95th, 3/95th,
17th Line, 1st and 3rd Caçadores,

Cavalry,   6,490
Fane's Brigade,
13th Light Dragoons, 14th Light
  Dragoons
Vivian's Brigade,
18th Hussars, 1st Hussars KGL
Somerset's Brigade,
7th Hussars, 10th Hussars, 15th Hussars
Manners's Brigade,
5th Dragoon Guards, 3rd Dragoons,
  4th Dragoons
Clifton's Brigade,
3rd Dragoon Guards, 1st Dragoons
Bulow's Brigade,
1st and 2nd Dragoons KGL

Artillery, British, 1,510,
Portuguese 550

Waterloo

June 18th 1815

British troops leave Brussels in the early hours of June 16th 1815. The officers at left are emerging from the Duchess of Richmond's Ball, many of them fighting and dying later that day wearing their fine undress uniforms.

On February 26th 1815, barely ten months after the end of the Peninsular War, Napoleon sailed from Elba to bring about the end of his brief period of exile. It was the beginning of the final, momentous chapter of the Napoleonic Wars that would culminate in the great battle of Waterloo and Napoleon's final downfall. The campaign was also to result in a head to head between the two great commanders of the age, Wellington and Napoleon, two men who had yet to face each other in battle.

Napoleon landed in France on March 1st and entered Paris on March 20th. He immediately set to work raising an army, the so-called Army of the North which, by the time of the Waterloo campaign consisted of 125,000 men. Facing Napoleon were the armies of the Seventh Coalition – it had declared Napoleon 'an enemy and disturber of the world' – which numbered as many as 800,000 men. But of the various armies opposed to him it would be the Anglo-Dutch army, under Wellington, and Marshal Blucher's Army of the Lower Rhine that would be the object of Napoleon's thrust in June 1815.

Wellington's Anglo-Dutch army was a marked contrast to that which had triumphed in the Peninsula, that particular army having been dispersed and scattered around the world, mainly to America, and only a handful of his Peninsular regiments would be present with him at Waterloo. Many of these were already in Holland having served with Sir Thomas Graham's force which had taken part in the campaign against Bergen-op-Zoom in 1813 and 1814. In fact, only 34,000 of the 100,000 troops under Wellington were British, the rest consisting of Germans, Hanoverians and Brunswickers, all good troops, and a large contingent of Nassauers, Dutch and Belgians. It was, as Wellington was moved to write, 'an infamous army, very weak and ill-equipped.' His staff was very inexperienced, although he did have several 'old heads' from the Peninsula, such as Hill, Picton, Alten, Kempt, Pack and Somerset. He also had the services of the Earl of Uxbridge as commander of the Allied cavalry. Uxbridge had eloped with Wellington's sister-in-law early on in the Peninsular campaign and following the Corunna campaign of 1808–09 saw no further service. As a result of this the British cavalry in the Peninsula was deprived of the only real cavalry commander

the British Army possessed. Nevertheless, old differences having been settled, Uxbridge was to lead the cavalry with distinction during the Waterloo campaign.

On June 15th 1815 Napoleon's army crossed the Sambre, catching Wellington, who was dancing the night away with his officers at the now-famous ball, given by the Duchess of Richmond, by surprise. His army had concentrated to the south of Brussels with Blucher's Prussians on its left. Napoleon's plan was to drive a wedge between the two and fight each army separately. It was vital, therefore, to prevent co-operation between the two and on June 16th the two battles designed to ensure this were fought. At Ligny, Napoleon himself attacked Blucher and gave him a severe mauling while Ney, with about 42,000 men, attacked Wellington at the crossroads at

Wellington and his staff at Waterloo. Depicted here with Wellington are Lord Henry Somerset, Viscount Hill, Sir William Ponsonby, the Marquis of Anglesey, Sir Thomas Picton and Sir John Byng.

Quatre Bras. The end result of a day of hard, confused fighting was that Blucher, having been forced to retreat north, in turn forced Wellington to withdraw in the same direction, marching parallel with the Prussians and keeping in close contact with them throughout.

By the evening of June 17th Wellington had drawn his army up along a ridge barring the road to Brussels, just south of the village of Mont St Jean. The position was a good one and afforded Wellington a 'reverse slope', upon which the majority of his troops were deployed, out of sight of the French. On Wellington's left flank were the farms of Papelotte and La Haye and the village of Frischermont. The centre was protected by the farm of La Haye Sainte, and the right wing by the chateau of Hougoumont, a particularly strong position held by the light companies of the Foot Guards. Both of these latter two positions lay a good distance in front of the main Allied position on the ridge. Wellington's troops numbered 68,000 including 12,000 cavalry. He had 156 guns with him also. A further 17,000 Allied troops were left at Hal, a few miles away to the west, in order to protect his right flank against any outflanking manoeuvre Napoleon might attempt in order

to cut him off from his base at Antwerp. Napoleon's army numbered 72,000 including 16,000 cavalry. With 256 guns at his disposal he outnumbered Wellington by nearly 100.

Wellington's decision to fight was based on assurances given him by Blucher that the Prussians, rather than retreat away from him, would march west in order to fall upon the French right flank. In order to prevent such a move Napoleon sent Marshal Grouchy with 30,000 men to pursue the Prussians and keep them from coming to Wellington's assistance The absence of these 30,000 troops would be a significant factor in the outcome of the battle.

The battle of Waterloo began at some time between 11.30 and noon on Sunday, June 18th, with an assault by Jerome Bonaparte's division upon the chateau of Hougoumont, held by the light companies of the Foot Guards. The attack was intended to be merely a feint, the intention being to draw troops away from the Allied centre which was to be the real target for Napoleon. Jerome, however, threw more and more men into the attack until the fight for Hougoumont became almost a battle within a battle, the Guards hanging on grimly throughout the day in the face on intense French pressure. The most dangerous moment for the defenders of

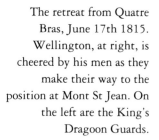

The retreat from Quatre Bras, June 17th 1815. Wellington, at right, is cheered by his men as they make their way to the position at Mont St Jean. On the left are the King's Dragoon Guards.

The eve of Waterloo. British infantrymen warm themselves around a camp fire on the eve of the great battle.

Hougoumont came at around 12.30 when Jerome's men forced open the north gates of the chateau and were only ejected after a desperate piece of defending led by Lieutenant Colonel James Macdonnell, of the Coldstream Guards. The chateau would remain in British hands for the rest of the day, even as flames burnt most of it to the ground following the French artillery bombardment.

At about 1.30pm the second phase of the battle began when Napoleon launched D'Erlon's corps against the Allied centre and left. The attack was preceded by a massive artillery bombardment from 80 guns of Napoleon's 'grand battery'. The attack demonstrated that the French had learned little from the Peninsular War as they came on in bulky, unwieldy columns. 'They came on in the old style and were driven off in the old style,' Wellington remarked later, although at first D'Erlon was successful. Indeed, Bylandt's Belgian brigade was broken and the steady volleys from both Pack's and Kempt's brigades could not halt the columns. The French reached the top of the ridge only to be met by Picton's division which burst through

'Now Maitland! Now's your time!' Wellington briefly assumes personal command of the 1st Foot Guards as Napoleon's Imperial Guard reaches the crest of the ridge. The Foot Guards delivered a few devastating volleys into the French ranks to send the Guard staggering backwards, having been defeated for the first time in battle.

some hedges and unleashed a terrific volley into the massed ranks of muddy, blue-jacketed Frenchmen. The attack came shuddering to a halt in the face of a withering fire from Picton's men, most of whom were veterans of the Peninsula. Tragically, Picton was killed at the moment of triumph, for he fell dead from his horse with a musket ball in his forehead. He died cheering his men on, cursing them as usual as he had done so often in Spain and Portugal. It is perhaps fitting that Picton, the veteran of so many of Wellington's great victories in the Peninsula, should meet his end at the greatest triumph of them all.

While Picton's men stepped over his dead body to press home their attack, Uxbridge chose the moment to launch his cavalry against the disorganised Frenchmen. D'Erlon's commanders tried desperately to reorganise their men but were suddenly swept away by an avalanche, formed of Uxbridge's Union Brigade, consisting of the 1st (Royals), 2nd (Scots Greys) and the 6th (Inniskilling) Dragoons. The Scots Greys had seen no active service since 1795 but made up for this absence with a vengeance as they smashed into the shocked ranks of terrified Frenchmen who surrendered in their thousands. During the charge Sergeant Ewart, of the Greys, captured the eagle of the French 45th Ligne Regiment, whilst on the brigade's right the Household Brigade charged, delivering an equally devas-

tating attack against D'Erlon's battered columns. During its attack the Household Brigade also took an eagle. Unfortunately, the triumphant cavalrymen, the Union Brigade in particular, became carried away with their success and charged on despite the sounding of the recall. The Scots Greys charged right up to Napoleon's guns, slaughtering the gunners and spiking many guns but their horses were soon blown and the Scotsmen suffered a severe mauling following a counter-attack by enemy cavalry, during which Major General Sir William Ponsonby, the brigade commander, was killed. Nevertheless, the attack had completely smashed D'Erlon's corps, some 3,000 Frenchmen being killed or wounded, while a further 3,000 were herded over the ridge towards Brussels as prisoners.

At about 4pm Wellington ordered the Allied line to pull back a short distance in the face the continuous heavy French artillery bombardment. This order was perceived by Marshal Ney to be a withdrawal upon which he ordered a massive cavalry attack by up to 10,000 French cavalry who cantered up – charging was almost impossible over the muddy ground – time and time again to engulf the Allied infantry squares which stood steady on the reverse slope of the ridge. These attacks continued for about two hours and yet achieved nothing, mainly due to the fact that the cavalry were unsupported by artillery. In

Opposite: Sergeant Charles Ewart, of the Royal Scots Greys, capturing the eagle of the French 45th Regiment at Waterloo. A Polish lancer is slain while Ewart prepares to deal with an enemy infantryman.

Caton Woodville's depiction of the defence of Hougoumont by the Foot Guards, June 18th 1815.

'The line will advance!' With Napoleon's Guard streaming away to the rear and with Blucher's Prussians arriving in ever-increasing numbers, Wellington takes off his hat and waves it in the air as the signal for his army to advance.

fact, the infantry squares welcomed the attacks as they gave then some release from the tortuous artillery bombardment that rained down upon them throughout the day and as long as the squares held firm there was little danger.

Even as Napoleon's cavalry thundered up the ridge of Mont St Jean the Emperor looked eastward in dismay as dark columns of troops began to appear on his right flank. They were Blucher's Prussians. Napoleon despatched his Young Guard and Middle Guard to the village of Plancenoit where bitter fighting raged as both French and Prussian fought to the death. The village changed hands several times before Blucher's men finally held on to the place.

In the centre of Wellington's position, meanwhile, a crisis had occurred with Ney's capture of the farmhouse of La Haye Sainte. The defenders, the 2nd King's German Legion Light Battalion, had put up a magnificent resistance all day but when their ammunition finally ran out they were forced to abandon the farmhouse. Major Baring, the commanding officer, and barely forty men made it back to the main Allied position. The fall of La Haye Sainte enabled the French gunners to bring their pieces to within just a few hundred yards of the centre of Wellington's line which reeled under the weight of this new onslaught and even Wellington's seasoned British troops

found it difficult to remember anything worse happening to them in the Peninsula. The climax of the battle had finally arrived.

The effect that the fall of the farmhouse had on the Allied line was not lost on Napoleon who realised that now was the time to launch his Imperial Guard into the attack. It was now or never, for if he could not defeat Wellington before the Prussians made their presence felt then the consequences for him and his empire would be catastrophic.

Napoleon duly turned to his Imperial Guard, those faithful warriors who had been kicking at his heels for years as together they had marched to glory after glory. The Imperial Guard had yet to taste defeat and it was with great confidence that seven battalions of the Guard, supported by guns, set out across the muddy fields, churned up by the earlier cavalry attacks. It is somewhat surprising that the Guard took this route as it would, possibly, have been easier to march directly up the Brussels road and smash through Wellington's centre. However, Napoleon's veterans turned off the main road and headed for that part of the ridge held by Maitland's Brigade of Guards. It is perhaps fitting that the decisive chapter of the final, great battle of the Napoleonic Wars should come down to a clash between the finest troops that both Napoleon and Wellington could offer, the Imperial Guard and the 1st Foot Guards.

The Imperial Guard advanced across the muddy ground in squares, the Guard not wanting to taste what D'Erlon's troops had tasted earlier in the day. From ground level, of course, these dense squares gave the appearance of being columns and thus gave rise to the endless arguments as to just exactly what was the Imperial Guard's formation. As the French approached the ridge they separated into two, one body of troops heading for the 30th and 73rd Regiments and the other heading straight towards Maitland's Foot Guards. The attack was in many ways a repetition of so many of the French infantry attacks in the Peninsula. To the Imperial Guard the ridge looked deserted but just before them, lying in the corn, were two battalions of the 1st Foot Guards and just at the moment when the French saw victory within their grasp Wellington shouted, 'Up Guards, Make Ready, Fire!' All at once the Imperial Guard saw its path blocked by a long red barrier which seemed to spring up from the ground itself. The French hardly had time to gather their wits about them before a series of devastating volleys tore them to shreds, sending them reeling and staggering backwards. The Foot Guards advanced to press home their attack, many of them 'firing from the hip', so close was the range. As the Imperial Guard

began to fall back Sir John Colborne's 52nd Light Infantry wheeled round to pour more musketry into its shocked ranks, the enfilade fire of the Peninsular veterans finally breaking the Frenchmen's resolve and sending them streaming away to the rear.

The other unit of the Imperial Guard met with initial success, pushing back the 30th and 73rd Regiments, but it too was checked, this time by Dutch infantry, and when the French troops saw Maitland's Foot Guards in pursuit of the other column of the Imperial Guard, cries of 'La Garde recule!' swept along their entire line. These were followed by 'sauve qui peut' as the repulse of the Imperial Guard turned into a total rout, reminiscent of the closing stages of the battle of Vittoria, almost two years earlier.

With Napoleon's troops falling back everywhere Wellington raised himself in his saddle and waved his hat in the air which was the signal for a general advance. At the same time the Prussians emerged from the burning remains of Plancenoit at which point the French army disintegrated. Wellington and Blucher met at La Belle Alliance and between them decided to leave the pursuit of the French to the Prussian Army.

Back on the ridge of Mont St Jean Wellington's exhausted soldiers congratulated themselves on their survival and simply fell down where they stood. Many fell asleep

The death of Sir Thomas Picton at the battle of Waterloo.

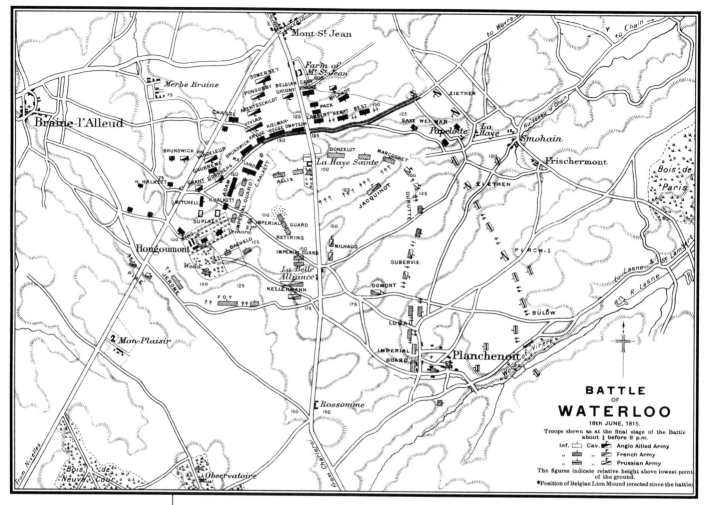

whilst others wandered around looking for comrades or saw to the wounded. Many others were just too excited to sleep and instead tried to look for food or drink, although little was to be found on the battlefield. The cost had been immense. Napoleon had lost his army at Waterloo where about 30,000 Frenchmen had been either killed, wounded or taken prisoner. Wellington himself had seen 15,000 of his men become casualties whilst the Prussians lost 7,000.

That night, back in the small village of Waterloo, Wellington sat down in his headquarters and began to write his despatch. As he did so, tears fell down onto the paper as he reflected sadly on the colossal casualty list. Once before, when visiting the breaches on the morning after the storming of Badajoz, he had wept and now he did so again. As himself said, 'Well, thank God, I don't know what it is to lose a battle; but certainly nothing can be more painful than to gain one with the loss of so many of one's friends.'

The battle of Waterloo marked not only the

end of a campaign but the end of an era. On June 22nd 1815 Napoleon abdicated and on July 7th Wellington entered Paris. Napoleon was later exiled to the island of St Helena where he died in 1821. Wellington himself had also fought his last battle. His reputation had been assured with his triumph in the Peninsula and his victory at Waterloo had raised him to even greater heights. His subsequent career as a politician was an undistinguished one but even that could not cloud his achievements as a military commander and when he died in 1852 he did so as one of the greatest Briton's ever to have lived, possibly *the* greatest. As Sir A. Alison later wrote, 'Long and severe was Wellington's trial, but great and glorious was his reward. He found it in the smiling and prosperous realms which he had protected by his arms; he found it in the wasted and desolate kingdoms which he had wrested from the enemy; he found it in the universal gratitude of the world.'

A fine tribute indeed, but it is one which he could not have earned without his army. The army at Waterloo may well have been 'an infamous one', albeit ultimately victorious, but his old Peninsular army, with which he achieved much of his reputation, was paid the very high compliment by Wellington who said it was, 'the most complete machine for its numbers now existing in Europe,' and added that he 'could have done anything with that army. It was in such perfect order.' Coming from the Great Duke himself this is, possibly, the finest tribute that Wellington's Regiments were accorded.

WELLINGTON'S BRITISH DIVISIONS AT WATERLOO
(Including attached KGL and Hanoverian troops)

1ST CORPS: THE PRINCE OF ORANGE
25,233 infantry, 56 guns
1ST BRITISH DIVISION,   4061
1st British Brigade: Peregrine Maitland,
2/1st Foot Guards, 3/1st Foot Guards
2nd British Brigade, Byng
2/Coldstream Guards, 2/3rd Foot
    Guards

3RD BRITISH DIVISION,   6970
5th British Brigade, Colin Halkett,
2/30th, 33rd, 2/69th, 2/73rd
2nd KGL Brigade, Ompteda,
1st Light Btn, 2nd Light Btn, 5th Line
    Btn, 8th Line Btn.
1st Hanoverian Brigade, Kielmansegge,
Bremen Btn, Verden Btn, York Btn,
    Luneberg Btn, Grubenhagen Btn,
    Jaeger Corps

2ND CORPS, HILL,   24,033 infantry
**2ND BRITISH DIVISION,
    CLINTON,   6833**
3rd British Brigade, Adam,
1/52nd, 1/71st, 6 coys 2/95th,
    2 coys, 3/95th
1st KGL Brigade, du Plat,
1st Line Btn, 2nd Line Btn, 3rd Line
    Btn, 4th Line Btn,
3rd Hanoverian Brigade, Hew Halkett,
Bremervorde Landwehr Btn, Osnabruck
    Landwehr Btn, Quackenbruck
    Landwehr, Salzgitter Landwehr

**4TH BRITISH DIVISION,
    COLVILLE,   7212**
4th British Brigade, Mitchell,
3/14th, 1/23rd, 51st
6th British Brigade, Johnstone,
2/35th, 1/54th, 2/59th, 1/91st
6th Hanoverian Brigade, Lyon,
Lauenburg Btn, Calenberg Btn,
    Nienburg Landwehr, Hoya Landwehr,
    Bentheim Landwehr

**WELLINGTON'S RESERVE,
    20,563**
**5TH BRITISH DIVISION, PICTON,
    7158**
8th British Brigade, Kempt,
1/28th, 1/32nd, 1/79th, 1/95th
9th British Brigade, Pack,
3/1st, 1/42nd, 2/44th, 1/92nd
5th Hanoverian Brigade, Vincke
Hameln Landwehr Btn, Gifhorn
    Landwehr Btn, Hildesheim Landwehr
    Btn, Peine Landwehr Btn

**6TH BRITISH DIVISION, COLE[1],
    5149**
10th British Brigade, Lambert,
1/4th, 1/27th, 1/40th, 2/81st
4th Hanoverian Brigade, Best,
Verden Landwehr Btn, Luneburg
    Landwehr Btn, Osterode Landwehr
    Btn, Munden Landwehr Btn

**BRITISH AND HANOVERIAN
    CAVALRY: UXBRIDGE, 10,155**
1st British Brigade, Somerset,
1st Life Guards, 2nd Life Guards, Royal
    Horse Guards, 1st Dragoon Guards
2nd British Brigade, Ponsonby,
1st Dragoons (Royals), 2nd Dragoons
    (Scots Greys), 6th Dragoons
    (Inniskilling)
3rd British Brigade, Dorneberg,
1st Lt Dragoons KGL, 2nd Lt Dragoons
    KGL, 23rd Light Dragoons
4th British Brigade, Vandeleur,
11th Light Dragoons, 12th Light
    Dragoons, 16th Light Dragoons
5th British Brigade, Grant,
2nd Hussars KGL, 7th Hussars,
    15th Hussars
6th British Brigade, Vivian,
1st Hussars KGL, 10th Hussars,
    18th Hussars
7th British Brigade, Arentschild,
3rd Hussars KGL, 13th Light Dragoons
1st Hanoverian Brigade, Estorff,
Cumberland Hussars, Prince Regent's
    Hussars, Bremen and Verden Hussars

ARTILLERY
British: 90 pieces,   4630 men
KGL: 18 pieces,   526 men
Hanoverian: 12 pieces,   465 men

[1] Lowry Cole was married on June 15th and so missed the battle on June 18th

WELLINGTON'S REGIMENTS

O ver 90 different British cavalry and infantry regiments fought under Wellington between 1808 and 1815. Some of the infantry regiments sent both 1st and 2nd Battalions whilst some, such as the 27th and 95th sent three battalions to war. The service records of Wellington's regiments are set out in this section of the book. It has, of course, been impossible to recount every single action within these short histories as every British unit at some point engaged the French in some minor skirmish or other, which the respective regiment today deems as being worthy of inclusion in its regimental history. The following histories are merely intended to be a sketch of each regiment's service record between 1808 and 1815, whether it embarked for the Peninsula or Belgium and the date of embarkation, its main actions, some casualty figures and the date of departure from the respective theatre of war, and whether it returned to England, Ireland or America. Also, the length of each history is in no way a reflec-

tion of its service between 1808 and 1815. It would certainly be unfair to draw comparisons between the 95th Rifles, one of the busier regiments, for example, and the 69th South Lincolnshire Regiment, present during the Waterloo campaign only.

Some battalions served under Wellington but saw no action at all, notably the 2/35th and 1/54th from Johnstone's 6th British Brigade during the Waterloo Campaign. This particular brigade, consisting of the 2/35th, 1/54th, 2/59th and 1/91st, spent June 18th 1815 away to the west of the battlefield of Waterloo, at Hal and Tubize, and was not engaged. Hence no service record of the 35th or 54th, the 59th and 91st having at least served in the Peninsula. The 35th and 54th did, however, see service under Sir Thomas Graham in Holland, in 1813–14, but as Wellington was not present their service records have not been included here.

Regimental pride and tradition are remarkable things and it is quite extraordinary just how many regiments claim to have been the first to land in the Peninsula, the last to embark at Corunna or to have delivered the most devastating attack of the war. Several others claim a hand in the defeat of the Imperial Guard at Waterloo, to have made the finest charge witnessed by Wellington, whilst others claim the honour of having been the first to set foot inside Badajoz. These points provide us with a glimpse of the fierce regimental pride that still exists amongst the regiments' descendants today. One could fill a book itself in discussing these claims but it is not the purpose of this volume to do so. We should reflect instead upon the tremendous combined achievements of Wellington and his men, of their feats of glory, and of the battles that made each regiment proud to boast that it one of Wellington's regiments.

Lieutenant Colonel Richard Fitzgerald, 2nd Life Guards, killed at Waterloo.

The 1st and 2nd Life Guards

Two squadrons from each of the 1st and 2nd Life Guards were sent to Portugal at the end of October 1812, disembarking at Lisbon on November 23rd. Together with the Royal Horse Guards, they formed the Household Cavalry Brigade, which was commanded by Major General Rebow of the 2nd Life Guards. The brigade was inspected by Wellington on May 23rd 1813 and on June 21st took part in the battle of Vittoria. The Life Guards entered the battle late in the afternoon as Joseph's army collapsed. The 1st Life Guards entered Vittoria itself whilst the 2nd Life Guards busied themselves driving off enemy infantry. During the operations in the Pyrenees there was, naturally, little scope for the Life Guards and both regiments spent the autumn and winter of 1813 in quarters at Logroño. The two regiments remained here until March 1814 when they advanced into France. Three more squadrons of Life Guards came out from England to join them and on April 10th 1814 were present at Toulouse, although they took no part in the actual battle itself. On July 22nd both regiments embarked at Boulogne for England. On April 27th 1815 two squadrons from each of the two regiments of Life Guards marched from London to join Wellington in Belgium. They landed at Ostend on May 3rd and were brigaded with the Royal Horse Guards and the 1st (King's) Dragoon Guards to form the 1st Cavalry Brigade, or 'Household' Brigade, under Major General Lord Edward Somerset. The 1st Life Guards were commanded by Lieutenant Colonel Ferrier and the 2nd Life Guards by Lieutenant Colonel the Hon. E.P. Lygon. The two regiments took part in Uxbridge's charge

against D'Erlon's corps at Waterloo and did great damage at a cost of 18 killed and 43 wounded in the 1st Life Guards, and 17 killed and 41 wounded in the 2nd Life Guards. Both regiments entered Paris on July 7th and remained in France until January 17th 1816 when they embarked at Boulogne for England. The two regiments were back in London by February 8th 1816.

The Life Guards in action at Waterloo, June 18th 1815.

The Royal Horse Guards (Blue)

Two squadrons of the Royal Horse Guards, numbering 21 officers, 24 NCOs, 4 trumpeters and 294 men, embarked at Portsmouth on November 10th 1812, disembarking at Lisbon on November 23rd. On January 10th 1813 the Royal Horse Guards marched to join Wellington's army, the regiment being commanded by Lieutenant Colonel Sir Robert Hill. The regiment first saw action at Vittoria, on June 21st 1813, although it did not enter the

battle until late in the day in support of the advancing infantry. The Royal Horse Guards went into quarters at Logroño on August 12th and due to the rugged nature of the Pyrenees saw no further action in 1813. The regiment remained at Logroño, in fact, until March 1814 when it crossed into France. At the close of the war the Royal Horse Guards marched to Boulogne where they embarked for England on July 23rd 1814, arriving at Dover on the

Captain Sir William Robert Clayton, Royal Horse Guards, 1816, wearing his Waterloo Medal. Clayton was also awarded a Military General Service Medal clasp for Vittoria.

25th. On May 2nd 1815 two squadrons of the Royal Horse Guards embarked at Ramsgate, bound for the Continent in consequence of Napoleon having escaped from Elba. The regiment marched to Brussels and was brigaded with the 1st and 2nd Life Guards and the 1st (King's) Dragoon Guards, to form the 1st Cavalry Brigade, or 'Household' Brigade, under Major General Lord Edward Somerset. During the battle on June 18th the regiment took part in the charge against D'Erlon's corps, suffering at the hands of French cavalry afterwards when it got out of control. Losses sustained during the day totalled 17 killed and 60 wounded. The regiment marched to Paris in July 1815 and remained there until January 16th 1816 when it began its march north to Calais, embarking there on January 31st. The regiment landed at Dover and Ramsgate on February 1st and 2nd 1816.

The 1st King's Dragoon Guards

The 1st King's Dragoon Guards played no part in the Peninsular War, spending the period at home on duty in England. On April 24th 1815, however, four squadrons of the regiment landed at Ostend to take part in the Waterloo campaign. As part of Lord Edward Somerset's 1st Cavalry Brigade, the regiment took no part in the battle of Quatre Bras on June 16th but formed part of the rearguard covering the retreat to the main position of the Allied army at Mont St Jean. During the battle of Waterloo on June 18th the regiment distinguished itself, particularly in fighting against the French curassiers. The battle cost the regiment 7 officers, 122 men and 269 horses killed. Four officers and 130 men were wounded. The regiment returned home in May 1816.

The 3rd (Prince of Wales's) Dragoon Guards

Eight troops of the 3rd Dragoon Guards, under the command of Lieutenant Colonel Sir Granby Calcraft, embarked at Portsmouth on April 3rd-4th 1809 and disembarked at Lisbon on April 26th-27th. The regiment formed part of Fane's cavalry brigade along with the 4th Dragoon Guards and on May 4th 1809 marched north to join Wellesley's army. The regiment was present at Talavera on July 27th-28th where Captain Brice was severely wounded. The 3rd Dragoon Guards formed part of the rearguard during the retreat from Talavera and closed the year in quarters in the Mondego valley. The regiment was present at Busaco although was not engaged in any of the fighting. When Massena retired towards Santarem following his sojourn in front of the Lines of Torres Vedras the 3rd Dragoon Guards took part in the pursuit, taking a number of French troops prisoner. The regiment skirmished frequently with Massena's rearguard and on April 16th 1811, near Los Santos, took over 200 prisoners. On May 16th 1811 the 3rd Dragoon Guards fought with distinction at Albuera to gain its second battle honour of the war. The regiment again distinguished itself at Usagre on May 25th and the following month formed part of the force covering the siege operations at Badajoz. A similar duty was performed by the regiment in January 1812, at Ciudad Rodrigo, and in March and April the same year, once more at Badajoz. The 3rd Dragoon Guards were present at Salamanca and saw out the year as part of the force covering the retreat from Burgos. The regiment's next action came at Vittoria on June 21st 1813. The regiment on this occasion was commanded by Lieutenant Colonel Holmes and it made several charges late in the day to hasten the retreat of the French army. 4 men and 6 horses were killed. The regiment took part in the blockade of Pamplona and was in reserve during the battle of the Pyrenees, although the country was unsuitable for cavalry operations. The 3rd Dragoon Guards crossed into France in the spring of 1814 and although present at Toulouse on April 10th 1814 were not engaged. On June 2nd the regiment began its march north, arriving at Calais where it embarked on July 20th. The regiment disembarked at Dover and Ramsgate the following day.

4th (Royal Irish) Dragoon Guards

On July 24th 1811, six troops of the 4th Dragoon Guards embarked at Portsmouth, disembarking at Lisbon on August 4th. The regiment was commanded by Lieutenant Colonel Sherlock and was posted to Major General Le Marchant's brigade of heavy cavalry. The regiment joined Wellington's field army in September 1811 and in January 1812 formed part of the force covering the siege operations at Ciudad Rodrigo. Shortly afterwards the regiment was removed to Major General Slade's brigade, consisting of the 4th Dragoon Guards, the 3rd Dragoon Guards and the 1st (Royal) Dragoons. A similar covering operation was carried out by the 4th Dragoon Guards at Badajoz in March and April 1812 after which Slade's brigade was attached to Hill's force, acting independently from the main army. As a consequence of this, the regiment missed the battle of Salamanca. Whilst Wellington proceeded north to Burgos the 4th Dragoon Guards remained in Madrid which they entered on August 1812. On March 13th 1813 the regiment was ordered home to England and after transferring all of its horses to the 1st (Royal) Dragoons and the 3rd Dragoon Guards it embarked at Lisbon on April 15th, disembarking at Portsmouth on June 3rd.

5th (Princess Charlotte of Wales's) Dragoon Guards

The 5th Dragoon Guards embarked at Portsmouth on August 12th 1811 and disembarked at Lisbon on September 7th. The regiment consisted of six troops numbering 544 all ranks. The regiment spent the winter of 1811-12 in quarters at Thomar before marching to Badajoz where it formed part of the covering force watching the movements of Soult's army during the siege operations in April 1812. Soon after the fall of Badajoz the 5th engaged the French for the first time, at Llerena on April 11th. Here, the dragoons inflicted over 100 casualties on a superior French cavalry force and took 140 prisoners. The regiment's first major action came at Salamanca on July 22nd 1812. On the eve of the great battle twenty men of the regiment were disabled when their horses trampled on them during the violent storm on the night of the 21st. During the battle the regiment, commanded by Colonel The Hon. William Ponsonby, was brigaded with the 3rd and 4th Dragoons to form the Heavy Cavalry Brigade under Le Marchant and caused havoc when launched against the French shortly after Pakenham's initial attack. The 5th Dragoon Guards lost 15 men killed and 17 wounded in gaining their first battle honour of the war. The regiment entered Madrid on August 12th and remained there for six days before marching north to cover the siege operations at Burgos. Following the failure of the siege the regiment retreated to Portugal along with the rest of the Allied army and went into winter quarters at Goes. In the spring of 1813 the 5th Dragoon Guards advanced into Spain once more and on June 21st took part in the battle of Vittoria, entering the fray during the latter stages of the battle in pursuit of the French army. The regiment took no part in the operations in the Pyrenees and on August 11th 1813 marched to Estella and remained there until December 27th. In February 1814 the regiment advanced into France and on April

The 5th Dragoon Guards advancing on Vittoria, 1813.

10th, under the command of Lieutenant Colonel Lord Charles Manners, took part in the final battle of the war at Toulouse. The regiment remained at Bordeaux at the close of the war before marching to Boulogne where it embarked on July 17th and 18th, landing at Dover between the 19th and 20th.

1st Royal Dragoons

The 1st Royal Dragoons sailed for Portugal on September 2nd 1809 and disembarked on the 12th and 13th of the same month. The regiment consisted of eight troops of 80 men each. It spent the spring and summer of 1810 on the Portuguese border where it skirmished occasionally with the French, notably at Frexadas where the regiment lost two men killed. The 1st Royal Dragoons covered Wellington's retreat to Busaco and Torres Vedras and spent the winter of 1810–11 in quarters close to Santarem. When Massena's army withdrew from here in March 1811 the regiment took part in the pursuit and clashed frequently with the French rearguard, taking over 70 prisoners on one occasion near Pombal

'The Captive Eagle'. Corporal Styles, of the 1st Royal Dragoons, holds aloft the eagle of the 105th French Regiment, taken by him and Clark-Kennedy at Waterloo.

on March 11th. The regiment's first action came on May 3rd-5th at Fuentes de Oñoro where, commanded by Lieutenant Colonel Clifton, it suffered 40 casualties, mainly in charges made on May 5th. Several minor actions took place in the summer of 1811 in which the 1st Royal Dragoons were involved, principally at Alfayates and Aldea de Ponte. During the sieges of Ciudad Rodrigo and Badajoz, between January and April 1812, the 1st Royal Dragoons formed part of the covering force. The regiment was attached to Hill's force at this time and so missed the battle of Salamanca in July 1812 and it was not until November that year that the regiment rejoined the main body of the army which was retreating from Burgos. The regiment spent the winter in Estremadura and did not see any further action until May 26th 1813 when, during the advance upon Vittoria, the 1st Royal Dragoons clashed with a French force at Alba de Tormes, capturing 143 prisoners. At the battle of Vittoria on June 21st 1813 the regiment was only required during the pursuit of the retreating French army. The regiment

saw no action in the Pyrenees but was part of the force blockading Pamplona. The 1st Royal Dragoons did not enter France until March 9th 1814 and although present at Toulouse on April 10th took no part in the battle itself. At the close of the war the regiment marched north to Calais where it embarked on July 18th, disembarking at Dover on the 19th. When news was received of Napoleon's escape from Elba the 1st Royal Dragoons were despatched to Belgium, where the regiment arrived in mid-May 1815. The regiment took no part in the battle of Quatre Bras but covered the retreating infantry on June 17th. At Waterloo, on June 18th, the regiment took part in the great charge against D'Erlon's corps, during which Captain A.K. Clark and Corporal Styles between them captured the eagle of the 105th Regiment. The 1st Royal Dragoons lost 97 men killed during the battle and, curiously, 97 wounded. The regiment entered Paris in early July and remained in France until January 1816 when it embarked at Calais, arriving at Dover on January 16th.

Private, 1st Royal Dragoons, 1815.

2nd (Royal North British) Dragoons

The 2nd Royal North British Dragoons, or Scots Greys to give them their more popular title, saw no overseas service from 1795 until 1815 when the regiment left British shores to take part in the Waterloo Campaign. On the great day of June 18th 1815 the Scots Greys achieved great fame when it captured one of the two French eagles taken during the battle of Waterloo. Six troops of the regiment under the command of Lieutenant Colonel Hamilton landed at Ostend in April 1815 and after proceeding to Ghent were brigaded with the Royals and Inniskillings to form the 2nd British Cavalry Brigade under Major General Sir William Ponsonby. The regiment did not fight on June 16th at Quatre Bras but along with the other British cavalry regiments covered the retreat of the Allied army on June 17th. At Waterloo on June 18th the regiment performed one of the great charges of military history when launched against D'Erlon's corps during the early afternoon. The Greys' charge has passed into legend but it is remembered as much for the tragic aftermath – during which the regiment, sadly out of control, was badly

mauled by fresh enemy cavalry – as it is for the moment when Sergeant Charles Ewart captured the eagle of the French 45th Regiment.

Private, Royal Scots Greys, 1815.

The devastating charge cost the Greys 104 killed and 97 wounded. After the battle the regiment marched to Paris which it entered in July 1815. On January 10th 1816 the regiment embarked at Calais for Dover, disembarking there and at Ramsgate on January 12th.

Captain the Honourable H. Cecil Lowther, 7th Hussars, 1810. Lowther saw action at Sahagun, Benavente, Orthes and Toulouse.

3rd (King's Own) Dragoons

The 3rd Dragoons landed at Lisbon in July 1811 under the command of Lieutenant Colonel Mundy and marched to join Wellington's army in September the same year. The regiment spent the latter part of 1811 on the Portuguese border before marching to Ciudad Rodrigo in January 1812 where it formed part of the force covering the siege operations there. There were numerous clashes with French cavalry during the next few months, particularly in the period leading up to the battle of Salamanca on July 22nd 1812. Here, the 3rd Dragoons took part in their first major action of the war as part of Le Marchant's Heavy Cavalry Brigade which wrought havoc amongst the French columns, destroying several enemy battalions. The battle was awarded to the regiment as its first honour of the war at a cost of just 20 killed and wounded. The 3rd Dragoons entered Madrid on August 12th and the following month formed part of the force covering the siege operations at Burgos. By the end of the year the regiment had retreated to Portugal with the rest of the Allied army and went into quarters at Saixho, Arganil and Soure until April 1813. The regiment took part in the closing stages of the battle of Vittoria on June 21st and in the pursuit of the French afterwards. The 3rd Dragoons took no part in the operations in the Pyrenees and did not enter France until March 1814. The regiment was present at Toulouse on April 10th although it did not see much fighting. In June 1814 the regiment began its march north to Boulogne where it embarked on July 19th, arriving at Dover the following day.

4th, or Queen's Own Dragoons

The 4th Dragoons arrived at Lisbon on April 25th 1809 with a strength of 29 officers, 37 sergeants and 674 other ranks. Commanding the regiment was Lieutenant Colonel Lord Edward Somerset. The regiment formed part of Fane's cavalry brigade along with the 3rd Dragoons. The regiment's first action came at Talavera on July 27th-28th 1809 where it took part in the charge that saw the 23rd Light Dragoons plunge headlong into a hidden ditch. The 4th Dragoons, however, advanced at a much more leisurely pace and came through unscathed. The regiment saw no further action until September 27th 1810 at Busaco although the regiment was held in reserve. Soon afterwards the regiment retreated along with the rest of the Allied army to the Lines of Torres Vedras. When Massena withdrew to Santarem in November 1810 the 4th Dragoons took part in the pursuit and frequently clashed with the French rearguard. In April 1811 the 4th Dragoons were sent to assist in the operations around Badajoz and when Soult advanced to relieve the place the battle of Albuera was fought during which the 4th Dragoons attacked the Polish lancers who had earlier overwhelmed Colborne's brigade. The regiment lost 29 men during the battle. On May 25th 1811 the 4th Dragoons took part in the victory at Usagre and for the remainder of the year saw much skirmishing around Ciudad Rodrigo which was besieged in January 1812, the regiment forming part of the covering force during the operations. In February 1812 the 4th Dragoons became part of Le Marchant's Heavy Brigade of Cavalry and the following month again formed part of the force covering the siege operations, this time at Badajoz. On July 22nd 1812 the 4th Dragoons fought at Salamanca where, as part of Le Marchant's brigade, it helped smash several French battalions. The regiment lost 8 men killed and 20 wounded during the day. Following Le Marchant's death at Salamanca command of the brigade passed to William Ponsonby who led it into Madrid on August 12th 1812. Shortly afterwards it marched north to cover the siege operations at Burgos and retreated to Portugal when the operation failed. The 4th Dragoons were present at Vittoria on June 21st 1813 although they took no part in the battle itself. The regiment remained in quarters close to Vittoria until February 1814 when it marched north and entered France. The 4th Dragoons were present at Toulouse on April 10th and on June 1st, the war having ended, paraded before marching north to Calais, arriving back in England on July 20th 1814.

6th (Inniskilling) Dragoons

The 6th (Inniskilling) Dragoons played no part in the Peninsular War but in April 1815 six troops embarked at Gravesend for Ostend in order to join Wellington's army in Belgium. The regiment, numbering 450 men under the command of Colonel Joseph Muter, was brigaded with the 1st Royal Dragoons and the Scots Greys to form the 2nd British Cavalry Brigade under Major General Sir William Ponsonby. At Waterloo on June 18th 1815 the Inniskillings formed up on the left of the Brussels road in support of Picton's division and when D'Erlon's corps attacked early in the afternoon the regiment took part in the great charge that shattered the advancing French columns. Like the rest of Ponsonby's brigade the Inniskillings got out of control and were badly cut up by enemy cavalry. Losses during the day were 86 killed and 107 wounded including Muter. The regiment marched to Paris afterwards and remained in France until January 1st 1816 when it embarked at Calais for Dover, which was reached the following day.

'The Night Before Waterloo.' The 6th (Inniskilling) Dragoons in camp on the eve of the battle.

7th (Queen's Own) Hussars

The 7th Hussars, commanded by Lieutenant Colonel R. Hussey Vivian, arrived at Corunna in November 1808. The regiment consisted of eight troops, numbering 750 all ranks. The regiment joined Sir John Moore's army and took part in the retreat to Corunna. On December 21st 1808 the regiment fought at Sahagun where, along with the 10th and 15th Hussars, the regiment took part in Lord Paget's attack on a superior number of French cavalry. Eight days later, the 7th again saw action, this time at Benavente, where a piquet of the regiment engaged the French, every single man of the piquet being either killed or wounded. On January 16th 1809, at Corunna, the 7th embarked aboard the ships taking the army back to England and the regiment did not return to the Peninsula until September 1st 1813 when eight troops, again commanded by Hussey Vivian, disembarked at Bilbao. The regiment supported the infantry during the crossing of the Bidassoa in October 1813 and shortly afterwards marched to Pamplona where it went into quarters for the next seven weeks. In December 1813 the 7th Hussars entered France and spent the winter in quarters near Bayonne. The regiment's first major action upon its return came at Orthes on February 27th 1814 where it made several charges. Four men were killed and 12 wounded during the day. The 7th Hussars were present at Toulouse on April 10th 1814 although the day was spent in support of the infantry. The regiment returned to England

in July 1814. In March 1815 the regiment was ordered to Belgium to join Wellington's army. On June 17th the regiment skirmished continually with the French cavalry during the Allied retreat from Quatre Bras. At the battle of Waterloo, on June 18th, the 7th Hussars were brigaded with the 2nd Hussars King's German Legion and the 15th Hussars, as part of Grant's 5th British Cavalry Brigade. The regiment made several charges during the day and casualties between June 17th and 18th were 56 killed and 99 wounded. In July the regiment reached Paris and remained close by until the summer of 1816 when it marched north to Calais and returned to England.

10th, or Prince of Wales's Own Hussars

The 10th Hussars departed from England on October 19th 1808, arriving at Corunna on November 10th. The regiment consisted of eight troops comprising three officers, one quartermaster, four sergeants, one trumpeter and eighty-four men each. The regiment

A private of the 7th Hussars on patrol in Spain during the Peninsular War.

Left: Lieutenant Andrew Finnucane, 10th Hussars, 1811.

Right: Sir Bellingham Graham, 10th Hussars, 1810.

joined Moore's army at Zamora on December 9th and almost immediately found itself embroiled in the retreat to Corunna. On December 20th the 10th, along with the 15th and 7th Hussars, surprised a body of French cavalry at Sahagun and took over 150 prisoners. A similarly fine action took place on December 29th at Benavente where the French lost around 55 killed and wounded as well as 70 prisoners, amongst whom was the French general, Lefebvre Desnouettes. When the regiment embarked at Corunna only thirty horses were put aboard the ships, the rest either being given to the Commissariat or slaughtered. The 10th Hussars did not return to the Peninsula for another four years, sailing from Portsmouth in January 1813 and arriving in the middle of February. In May 1813, the 10th advanced with the rest of Wellington's army and on June 2nd the regiment, supported by the 15th and 18th Hussars, engaged an enemy cavalry force at Morales and broke them, taking over two hundred prisoners. On June 21st the 10th Hussars took part in the battle of Vittoria where the regiment played its part during the fighting and in the short pursuit of the enemy afterwards. The battle cost the regiment four men killed and ten wounded. The nature of the ground fought over during the Pyrenees campaign precluded

any serious action by Wellington's cavalry although some skirmishing occurred between British and French piquets. On December 19th 1813 the 10th crossed the Bidassoa and entered France. The regiment's next action came on February 27th 1814 at the battle of Orthes but although the regiment took part in the operations there astride the Gave de Pau it played no direct part in the actual battle itself. The final action of the war, at Toulouse on April 10th 1814, saw the 10th Hussars form up with the 4th Division in support of the infantry and artillery under Beresford. During the battle the regiment came under heavy artillery fire and one officer and four men were killed and one officer and six men wounded. In July 1814, after the close of the war, the regiment sailed for Dover but less than a year later was back on foreign soil as part of Wellington's Anglo-Dutch Army during the Waterloo Campaign. The 10th Hussars played their part in the retreat from Quatre Bras on June 16th and two days later at Waterloo itself the regiment, commanded by Colonel Quentin, made several charges and covered itself with glory at a cost of two officers and 19 men killed and six officers and 26 men wounded. The 10th Hussars rode on to Paris after the battle with the Wellington's army and returned to England in January 1816.

A dismounted private of the 15th Hussars, 1810.

15th, The King's Hussars

The 15th Hussars disembarked at Corunna between November 12th and 15th 1808. The regiment consisted of eight troops, each of 85 men, under the command of Lieutenant Colonel Colquhoun Grant. On December 21st the regiment fought its first action, at Sahagun, as part of Lord Paget's hussar force that defeated a French force twice its own size. 22 casualties were sustained during the short but brilliant action which earned the regiment its first battle honour of the war. During the retreat to Corunna the 15th Hussars skirmished frequently with French cavalry until Corunna itself was reached in January 1809. The 15th embarked here on the afternoon of January 16th and reached England later the same month. The 15th Hussars returned to the Peninsula in February 1813, disembarking at Lisbon between the 3rd and 7th of that month. The regiment numbered 560 officers and men

and saw its first major action upon its return at Vittoria on June 21st 1813. here, the regiment crossed the Tres Puentes bridge and advanced against the French right-centre. The regiment made several charges during the day and lost 61 killed and wounded. On July 28th 1813 the 15th Hussars were present at Sorauren although they were not seriously engaged. The regiment took part in the operations to cross the Bidassoa and Nivelle rivers and on December 15th entered France, going into quarters until February 1814. The regiment crossed the Gave de Pau on February 26th, skirmishing with the French as it did so, and the following day was in support of the 3rd Division at the battle of Orthes. The 15th Hussars' final action of the war came on April 10th 1814 at Toulouse where they spent the day under enemy artillery fire, the nature of the ground preventing any direct combat with

'On the March in the Peninsula.' Waggons being escorted by the 15th Hussars on a filthy day in the Peninsula.

Captain Sir William Loftus Otway, 18th Hussars. Otway fought at Sahagun, Benavente, Busaco and Albuera where he commanded three regiments of Portuguese cavalry.

the French. The regiment marched north in June 1814 and on July 17th disembarked at Dover. In April 1815, six troops of the 15th Hussars were ordered to Belgium to join Wellington's army. 444 men, under the command of Lieutenant Colonel L.C. Dalrymple, duly arrived at Ostend on May 19th and on June 18th 1815 fought at Waterloo where they suffered from French artillery fire throughout the day. 22 officers and men were killed and 49 wounded, including Dalrymple who lost a leg. The regiment proceeded to Paris in July 1815 and in May 1816 embarked at Calais, disembarking at Dover on May 15th.

18th King's Irish Hussars

On July 26th 1808 eight troops of the 18th Hussars, numbering 672 men, embarked at Northfleet for Lisbon, where they disembarked on September 1st. The regiment was immediately embroiled in the retreat to Corunna during which it clashed several times with enemy cavalry, notably at Valladolid and at Benavente where, on December 29th, the regiment engaged Lefebvre's French cavalry beneath the very eyes of the watching Emperor Napoleon himself. The regiment embarked at Corunna on January 14th 1809, reaching England a few days later. On January 13th and 14th 1813 six troops of the regiment, under the command of Lieutenant Colonel the Hon. Henry Murray, again sailed for the Peninsula, disembarking at Lisbon on February 10th. The regiment was reviewed by Wellington at Frescadas on May 18th along with the 10th and 15th Hussars. On June 1st 1813 the 18th Hussars took part in the attack on the French rearguard at Morales, taking 200 prisoners. On June 21st the regiment took part in the closing stages of the battle of Vittoria and in the pursuit of the French afterwards. Here, several men of the 18th Hussars captured part of King Joseph's baggage and narrowly missed capturing Joseph himself. The 18th Hussars were present at the battle of Sorauren on July 28th 1813 and in December the same year took part in the battle of the Nive. The regiment saw a good deal of skirmishing with the French during the winter of 1813-14 and was present in support of the 7th Division at the battle of Orthes on February 27th 1814. More skirmishing followed, notably at Tarbes, St Martin de la Touch and at the bridge of Croix d'Orade. The 18th Hussars were only lightly engaged at Toulouse on April 10th and in June the same year marched north to Calais where they embarked on July 12th. On April 19th 1815 six troops, some 390-strong, sailed from Ramsgate for Ostend to take part in the Waterloo campaign. The regiment helped cover the retreating Allied army on June 17th and the following day, at Waterloo, distinguished itself during the day making several charges against enemy cavalry. Losses were 13 killed and 74 wounded. The 18th Hussars entered Paris on July 7th 1815 and remained in France until November 1816 when they returned to England.

9th Light Dragoons

The 9th Light Dragoons arrived at Lisbon on July 17th 1811, some six troops strong. The regiment was sent to join the force under Rowland Hill and was brigaded with the 13th Light Dragoons and the 2nd Hussars King's German Legion under Major General Long. On October 28th 1811 the regiment took part in Hill's surprise of Girard at Arroyo dos Molinos. During the fight Brigadier Bron, commanding the French cavalry, was taken prisoner and surrendered his sword to Trumpeter Martin of the 9th Light Dragoons. The regiment lost 2 men killed and one man wounded. The regiment remained with Hill into 1812 and engaged the French in several skirmishes during the next few months, notably at Villafranca and Merida. In April 1812 the regiment formed part of the force covering the siege operations at Badajoz and fought minor actions at Polomar and Ribera. As a consequence of remaining with Hill the 9th missed the battle of Salamanca. When the army retreated to Portugal following the abortive siege of Burgos the 9th Light Dragoons formed part of the rearguard. Following this the regiment went into winter quarters at Fronteira where it remained until March 13th 1813 when a General Order was issued ordering the regiment to return to England. After transferring all its horses to the 13th and 14th Light Dragoons the regiment marched, unmounted, to Lisbon where it embarked on April 17th 1813, arriving in England on May 17th the same year.

Lieutenant Colonel Sir Henry Webster, 9th Light Dragoons.

11th Light Dragoons

Eight troops of the 11th Light Dragoons sailed for the Peninsula on May 4th 1811 with a total strength of 723 all ranks. They joined Wellington's army during the summer of that year when he was engaged in besieging the fortress of Badajoz, an operation which on this occasion proved unsuccessful. Their first action came on June 22nd when a strong French cavalry force attacked them near Campo Mayor. The 11th were surprised after a piquet of German hussars had failed to warn it of the approaching French and in the ensuing fight 8 men were killed, one officer and 21 men wounded and two officers and 75 men taken prisoner. On September 25th 1811 two squadrons of the 11th were involved in a hard fight at El Bodon. Not a major action, it did, nevertheless, see the 11th lose ten killed and twenty-four wounded and the good conduct of the regiment was mentioned by Wellington in his despatches. The remainder of 1811 saw the 11th involved mainly on patrol duties whilst March and April 1812 were spent covering the Allied army as it lay siege to Badajoz. On July 22nd the 11th Light Dragoons took part in the victory at Salamanca where, as part of Anson's light cavalry brigade, they helped rout Marmont's army and were involved in the pursuit afterwards. The 11th lost just two men on this great occasion. After the abortive siege of Burgos the 11th formed part of the rearguard of Wellington's retreating army. At the Pisuerga river the rearguard was attacked by Souham's French advanced units and a hard fight ensued during which the 11th lost 15 men killed and 3 officers and 26 men wounded. The regiment finally reached Ciudad Rodrigo, which marked the end of the retreat from Burgos, on November 19th. Such was the reduced state of the 11th due to sickness and to losses sustained during the retreat that they were forced to give up their horses and return to Lisbon in order to embark for England. Throughout their service in the Peninsula the 11th Light Dragoons had lost 417 men and 555 horses. The 11th returned to service with Wellington's army during the Waterloo campaign of June 1815. The regiment arrived at Ostend in April of that year numbering 453 all ranks and 396 horses and witnessed the arrival of Louis XVIII in Ghent. The 11th, part of Vandeleur's Brigade, arrived at Quatre Bras too late to join in the battle but played a part in the withdrawal the next day when they continually saw off French cavalry who threatened the retreating Allied army. At Waterloo the 11th numbered three troops of 320 men altogether and were drawn up on Wellington's left flank. The 11th helped rescue the remnants of the Union Brigade after their charge early in the afternoon and later broke a French infantry square as Napoleon's army fled from the battlefield. The 11th lost one officer and eleven men killed and four officers and 37 men wounded. 23 men were reported missing. The 11th entered Paris on July 2nd and formed part of the army of occupation in France. The regiment returned home to England in November 1818.

12th (Prince of Wales's) Light Dragoons

The 12th Light Dragoons served in the Walcheren campaign of 1809 but did not arrive in the Peninsula until July 25th 1811. The regiment was brigaded with the 1st Royal Dragoons under Major General Slade and saw some skirmishing in September 1811 at El Bodon and Aldea da Ponte. In February 1812 the regiment marched south to cover the siege operations at Badajoz which began the following month. The 12th Light Dragoons at this time were brigaded with the 14th and 16th Light Dragoons to form Anson's cavalry brigade. The regiment subsequently took part in the action at Llerena on April 11th 1812 but its first battle honour of the war was gained on July 22nd 1812 at Salamanca, where the regiment charged twice. The regiment formed part of the rearguard during the retreat from Burgos in October and November 1812 and spent the winter in quarters on the Portuguese border. At Vittoria, on June 21st 1813, Anson's brigade, including the 12th Light Dragoons, was ordered to cut the road leading to Pamplona at Gamara Mayor. A strong body of enemy infantry and cavalry had to be driven off before this was accomplished.

The regiment played little part in the operations in the Pyrenees in the summer of 1813 but in October was attached to Hay's column which crossed the Bidassoa at Fuenterrabia. The following month the regiment was again present at the battle of the Nivelle and in December 1813 saw action on the Nive when Soult counter-attacked on the 13th. The 12th Light Dragoons spent the winter in quarters at St Jean de Luz but in February 1814 advanced across the Adour to take part in the blockade of Bayonne. At the close of the war the regiment marched north and after embarking at Calais arrived back in Dover in July 1814. In April 1815 the 12th Light Dragoons were despatched to Ostend to join Wellington's army in Belgium following Napoleon's escape from Elba. The regiment was brigaded with the 11th and 16th Light Dragoons to form the 4th British Cavalry Brigade under Major General Sir John Vandeleur. The regiment was still on its way south when Ney attacked at Quatre Bras on June 16th and arrived only at the battle's close. At Waterloo, on June 18th 1815, the regiment, commanded by Lieutenant Colonel the Hon. Frederick Ponsonby, charged in order to assist the beleaguered Union Brigade. In the subsequent charge Ponsonby was seriously wounded and the stories of his ordeal and eventual survival as he lay out on the battlefield have become part of Waterloo folklore. The regiment lost 46 killed and 60 wounded during the day. The regiment remained in France until November 1818 when it sailed for England.

13th Light Dragoons

In February 1810, six squadrons of the 13th Light Dragoons, under the command of Lieutenant Colonel Michael Head, sailed for the Peninsula. After disembarking at Lisbon the regiment was attached to Rowland Hill's division. The regiment first saw action at Busaco on September 27th 1810 although it was not involved in any of the fighting. After spending the winter of 1810–11 close to the lines of Torres Vedras, the 13th Light Dragoons emerged in pursuit of the French army and on March 25th 1811 two squadrons of the regiment took part in the fight at Campo Mayor. During the action a French colonel, Chamarin, was killed in single combat by Corporal Logan of the 13th Light Dragoons. The regiment won its first honour of the war at Albuera on May 16th 1811 and later was present at Lumley's action at Usagre. Later on in 1811 the 13th Light Dragoons were attached to Hill's independent force and with the 9th Light Dragoons and 2nd Hussars KGL, formed Major General Long's cavalry brigade. On October 28th 1811 the regiment took part in Hill's surprise of Girard at Arroyo dos Molinos and was mentioned in Hill's subsequent despatch. The regiment remained with Hill's force throughout the early months of 1812 and saw much skirmishing with the enemy during the operations covering the sieges of both Ciudad Rodrigo and Badajoz. On May 19th 1812 the 13th Light Dragoons marched to Almaraz with Hill and took part in the raid on the bridge and the works there. The regiment finally rejoined the main Allied army at Salamanca following the retreat from Burgos in October 1812. Its next major action came on June 21st at Vittoria. During the aftermath of the battle the 13th Light Dragoons enjoyed themselves – as did most of the cavalry regiments – in pursuing the routed French, during which Captain Doherty led a party of the regiment which captured some of Joseph's royal carriages. In July 1813 one squadron of the regiment was detached to take part in the blockade of Pamplona whilst the remainder of the regiment moved forward in support of the 6th Division during the battle of the Pyrenees. The regiment took part in the passage of the Nive in December 1813 and during the fighting on December 13th Private James Armstrong distinguished himself to the extent that he was promoted by Hill soon afterwards. On February 27th 1814 the 13th Light Dragoons fought at Orthes, sustaining light casualties, and on April 10th were present at Toulouse although the regiment was not involved in any of the fighting. At the close of the war the regiment marched to Boulogne and embarked aboard ships for England, arriving at Ramsgate on July 7th 1814. In May 1815 the 13th Light Dragoons again found themselves back on Continental soil following Napoleon's escape from Elba.

The regiment was brigaded with the 3rd Hussars KGL, under Colonel Sir Frederick Arentschildt, to form the 7th Cavalry Brigade. The regiment took part in covering the retreat of Wellington's army on June 17th and on June 18th, at Waterloo, was positioned behind Hougoumont throughout the day, engaging French cavalry. Losses during the battle were 14 killed and 78 wounded. The regiment remained in France until the spring of 1816 when it embarked at Calais for Dover, arriving there on May 13th 1816.

14th, or Duchess of York's Own Light Dragoons

The 14th Light Dragoons, some four squadrons strong, arrived at Lisbon on December 23rd 1808 under the command of Colonel Hawker. The regiment was spared the retreat to Corunna and did not begin campaigning until April 1809 following Wellesley's return to the Peninsula. The regiment was brigaded with the 16th Light Dragoons, 20th Light Dragoons and 3rd Hussars King's German Legion, under Brigadier General Cotton. On May 12th 1809 the 14th Light Dragoons crossed the Douro three miles up-river from Oporto and came down upon the enemy as they retreated from there. The regiment thus became the only cavalry regiment to win the honour 'Douro'. The 14th Light Dragoons next saw action on July 27th–28th at Talavera. Here, the regiment played a vital part in checking the French advance and gained its second battle honour of the war in doing so. There was no serious fighting for nearly a year, although on July 11th 1810, the regiment was embroiled in Craufurd's unsuccessful attack on a French infantry unit at Barquilla where the 14th lost 13 men killed and 23 wounded. Amongst the dead was Lieutenant Colonel Talbot, commanding the regiment. Two weeks later the regiment was again involved in a controversial action, this time on the Coa river on July 24th. The 14th Light Dragoons were present at Busaco on September 27th 1810 but were held in reserve. During the retreat to the Lines of Torres Vedras the regiment had a sharp engagement with the French at Rio Mandevilla, losing 23 men. The regiment's next major action came at Fuentes de Oñoro on May 3rd–5th 1811 where 51 men were lost including Captain Knipe, who died whilst leading his squadron against a battery of enemy artillery. From January to April 1812 the 14th Light Dragoons were involved in covering the siege operations at Ciudad Rodrigo and Badajoz following which they advanced to Salamanca and took part in the battle there on July 22nd. The regiment sustained slight losses here although 55 men were lost during a skirmish at Castrillos, four days earlier. The regiment formed part of Wellington's rearguard during the retreat from Burgos in November 1812 and on June 21st 1813 was present at Vittoria where men of the regiment captured King Joseph's silver chamber pot, thus ensuring the regiment's future nickname, 'The Emperor's Chambermaids'. The regiment saw some skirmishing in the Pyrenees in July 1813 and entered France on November 10th following the battle of the Nivelle. The 14th Light Dragoons were also present at the battle of the Nive in December 1813 but only in support of the infantry. The regiment saw much skirmishing in March 1814 and on April 10th was present at Toulouse although it was not seriously engaged. The 14th Light Dragoons marched to Calais in June 1814 and arrived at Dover on July 17th.

16th, or Queen's Light Dragoons

On March 31st 1809, the 16th Light Dragoons, commanded by Colonel George Anson, sailed from Falmouth and disembarked at Lisbon on April 13th. The regiment was immediately brigaded with the 14th Light Dragoons, the brigade being commanded by Major General Stapleton Cotton. The regiment first saw action during the operation to cross the Douro in May 1809 and on May 16th the attacked the French rearguard at Salamonde. The 16th Light Dragoon earned its first battle honour of the war at Talavera on July

27th–28th 1809 where 13 men were lost. The regiment spent the winter on the Tagus and in spring 1810 was attached to Robert Craufurd's Light Division. During July of that year the regiment skirmished frequently with the enemy outposts and on July 11th was involved in the ill-fated attack on a small French unit at Barquilla. During the retreat to the position at Busaco the regiment played an active part in covering the movements of the army and again clashed with French cavalry. The 16th Light Dragoons were present at Busaco on September 27th 1810 but took no part in the battle. When the Allied army reached Torres Vedras in October 1810 the 16th Light Dragoons were stationed in quarters in Mafra and later at Ramalhal. The regiment pursued Massena's retreating army in November 1810 when it withdrew from in front of the lines and during the next few months clashed with the French rearguard. The regiment's next major action came on May 3rd–5th at Fuentes de Oñoro, where casualties were light, following which it went into quarters on the Spanish border. The period between January and April 1812 was spent covering the siege operations at Ciudad Rodrigo and Badajoz respectively, a task undertaken by many of Wellington's cavalry regiments. On April 11th 1812 the regiment took part in the cavalry action at Llerena taking scores of prisoners and was mentioned in Cotton's despatch. The regiment took part in the battle of Salamanca on July 22nd 1812 and afterwards went into cantonments on the Douro while Wellington marched on to Madrid. In October 1812 the 16th Light Dragoons found themselves covering the siege operations at Burgos and during the retreat from there fought a hot action on October 23rd on the Pisuerga river, losing some 62 officers and men. During the winter of 1812-13 the regiment occupied quarters at Aveiro and did not enter Spain again until May 1813 when Wellington began the advance that would take him to Vittoria. On June 21st 1813 the 16th Light Dragoons fought in the great battle there, losing 21 men during the day. There was little scope for any serious action for the regiment during the operations in the Pyrenees but on November 10th 1813 it took part in the battle of the Nivelle, acting in support of the infantry on the left wing of the army around St Jean de Luz. The following month the 16th Light Dragoons saw action during the battle of the Nive following which they went into winter quarters. When Wellington pushed on towards Toulouse the 16th Light Dragoons remained at Bayonne as part of the force blockading the town and the regiment was still there when the Peninsular War ended in April 1814. Two months later the regiment marched north to Calais and arrived back in England in July. When news of Napoleon's escape from Elba was received in March 1815 three squadrons of the 16th Light Dragoons, under Lieutenant Colonel James Hay, were despatched to Ostend to join Wellington's army. The regiment formed part of Major General Sir John Vandeleur's brigade along with the 11th and 12th Light Dragoons. The regiment took part in covering the retreat of the Allied army from Quatre Bras on June 17th and on June 18th, at Waterloo, made several charges to drive back enemy cavalry at a cost of 10 dead and 22 wounded, including Lieutenant Colonel Hay. The 16th Light Dragoons marched to Paris after the battle and remained in France until December 1815 when it embarked at Calais for Dover.

Major Craven,
16th Light Dragoons, 1815.

20th Light Dragoons

In August 1808 six troops of the 20th Light Dragoons arrived in Portugal having sailed from Portsmouth the previous month. The regiment was present at the first battle of the war, at Roliça on August 17th 1808, but was not involved in any of the fighting. Four days later, however, the 20th Light Dragoons took part in the battle of Vimeiro and presented the British army with the first in a series of inglorious cavalry charges. Commanding the regiment was Colonel Taylor who, when Wellesley called out, "Now 20th! Now's your chance", led them against a body of French cavalry. The charge was partially successful but the regiment got out of control, charged too far and was badly mauled in consequence. Colonel Taylor was killed during the charge as well as 19 men. 22 were wounded. The regiment remained in the Peninsula until the end of 1809 although it saw little action. At the end of the year the 20th Light Dragoons were sent to Sicily although part of the regiment returned in 1812 and saw action on the east coast of Spain at Vincente. In 1813 the remainder of the regiment arrived from Sicily and likewise saw action on the east coast, notably at Castalla and Villafranca. In 1814 the regiment left the Peninsula and sailed for Italy where it took part in the capture of Genoa, and returned to England in 1815.

23rd Light Dragoons

The 23rd Light Dragoons arrived at Lisbon on June 23rd 1809 and had been in the Peninsula barely a month before it fought its first battle, at Talavera on July 27th-28th 1809. The regiment formed part of Anson's Light Cavalry Brigade along with the 1st Light Dragoons King's German Legion. On the afternoon of July 28th the regiment was launched against Ruffin's division but lost control and failed to see a dry water-course into which scores of men and horses plunged. A total of 207 all ranks were lost during the afternoon out of 480 present. It was the last occasion upon which a British cavalry regiment bore its colours into battle. Such were the losses sustained at Talavera that the 23rd Light Dragoons were ordered home to England, arriving there in January 1810. The regiment was not to return to the Peninsula and in fact saw no further service overseas until April 1815 when it was ordered to embark for Ostend to join Wellington's army in Belgium. The 23rd Light Dragoons, some 397-strong, formed part of Dornberg's cavalry brigade with the 1st Light Dragoons KGL and the 2nd Dragoons KGL. At Waterloo, on June

The disastrous charge of the 23rd Light Dragoons at Talavera on July 28th 1809. The regiment, out of control and charging much to fast, failed to see a dry watercourse in front of it, into which scores of men and horses tumbled.

18th 1815, the regiment was commanded by Lieutenant Colonel the Earl of Portington. It lost 77 men killed, wounded and missing during the battle. At the end of the day a group of the 23rd escorted the wounded Earl of Uxbridge from the field. The regiment remained in France until December 1815 when it embarked at Calais, arriving at Ramsgate and Dover on December 21st, 23rd and 24th.

The 1st Regiment of Foot Guards

On September 8th 1808 nearly 2500 men of the 1st and 3rd Battalions 1st Foot Guards embarked at Ramsgate for the Peninsula, disembarking at Corunna at the end of October. The 1st Foot Guards, forming part of the force under Sir David Baird, had hardly joined the main British army when Moore began his retreat to Corunna. The retreat began on Christmas Eve 1808 and finally ended with the battle of Corunna on January 16th 1809. During the terrible retreat the 1st Foot Guards was one of the few units that maintained discipline and when the two battalions marched into Corunna at the end of the retreat in step as if on parade, something which was remarked upon by Moore. The 1st Foot Guards were not to return to the Peninsula until the spring of 1810. In March 1811 six companies of the 1st Guards formed part of a British force of around 4000 men under Sir Thomas Graham which clashed with the French at Barrosa on March 5th during which the 1st Foot Guards distinguished themselves in some fierce fighting. The 1st and 3rd Battalions of 1st Foot Guards eventually joined Wellington's main army during the retreat from Burgos during the autumn and winter of 1812. In November 1812, 800 men of the 1st Foot Guards were sent from England to Holland to take part in Graham's attack on Bergen-op-Zoom. The 1st Foot Guards next saw service during Wellington's advance into Spain in 1813 which culminated in the victory at Vittoria. The regiment was next involved at the siege of San Sebastian which fell on August 31st 1813. On October 7th 1813 the 1st and 3rd Battalions 1st Foot Guards spearheaded the crossing of the river Bidassoa and next took part in the crossing of the rivers Nivelle and Adour. The Peninsular War came to an end on April 12th although for the Guards there was still one more major action because on April 14th the governor of Bayonne, Thouvenot, launched a sortie during which the two Brigades of Guards suffered

some 508 men killed, wounded or taken prisoner. The 1st Brigade of Guards eventually sailed from France on July 26th and 27th 1814. During the Waterloo campaign of 1815 the 2nd and 3rd Battalions of the 1st Foot Guards, under Peregrine Maitland, constituted the 1st Brigade of Guards. At Quatre Bras on June 16th the light companies of the regiment were heavily involved in the fighting in Bossu Wood. During the main battle on the 18th the light companies helped defend the post of Hougoumont although they were later withdrawn to rejoin their battalions on the main position atop the ridge of Mont St Jean where the 1st Foot Guards spent the day under fire. When Napoleon decided to commit his Imperial Guard to the attack at the crucial moment of the battle, the 1st Foot Guards bore the brunt of the attack. The Imperial Guard reached the crest of the Allied position but at the vital moment Maitland's

Alexander, Lord Saltoun, 1st Foot Guards, in the uniform of a lieutenant, light company, 1810. Saltoun won medal clasps for Corunna, Nivelle and the Nive. He also fought with great distinction at Waterloo.

Guards rose to deliver a series of devastating volleys into the ranks of Frenchmen who were driven back in disorder and the battle was as good as won. As recognition of their part played in defeating the Imperial Guard the Prince Regent bestowed upon the 1st Foot Guards the title of 'Grenadier' the full name of the regiment becoming the First of Grenadier regiment of Foot Guards. The 2nd Battalion returned to England in January 1816 while the 3rd Battalion returned in October the same year.

Lieutenant Colonel James Macdonnell, Coldstream Guards. One of the defenders of Hougoumont, Wellington later called Macdonnell 'the bravest man at Waterloo.' He also won clasps for Barrosa, Salamanca, Vittoria, Nivelle and the Nive.

The Coldstream Regiment of Foot Guards

The 1st Battalion of the Coldstream Guards arrived in the Peninsula between March and April of 1809. In May of that year the battal-ion took part in the crossing of the river Douro. Just over two months later the Coldstream was heavily involved at the battle of Talavera, on July 27th–28th, during which the battalion suffered 297 killed and wounded. The Coldstream was present at Busaco although the battalion was not involved directly in any of the day's fighting. In the south at Cadiz, two companies of the Coldstream took part in the battle of Barrosa on March 5th 1811 and distinguished themselves in some fierce fighting atop the hill of Barrosa losing 57 men. At Fuentes de Oñoro, on May 3rd–5th 1811, the Coldstream sustained similar casualties, 54 during the two days' fighting. In January 1812, the battalion took its turn in the trenches before Ciudad Rodrigo although it was not involved in the actual assault. On July 22nd 1812 the light companies of the battalion fought at the battle of Salamanca, being detailed to hold the vital position of the village of Los Arapiles. At Burgos the Coldstream performed well during the siege operations, something which was noted by Wellington in his despatches, adding that it was a pity the rest of the army had not performed likewise. In July and August 1813 the Coldstream was involved in the siege of San Sebastian which fell on August 31st and on October 7th spearheaded the crossing of the left wing of the army over the Bidassoa. Soon after the regiment took part in the crossing of the rivers Nivelle and Adour. During the crossing of this latter river, on February 23rd 1814 the Coldstream and 3rd Foot Guards made a bold crossing in small boats covered by some riflemen and a couple of salvoes of Congreve rockets. After the crossing of the Adour the main part of Wellington's army pressed on towards Toulouse while the Guards remained behind to lay siege to Bayonne. On April 12th the Peninsular War finally came to an end although on April 14th, the governor of Bayonne, Thouvenot, launched a sortie during which the Coldstream suffered some 34 killed, 128 wounded and 84 taken prisoner. It was a bloody and totally futile action. The 1st Battalion returned home on July 28th 1814. During the Waterloo campaign it was the 2nd Battalion of the Coldstream Guards that fought. It was brigaded with the 2nd Battalion 3rd Foot Guards in the 2nd Brigade of Guards, under Sir John Byng. On June 16th the battalion's light companies saw action at Quatre Bras and two days later, at the battle of Waterloo, the Coldstream defended the vital post of the chateau of Hougoumont, on Wellington's right flank. It was the Coldstream's finest hour as whole divisions of French troops were poured into the fight, only to be driven off. In spite of repeated heavy attacks from French infantry and artillery, which set the buildings alight, Hougoumont remained in British hands throughout the entire day. The 2nd Battalion lost 55 killed 249 wounded throught the day. The battalion returned to London in February 1816.

3rd Foot Guards

In January 1809, the 1st Battalion 3rd Foot Guards sailed for Portugal numbering 43 officers and 1,305 men, making it one of the strongest battalions in the Allied army. Its first action was at the crossing of the Douro in May 1809 and two months later, on July 28th, the battalion fought at Talavera where it lost 24 killed and 267 wounded in the battle. Far greater casualties were sustained by the regiment's 2nd Battalion at Walcheren where hundreds died through sickness. In 1810 three companies of the 2nd Battalion were despatched to Cadiz to reinforce the garrison there while the 1st Battalion was present at Busaco on September 27th 1810. On March 5th 1811 the three companies of the 2nd Battalion fought at the battle of Barrosa where it was noted, 'how gloriously the Brigade of Guards maintained the high character of His Majesty's Household troops.' On May 3rd-5th 1811 the 1st Battalion fought at Fuentes de Oñoro where the battalion lost 59 men. Although the battalion was present at the siege of Ciudad Rodrigo it took no part in the actual storming. The battalion was next in action at Salamanca on July 22nd 1812 where the battalion's light company, assisted by the light company of the Coldstream Guards, was involved in fierce fighting in the village of Los Arapiles. At the abortive siege of Burgos the battalion was one of the few to distinguish itself. The 3rd Foot Guards were present at the battle of Vittoria in June 1813 but took no part in the fighting. 25 men became casualties at the siege and storming of San Sebastian where the battalion provided volunteers for the assault. It was also present at the crossing of the Bidassoa in October 1813 and when the army entered France the battalion suffered 65 casualties at the battle of the Nive on December 9th-13th. At the crossing of the river Adour in February 1814 a few men of the Coldstream and 3rd Foot Guards crossed the river supported by rockets and held the bridgehead until reinforcements came across. The battalion's last action of the Peninsular War came at the siege of Bayonne where the governor of the town launched a futile sortie which cost the battalion some 203 men and officers either killed, wounded or taken prisoner. The 2nd Battalion, meanwhile, had been in action in Holland at Bergen-op-Zoom and following this operation was stationed near Brussels. Therefore, when Napoleon began his last campaign in June 1815, the battalion was thrown straight into the action, fighting at Quatre Bras on June 16th and at Waterloo two days later. During the battle the 2nd Battalion was positioned on the right of the line with its light company helping to defend the chateau of Hougoumont along with the light companies of the 1st Foot Guards and Coldstream Guards. Throughout the day the defenders of Hougoumont frustrated the attacks of over 30,000 Frenchmen who failed to take the position moving one historian to write, 'probably the gallantry of the defenders of this post has never been surpassed on any battlefield.' It was the crowning glory of their service under Wellington. The battalion returned to London in January 1816.

1st Regiment of Foot, or Royal Scots

The 3/1st arrived at Corunna in October 1808 as part of the force despatched to the Peninsula under Sir David Baird. The battalion fought in the battle there on January 16th where it was heavily engaged at the village of Elvina. The 3/1st returned to the Peninsula in 1810 after serving in the Walcheren campaign the year before. As part of the 5th Division the battalion saw action at Busaco where its losses were just two men wounded. At Fuentes de Oñoro in May 1811, the battalion suffered similarly low casualties. On February 11th 1812 the Prince Regent officially gave the regiment its name, 'The 1st Regiment of Foot, or Royal Scots.' In April of that year the battalion was present at the siege of Badajoz and although it took no part in the storming it did have the honour of being Wellington's personal guard. In July of 1812 the Royals fought at Salamanca sustaining 164 casualties. The battalion retreated to the Portuguese border along with the rest of Wellington's army in the autumn and winter of 1812 but in May the following year fought at Vittoria where the battalion was engaged in cutting off the French army's line of retreat after the battle. The Royal Scots suffered 11 casualties that day. At San Sebastian the 3rd Battalion played a particularly distinguished part. The battalion provided the assaulting force for the first attempt to secure a breach in the fortifications. Due to fierce resistance and constant bombardment this attempt failed however, although Sir Thomas Graham wrote that the distinguished gallantry of the battalion was most conspicuous. On August 31st the town was taken and again Graham praised the Royals, when he wrote, 'I conceive our ultimate success depended on the repeated attacks made by the Royal Scots.' San Sebastian having fallen, no obstacles remained before the French frontier and it was the Royal Scots who were the first British troops to cross the Bidassoa into France. Crossing the river Nive the battalion took part in the defeat of the French who counter-attacked before Bayonne. This concluded their part in the Peninsular War and in September 1814 the battalion sailed home. In May 1815, however, it returned to the Continent for the Waterloo campaign. On June 15th 1815 the battalion left their dinners uneaten in order to march straight to Quatre Bras where, on June 16th, the battalion repulsed several French cavalry attacks and were in the thick of the fighting, ending the day with 26 dead and 192 wounded. At Waterloo, on the 18th, the battalion was exposed to enemy bombardment for hour after hour and again stood steady in the face of repeated French cavalry attacks. During the battle, Ensign Kennedy, who was carrying the Colour in advance of the battalion, was shot but continued to advance until he was again wounded, this time mortally, but when a sergeant tried to retrieve the Colour Kennedy refused to let go. Such was the admiration of the French that they held their fire until the sergeant had returned safely to the battalion's square. The Royals suffered 15 killed and 126 wounded on June 18th. Four officers and a sergeant major in turn fell carrying the King's Colour. The 3rd Battalion Royal Scots marched on to Paris and returned to England in March 1817.

2nd (The Queen's Royal) Regiment of Foot

The 2nd (Queen's Royal) Regiment arrived in the Peninsula on July 30th 1808 and formed part of Acland's 8th Infantry Brigade. The Queen's first action came at Vimeiro on August 21st, where the regiment suffered minimal losses. During the retreat to Corunna in the winter of 1808-09 the Queen's formed part of Sir John Hope's division, protecting the march of the artillery during the march to Salamanca. At the battle of Corunna on January 16th the regiment, commanded by Lieutenant Colonel Kingsbury, formed part of the rearguard covering the embarkation of the troops. One member of the regiment, Private Edwards, was wounded during the battle but made it back to England, only to die on January 30th at Plymouth. A post mortem shortly afterwards showed that he had been shot through the heart but lived sixteen days with the wound Although the regiment had returned to England, a single company had remained behind in Portugal and when

Wellesley returned to the Peninsula in April 1809 the company formed part of the 2nd Battalion of Detachments, which formed part of Campbell's 4th Division. The company fought at Talavera before returning home in August that year. The Queen's returned to the Peninsula in March 1811 and formed part of the 6th Division. The regiment was present at the battle of Fuentes de Oñoro on May 3rd-5th but was not involved in any direct fighting. The Queen's next saw action at Salamanca on July 22nd 1812 during which it lost 109 men. The regiment was way below strength during the battle and was just 408-strong. Between the summer of 1812 and January 1813 the strength of the regiment fell so low in fact that six weak companies were sent home, the remainder being joined by four companies of the 53rd Regiment to form the 2nd Battalion of Detachments. The unit formed part of Anson's brigade of Cole's 4th Division and was present at Vittoria on June 21st 1813. The four companies next saw action at Sorauren, during the battle of the Pyrenees, where casualties were very light. On November 10th 1813 the Queen's, again as part of the 2nd Battalion of Detachments, took part in the battle of the Nivelle, suffering 53 casualties. The battalion saw no further action until the final battle of the war, at Toulouse on April 10th 1814. Again, as part of Cole's 4th Division, the unit suffered light casualties, just 33 killed and wounded. At the close of the war the four companies returned to England, arriving at Plymouth on July 30th 1814.

The 3rd (East Kent – The Buffs) Regiment of Foot

The 1/3rd (The Buffs) arrived in the Peninsula on September 1st 1808 just as the ships evacuating the French troops defeated after Vimeiro sailed away. When Moore began his march into Spain in October 1808 the Buffs brought up the rear, escorting the wagons and only the battalion's grenadier company ever caught up with the main body of the army. Therefore, whilst the army struggled through the snows during the retreat to Corunna Lieutenant Colonel Blunt, commanding the Buffs, extricated his battalion and managed to return to Lisbon although the battalion's grenadier company did carry on to fight at Corunna. The Buffs first saw action at Oporto during the bold crossing of the Douro. The Buffs were the first troops to cross the river in barges, beneath the eyes of the unwary French. At Talavera the Buffs lost 152 men killed and wounded with their commanding officer being among the former. The battalion took no part in the battle of Busaco but helped man the Lines of Torres Vedras during the winter of 1810-11. In April 1811, the Buffs formed part of the 2nd Division of the army under Beresford which was besieging Badajoz and on May 15th he fought the battle of Albuera during which the Buffs, caught in line and blinded by a hail and rain storm, suffered over 450 casualties, mainly at the hands of Polish lancers. At the end of the day only 85 of the battalion's 728 men remained unscathed.

During the battle Lieutenant Latham had defended the King's Colour in the face of a savage attack by enemy cavalry. He was later picked up off the field, almost unrecognisable, covered in blood and terribly wounded having lost one arm. But the colour was wrapped safely inside his jacket. The anniversary of the battle is now the regimental day. Although the ranks of the decimated battalion were filled it was to be another two years before the Buffs saw action again. This was at Vittoria on June 21st 1813 during which the battalion came through with little loss. During the actions in the Pyrenees at Roncesvalles and Sorauren between July 25th and 28th 1813 the Buffs lost 101 men killed and wounded. The Buffs next saw action at the battle of the Nivelle on November 10th 1813 and a month later crossed the River Nive to drive the French defenders from their positions on the northern bank. Both these operations cost the Buffs little cost. The Buffs were present at the two last battles of the war at Orthes and Toulouse in February and April 1814 but on both occasions the battalion suffered no casualties. The casualties sustained during the last six months of the war, therefore, had been in marked contrast to those sustained at Albuera. Shortly after the close of the war the Buffs were embarked for America and arrived back in Europe a month too late to take part in the battle of Waterloo.

The 4th, or the King's Own Regiment

The flag of the Hesse d'Armstadt Regiment, captured by Private George Hatton, 4th (King's Own) Regiment during the storming of Badajoz on April 6th 1812.

The 1/4th arrived off Portugal on August 19th having sailed from Sweden where it had taken part in Sir John Moore's campaign there. The battalion came ashore on August 25th and so missed the first two battles of the war at Roliça and Vimeiro. The 1/4th formed part of the force under Major General Frazer and subsequently took part in the retreat to Corunna and in the battle there on January 16th 1809. During the battle Sir John Moore was moved to remark about the battalion, 'I am glad to see a regiment there in which I can place so much confidence.' Lieutenant Colonel Wynch, commanding the battalion, was wounded during the battle along with 5 other officers. No accurate record was kept of casualties although it is thought that two men were killed and ten more wounded. The battalion returned to Portsmouth on January 31st and later the same year was despatched to Walcheren. The 2/4th sailed from England in January 1810 but saw service only as part of the garrison of Cueta. The 1st Battalion, meanwhile, returned to the Peninsula in October 1810 and was attached to Leith's 5th Division. The battalion had landed with a strength of about 1,000 men but was still suffering the effects of Walcheren fever. By May 1811 only 600 men were fit for service and yet the battalion had still to fight a major action. The 1/4th's first action came at the terrible storming of Badajoz on April 6th 1812. The battalion formed part of Leith's force which attacked the San Vincente bastion and as it moved along the ramparts to help clear them of enemy troops Private George Hatton captured the flag of the Hesse D'Armstadt regiment which formed part of the garrison. The flag was later presented to Wellington who rewarded him with some money and recommended him for promotion. The storming cost the battalion some 4 officers and 40 men killed and 15 officers and 173 men wounded. The 1/4th next saw action at Salamanca on July 22nd 1812 where both battalions of the regiment – the 2nd Battalion had arrived to join the army on May 10th 1812 – suffered one officer and 48 men killed and wounded between them. The retreat from Burgos took its toll on the regiment and on Christmas Eve 1812 the handful of fit men from the 2nd Battalion were transferred to the 1st Battalion, the cadre of the 2/4th returning home to recruit. During the Vittoria Campaign in May and June 1813 the 1/4th formed part of the force under Sir Thomas Graham which marched to the north of Wellington's main force. During the battle itself on June 21st the battalion saw fierce fighting, particularly at the village of Gamara Mayor which was taken only after a stiff fight. 2 officers and 11 men were killed and 6 officers and 72 men wounded. A further 5 officers and 117 men were left dead in the breach at San Sebastian on August 31st 1813 including Lieutenant Maguire, who had placed a white feather in his cap to make himself look more conspicuous. 6 officers and 170 men were wounded. The 1/4th was present at both the crossing of the Bidassoa on October 7th and the battle of the Nivelle on November 10th, although it was never really seriously engaged on either occasion. The battalion's last major battle of the Peninsular War came at the battle of the Nive, on December 9th-13th 1813. The battalion was part of Hope's force on the Allied left and suffered 182 casualties during the four days' of fierce fighting. The 1/4th saw out the war blockading Bayonne and on May 29th 1814 it sailed for North America. The 1/4th was one of the few battalions to serve at New Orleans and still return to Europe in time to play a part in the battle of Waterloo on June 18th 1815. Once again the battalion was commanded by Lieutenant Colonel Brook and was attached to Lambert's division. The 1/4th found itself in the centre of the Allied position which turned out to be one of the hottest spots on the battlefield. casualties during the day were 12 men killed and 8 officers and 113 men wounded. The battalion entered Paris on July 7th and subsequently formed part of the Army of Occupation. It remained in France for a further three years and did not return to England until October 30th 1818.

Sergeant – 71st (Highland) Light Infantry 1815   Officer – 51st (2nd Yorkshire, West Riding, Light Infantry) Regiment 1815.

10th, or Prince of Wales's Own Hussars 1808.   Officer – 11th Light Dragoons 1811

2nd (Royal North British) Dragoons 1815   The 1st Life Guards 1815.

Sergeant – The Coldstream Regiment of Foot Guards 1815   92nd (Highland) Regiment 1815.

Officer – The Royal Horse Guards (Blue) 1814   The 1st (Royal) Dragoons 1813.

15th, The King's Hussars 1815   Officer – 16th, or Queen's Light Dragoons 1814.

Officer – 5th Batt. 60th (Royal American) Foot 1812   27th (Inniskilling) Foot 1810.

5th, or Northumberland Foot 1809*   Officer – The 4th, or The King's Own Regiment 1809.

*The 5th won the distinction of wearing white feathers in their caps following an action against the French on the island of St Lucia in 1778.

5th, or Northumberland Foot

The 1/5th sailed for the Peninsula in July 1808, 1,017 strong under the command of Lieutenant Colonel Mackenzie. It formed part of Hill's 1st Brigade and on August 17th fought in the first battle of the Peninsular War at Roliça, where it sustained 46 casualties. Four days later the battalion was present at Vimeiro, although it took little part in the battle. During the retreat to Corunna the battalion suffered along with the rest of the army and at the battle itself, on January 16th 1809, Mackenzie was killed as he rode out in front of his men. Some 654 men of the battalion made it safely back to England. On its return to England the 1/5th had a short period of rest before being despatched to take part in the Walcheren Campaign. Meanwhile, a small detachment of the battalion, which had stayed behind in Portugal during the Corunna campaign was present at Talavera. That same month, July 1809, the 2/5th landed at Lisbon although it was to be over a year before it saw any action, at Busaco on September 27th 1810, where it formed part of Sir Thomas Picton's 'Fighting' 3rd Division. At Fuentes de Oñoro, on May 3rd-5th, only the battalion's light companies saw action, suffering seven men wounded. Later that month the battalion marched south to take part in the first siege of Badajoz which ended in failure after unsuccessful assaults on June 6th and 9th. On September 25th 1811 the 2/5th took part in the action at El Bodon. It was not a major battle that warranted an honour but it was, nevertheless, one in which the battalion greatly distinguished itself losing five men killed and one officer and 13 men wounded. The siege and storming of Ciudad Rodrigo, in January 1812, cost the battalion 102 casualties, 36 of whom were killed during the assault on the Greater Breach. At the siege of Badajoz, from March 16th to April 6th 1812, the battalion was spared the horrors of the two breaches although 45 men were either killed or wounded in the escalade of the Castle which won the town for Wellington. Major Ridge, commanding the 5th, is traditionally seen as the first man to enter the town only to be killed shortly afterwards. On June 24th 1812 the 1/5th landed at Lisbon to join their comrades of the 2nd Battalion. A month later at Salamanca, on July 24th, both battalions took part in the battle, the 1/5th losing 10 men killed and 6 officers and 110 men wounded, while the 2/5th lost one man killed and two officers and 21 men wounded. In November of 1812 the remnants of the 2/5th embarked at Lisbon and sailed home to England. The 1/5th remained in Spain and on June 21st 1813 fought at Vittoria, losing 4 officers and 22 men killed and 4 officers and 133 men wounded. The 1/5th next saw action at the battle of the Nivelle, on November 10th 1813, losing a further 127 men killed or wounded. Having taken part in the invasion of France the battalion fought at Orthes on February 27th 1814 and finally at Toulouse on April 10th, suffering very light casualties at both battles. On May 31st the battalion sailed for Canada.

'On Outpost Duty'. A piquet of the 5th Foot in the Peninsula, 1814.

6th (1st Warwickshire) Foot

The 1/6th Foot was already in Gibraltar when the Peninsular War broke out in 1808 and, as part of Sir Brent Spencer's force, joined Wellesley's field army on August 6th the same year. The 1/6th formed part of the 4th Infantry Brigade under Colonel Foord Barnes. The battalion fought at Roliça on August 17th although it was never seriously engaged, and four days later was present at Vimeiro where again, it saw little direct action. The battalion subsequently took part in the retreat to Corunna, where it embarked for England on January 17th 1809. The 6th lost around 300 men during the retreat. The 1/6th took part in the Walcheren campaign of 1809 and did not return to the Peninsula until November 15th the same year, when the battalion landed at Lisbon, some 1,169-strong. It marched to join Wellington's main field army in the spring of 1813 and was attached to Dalhousie's 7th Division. The battalion was present at Vittoria on June 21st but did not join in the battle until late in the day and as such suffered hardly any casualties. During the battle of the Pyrenees, however, the battalion finally got to grips with the enemy and on July 25th, at Roncesvalles, distinguished itself in the mountain pass, losing 3 officers wounded – one fatally – and 2 men killed and 17 wounded. On August 2nd at Echalar the 6th again distinguished itself in some fierce fighting, which prompted a Divisional Order from Wellington who called the 6th's action, 'the most gallant, and the finest thing he ever witnessed.' The battalion lost one officer and 12 men killed and 4 officers and 118 men wounded. The battalion's next action came at the battle of the Nivelle, on November 10th 1813, where the 6th carried French redoubts around St Pee. One man was killed and six wounded during the day. The battalion played no part in the battle of the Nive, although it was held in reserve. On February 27th 1814 the 6th fought its last battle of the war, at Orthes, where it was heavily engaged, particularly during the fighting in the village of St Boes. At one point the 6th was brought into action by Wellington himself. The battalion suffered 2 officers and 27 men killed and 10 officers and 114 men wounded. The 6th took no part in the battle of Toulouse, being employed in the region around the Garonne and Dordogne. The 6th embarked at Bordeaux on May 5th 1814 and arrived in Canada two months later.

7th (Royal Fusiliers)

The 2/7th (Royal Fusiliers) disembarked at Lisbon in April 1809 with a total strength of 650 officers men. The battalion joined Wellesley's army just after it had crossed the Douro at Oporto. Its first action came at Talavera where the 2/7th suffered 63 casualties. The battalion was joined by the 1st Battalion in the summer of 1810 and both fought at Busaco on September 27th that year. In May 1811, both battalions of the 7th found themselves part of the force under William Beresford laying siege to Badajoz and on the 16th of that month took part in the battle of Albuera. The two battalions took part in some of the bitterest and hardest fighting of the entire war as they fought the French to a standstill, refusing to give an inch. 'That astonishing infantry' was how Napier described the infantry at Albuera and the glorious conduct of the 7th during the battle established their reputation as a fighting force but at a terrible price. Out of a total of 1,282 all ranks, 705 were either killed or wounded, a 55% casualty rate in a battle still celebrated by the Royal Fusiliers today. After the battle the remains of the two battalions were formed into one and the officers of the 2/7th returned home to recruit. At Aldea de Ponte on September 27th 1811 the 1/7th lost 42 men in a small action before it settled down to besiege Ciudad Rodrigo in January 1812. The 1/7th took part in the storming with little cost, just 10 casualties but at Badajoz in April of that year 180 men were lost in taking the place. The 1/7th next saw action at Salamanca where as part of the 4th Division it suffered 198 killed and wounded. The 7th formed part of the reserve during the siege of Burgos and dragged itself back to the Portuguese border following the unsuccessful siege of the place in

September and October 1812. On June 22nd 1813 the 1/7th fought at Vittoria where it sustained only light casualties but during the battle of the Pyrenees from July to August 1813 it was involved in some fierce fighting, particularly at Sorauren where the battalion lost 217 officers and men. Two days before the battle, at Roncesvalles on July 25th, the 1/7th had fought and lost 31 men. At the storming of San Sebastian on August 31st 1813 the 1/7th supplied volunteers of whom 6 became casualties. After crossing the Nivelle at little cost the battalion pushed on into France and fought their final two actions in 1814, first on February 27th at Orthes, where it lost 68 men and finally at Toulouse on April 10th where the battalion lost just four men. On June 14th 1814 the battalion sailed from Pauillac for England where it arrived at the end of the same month. The 1/7th played no part in the Waterloo campaign for on October 4th 1814 the battalion sailed for North America where it fought at the disastrous battle of New Orleans in January the following year.

9th (East Norfolk) Foot

The 1/9th Regiment first saw action at Roliça on August 17th 1808. The battalion had sailed to Portugal as part of Sir Arthur Wellesley's first expedition to the Peninsula. During the battle the battalion withstood repeated French attacks, the 9th doing good work making several bayonet charges. Four days later the battalion won its second battle honour of the war at Vimeiro. With Wellesley's recall to England following the Convention of Cintra, Moore assumed command of the army and led it through the terrible retreat to Corunna in the winter of 1808-09, during which the 1/9th formed part of the rearguard. The battalion was one of the very last to leave Spain's shores and Captain Gomm of the 9th claimed to be the last British soldier to embark. After the disaster at Corunna the 1/9th returned home but it was not long before the battalion was part of another, this time at Walcheren in 1809. After the fiasco, the 1/9th returned to the Peninsula and under the command of Lieutenant Colonel Cameron did great execution at the battle of Busaco on September 27th 1810. Cameron, unwell on the eve of the battle, insisted on taking his place at the head of the regiment and during the battle had his horse shot dead under him and was badly bruised by the fall but when the battalion chased the French from the ridge at bayonet point Cameron was there, sword in hand at the head of his men. The flank companies of the 1/9th saw action at Barrosa on March 5th 1811 where 68 of their number became casualties. Two months later the battalion was present at Fuentes de Oñoro but took little part in the fighting, as was the case at the siege of Badajoz in March and April 1812. The 1/9th next saw action at the battle of Salamanca on July 22nd 1812. Once again the men were led into action by Cameron, sitting astride his horse waving his hat in the air exclaiming, "Now, boys, we'll at them!" Legend has it that when one of Wellington's staff told him to advance Cameron replied, "Thank you, sir, that is the best news that I have had today." The battalion spent the winter of 1812–13 on the Portuguese border following the retreat from Burgos and next saw action at Vittoria on June 22nd 1813. Further fighting followed during July and August of 1813 during the battles of the Pyrenees and at San Sebastian the 1/9th suffered 257 casualties during the siege and storming. A further 194 men became casualties at the crossing of the Nive in December

The 9th on active service in the Peninsula, 1811. This picture shows the battalion in Andalucia, southern Spain. Gibraltar can be seen in the distance.

1813 and as the Allied army pushed on into France the 1/9th saw its last spell of service in the Peninsular War at the blockade of Bayonne in southern France. At end of the war the battalion sailed for Canada to protect the border against attacks from American troops. The 9th did not arrive in time to fight at Waterloo in 1815 but formed part of the army of occupation in France until 1819.

Above: A very young looking officer of the 10th Regiment, c.1815.

Right: Lieutenant Colonel J.W.S. Ross, 10th Foot, 1813.

10th (North Lincolnshire) Foot

The 1/10th took no part in any of the main battles of the Peninsular War but was involved in the operations on the eastern side of the Iberian peninsula, mainly against the French Army under Marshal Suchet. The 10th had arrived in Spain after having been moved from Sicily to bolster the defence of Alicante in August 1812 and the following year, whilst serving under Lieutenant General Sir John Murray, the battalion was present at Tarragona although not directly in any of the fighting there. The battalion took part in the battle of Castalla, on April 13th 1813 and at Villafranca on September 13th 1813. These actions were enough to earn the 10th Regiment the battle honour 'Peninsula'. At the end of the war the battalion returned to Sicily.

11th (North Devonshire) Foot

The 1st Battalion 11th Regiment was stationed at Madeira when it received orders to proceed to Portugal, arriving at Lisbon on August 3rd 1809. The battalion was commanded by Major Newman and on March 8th 1810 was strengthened by a draft of 8 officers and 295 men from the 2nd Battalion. It was not until the battle of Busaco, on September 27th 1810, that the battalion saw its first action as part of Lowry Cole's 4th Division. The battalion was not involved in any direct fighting however and no losses were sustained. The 1/11th spent the winter months inside the lines of Torres Vedras, emerging with the rest of Wellington's army in November 1810 to begin the pursuit of Massena's starving army. While the 1st Battalion continued to keep watch on Massena the 2nd Battalion was also despatched to the Peninsula and arrived at Gibraltar in March 1811. The battalion took no active part in the war, however, and spent the remainder of the war as part of the Gibraltar garrison. The 1st Battalion, meanwhile, formed part of Hulse's brigade of Campbell's 6th Division. The battalion was present at Sabugal on April 3rd during the pursuit of Massena but did not see any action and no casualties were sustained. Nor were any at Fuentes de Oñoro on May 3rd-5th. In May 1811 the light company of the 2nd Battalion was sent to Tarifa to assist in the defence of that place, which ended with the withdrawal of the besieging French forces in January 1812. During the siege the company, which was commanded by Captain Wren, surprised a French piquet and took several prisoners as well as inflicting some casualties. Wren was mentioned in General Orders afterwards. Wren was later set upon by a French sergeant after having distanced himself from his men. He was accompanied by a British sergeant, Jones, who parried the Frenchman's thrust and ran him through with his own bayonet. Wren stripped the Frenchman of his pack, etc, and gave them to Jones, thanking him for his conduct. The battalion, took no part in the siege operations against either Ciudad Rodrigo or Badajoz but formed part of the covering force under Sir Thomas Graham. The 1/11th was present, however, at the battle of Salamanca, during which it earned itself the nickname, 'the Bloody Eleventh.' The battalion formed part of Clinton's 6th Division during the battle, again in Hulse's brigade, and were heavily involved during the latter stages of the battle when Clausel launched a counter-attack upon the Allied line. The 6th Division was drawn up by Wellington in a two-deep line which met the oncoming French columns halfway between the two hills, the Greater and Lesser Arapiles. A terrific firefight ensued between the two sides during which the 1/11th suffered grievous losses but the French were eventually driven back and the day ended in victory for the Allies. During the battle a round shot decapitated both sergeants standing with the Colours, and of a negro, furiously beating his cymbals at the time. The battalion took a green flag during the fighting, which is presumed to have belonged to one of the foreign regiments serving with the French army. The battalion also overran a battery of guns during the closing stages of the battle. The cost to the 1/11th was great. Of 516 officers and men present no fewer than 55 were killed and 295 were wounded, a total of 340. For his gallant conduct during the battle, Lieutenant Colonel Cuyler was awarded a gold medal while the regiment itself was awarded the battle honour, 'Salamanca', its first of the war. The battalion, although severely weakened by its exertions at Salamanca, took part in the

failed siege of Burgos in September and October 1812 during which a number of men from the 11th became casualties. The 1/11th retreated, along with the rest of Wellington's army, to the Portuguese border following the siege and did not march again until May 1813. The battalion was ordered to guard the magazines and supplies at Medina de Pomar, however, and therefore missed the battle of Vittoria on June 21st 1813. The battalion next saw action at Sorauren on July 28th–30th 1813 during which battle it sustained 74 casualties. During the storming of San Sebastian on August 31st a French Colour was hauled down by Lieutenant Gethin, a volunteer from the 11th. On November 10th 1813 the battalion took part in the battle of the Nivelle, where it sustained light casualties of just ten killed and wounded. During the battle the battalion, part of Lambert's brigade of the 6th Division, swept the French defenders from their redoubts around Ainhoe and around the important bridge at Amotz. Casualties were also light the following month during the battle of the Nive, where the light company of the 1/11th took the village of Villefranche. After a spell with the force blockading Bayonne the 1/11th rejoined the main body of the army on February 21st 1814 and six days later took part in the battle of Orthes, coming through unscathed with no casualties. On April 10th the battalion fought its last battle of the Peninsular War, at Toulouse, where it served with distinction, losing 142 men. At the close of hostilities the battalion marched to Bordeaux where it spent a month in cantonments. On June 21st 1814 the battalion sailed for Ireland where it disembarked on July 13th.

14th (Buckinghamshire) Foot

The 2/14th Regiment formed part of Hill's 4th Brigade, part of the 2nd Division of Moore's army which was commanded by Sir James Hope. Having arrived in the Peninsula in October 1808 the battalion soon found itself embroiled in the retreat to Corunna. The 2/14th, commanded by Lieutenant Colonel Jasper Nicholls, fought on the left wing of the army at the battle of Corunna on January 16th 1809 where it held the village of Palavia

Abaxo against repeated French attacks. The battalion got aboard ships bound for England at about 4pm on the afternoon of the 17th and arrived at Plymouth on the 23rd, having lost about 66 men during the ill-fated campaign. The 2/14th subsequently saw active service during another disastrous campaign, at Walcheren in 1809, and did not see any further active service during our period of 1808-1815. The 3/14th, on the other hand, fought at Waterloo where it was formed part of Mitchell's 4th Brigade, which in turn was part of Colville's 4th Division. The battalion had landed at Ostend on March 31st 1815 and when the campaign opened it found itself at Enghein and Nivelles. It took no part in the fighting on June 16th at Quatre Bras but on the 18th occupied a position on the extreme right of Wellington's line, on the Nivelles road. The 3/14th remained here whilst the attacks on Hougoumont raged in front of them. The battalion held this position throughout the day, forming square when the French cavalry attacked during the afternoon. The 3/14th lost seven men killed, and one officer and 20 men wounded during the day's fighting. After the battle the 14th marched to Paris where it remained until February 1816, arriving at Deal on the 2nd of that month.

20th (East Devonshire) Foot

The 20th sailed from Harwich on 18th July 1808 and arrived in Portugal one day after the battle of Roliça. Three days after landing the battalion fought at Vimeiro as part of Ackland's 8th Brigade. Casualties were light on this occasion, just one killed and six wounded. With Wellesley recalled to England following the Convention of Cintra the army was commanded by Sir John Moore who led it during the Corunna campaign of 1808–09. The 20th suffered terribly, as did all units of the army, although the losses of the battalion were never recorded. The 20th did not return to the Peninsula until November 1812, having served in the Walcheren Campaign in the meantime. Commanded by Colonel Ross, the 20th formed part of Lowry Cole's 4th Division. Its first battle upon its return came on June 21st 1813 at Vittoria where it saw only slight action, suffering just three men killed and two wounded. On July 25th the 20th was heavily engaged at the fight at the pass of Roncesvalles. The battalion barred the way of a heavy French column, an officer of which called upon the 20th to surrender. This was answered by Captain Tovey who ordered his company of the 20th to charge with fixed bayonets. The French were pushed back momentarily but came on in strength throughout the remainder of the day and heavy fighting ensued as they tried to force the pass. During the day's fighting the 20th suffered 30 men killed and 8 officers and 102 men wounded. Twelve men were listed as missing. A further one officer and 18 men were killed and six officers and 83 men wounded on July 28th at the battle of Sorauren. The conduct of the 20th on these two days was mentioned by Wellington in his despatches. On August 31st the 20th sent a detachment of 23 volunteer officers and men to take part in the storming of San Sebastian, all of whom were either killed or wounded in the assault. The 20th next saw action during the battle of the Nivelle on November 10th and although it was not awarded to the regiment as a Battle Honour it did good service during the day's fighting, carrying the Louis XIVth redoubt. The 20th was held in reserve during the passage of the Nive on December 9th and next saw serious action at the battle of Orthes on February 27th 1814. Here the 20th lost 3 officers and 6 men killed and 5 officers and 99 men wounded. After the battle the regiment numbered barely 200 men. The 20th's last action of the war came at Toulouse on April 10th where casualties were slight. After remaining in France for another two months the regiment sailed for Ireland on June 22nd 1814.

23rd (Royal Welsh Fusiliers)

The 2/23rd sailed for Spain on October 8th 1808 as part of the force under Sir David Baird. The battalion, 671-strong, disembarked on October 17th and was brigaded with the 2/14th, 2/43rd and 2/95th, under the command of Robert Craufurd. The battalion suffered the rigours of the retreat to Corunna and on January 16th 1809 took part in the battle there and is reputed to have been the last battalion to embark on the ships bound for England. The battalion returned to England and shortly afterwards was sent to Walcheren to take part in the campaign there, from whence it returned, 'almost as a skeleton'. The 1st Battalion of the 23rd arrived in the Peninsula on December 10th 1810 and was attached to Cole's 4th Division. The battalion's first action came at Albuera on May 16th 1811, during which it suffered severe losses of some 2 officers and 74 men killed as well as 12 officers and 245 men wounded, most of whom were struck down during Cole's crucial but decisive attack late in the day that won the battle for Beresford. The 1/23rd took its turn in the trenches before Ciudad Rodrigo in January 1812 but took no part in the storming of the place. At the storming of Badajoz, on April 6th 1812, the battalion formed part of Colville's 4th Division which was given the task of storming the breaches. The battalion suffered heavy losses in its efforts, a total of 172 men being lost, both in the siege and the actual storming. A further 101 casualties were sustained at Salamanca on July 22nd 1812 following which, on August 12th, the battalion entered Madrid. It took no part in the siege of Burgos but on the retreat from that place the 1/23rd fell back to the Portuguese border. The battalion next saw action at Vittoria, on June 21st 1813, where casualties on this occasion were light. On July 28th the 1/23rd fought at Sorauren where casualties reduced the effective strength of the battalion to just 160 men. A party of volunteers from the 1/23rd took part in the storming of San Sebastian on August

31st 1813 where 8 of their number became casualties. The next major action for the battalion came at the forcing of Soult's position along the line of the river Nivelle, the 1/23rd driving the French from the village of Sare. The battalion was to see no further action until February 27th 1814 at Orthes, where, as part of Cole's 4th Division, it drove the enemy from the village of St Boes on the enemy's right flank. Heavy fighting during the battle cost the battalion some 94 casualties. On April 10th 1814 the 1/23rd fought its last battle, at Toulouse. Just eight men were killed or wounded. On June 6th 1814 the battalion sailed for England, disembarking at Portsmouth on the 25th. The following year the battalion was again sent overseas to take part in the Waterloo campaign. The battalion sailed from Gosport on May 23rd and upon arrival at Ghent was again attached to the 4th Division. On June 18th 1815, the battalion was held in reserve although it suffered from enemy artillery fire throughout the day. 4 officers and 11 men were killed and 7 officers and 78 men wounded. The wounded included Colonel Sir Henry Ellis who was mortally wounded whilst cheering on his men from the centre of the battalion's square. On July 1st the battalion entered Paris and remained in France until November 1st 1818 when it embarked at Calais, arriving at Dover the following morning.

24th (2nd Warwickshire) Foot

The 2/24th Regiment arrived in Portugal in April 1809 shortly after Wellesley's return to that country following the inquiry into the Convention of Cintra. On July 28th the battalion found itself in the thick of the fighting at Talavera. When the Brigade of Guards and Langwerth's Germans were thrown back, following their initial successful repulse of the French, the 2/24th were called upon to hold the line as the two units mentioned fell back through their ranks. As the Guards reformed the 2/24th poured in several well controlled volleys until the pressure was taken off that part of the British line. The brigade commander, General Mackenzie, was killed during the battle and the 2/24th sustained 46% casualties, more than any other battalion other than

a unit of the King's German Legion. Following the battle of Talavera the 2/24th, now reduced to jut 360 men, was commanded by Major Chamberlain. A year later the battalion was in action again, this time at Busaco, where only the light company was directly involved in the battle. At Fuentes de Oñoro, on May 3rd-5th 1811, the 2/24th played a major part in driving the French from the village, accomplishing this task with little cost. This took place on the first day of the battle. There was little fighting on the 4th and on the 5th the battalion played a supporting role before Wellington finally forced Massena to withdraw. The battalion next saw service before Ciudad Rodrigo in January 1812, helping to construct batteries and dig trenches before that place, during which spell of duty the battalion lost 20 men when General Barrie launched a sortie. The battalion was not involved in the storming on January 19th. The next major action in which the 2/24th was engaged came on July 22nd 1812 at Salamanca which saw Marmont's army crushed. During the siege of Burgos, the 2/24th was one of the few battalions to come out of the episode with any credit when, on October 4th, the battalion was ordered to assault one of the breaches made in the castle's walls. No sooner had the Allies exploded a mine beneath the walls than the 198 men of the 2/24th raced forward led by Lieutenant Fraser. They charged through the smoke, dust and rubble to begin clearing away the defenders. A covering party led by Captain Lepper followed supported by another party led by Captain Coote. The 2/24th pressed home its attack on the breach but its efforts were ultimately to no avail. The regiment distinguished itself during the attack although the siege failed. Wellington later described the attack by the 2/24th as 'highly praiseworthy'. By the time Wellington began his 1813 campaign the battalion had been so reduced in numbers that it formed a provisional battalion with the 2/58th Regiment and next saw action at Vittoria. As the French fled northwards to France the 2/24th gained further battle honours at the battles of the Pyrenees, the Nivelle and finally at Orthes. When the 2/24th returned home in November 1814 it numbered just 300 men.

26th Cameronian Regiment

The 1/26th departed for the Peninsula from Cork on September 10th 1808 numbering 990 officers and men as well as 79 women and children. Due to various delays the battalion did not disembark at Corunna until November 4th upon which it formed part of Sir David Baird's force acting in conjunction with that under Sir John Moore. During the subsequent retreat to Corunna during the winter of 1808-09 the 1/26th was unfortunately one of the battalions to misbehave and lose discipline and in fact when it reached Betanzos on January 10th 1809, only 14 officers and 50 men were still with the colours, although many more stragglers came in later in the day. The battalion was sufficiently up to strength to fight in the battle of Corunna on January 16th and upon its return to England showed a deficiency in numbers of just 204. The battalion was despatched to Walcheren upon its return to England but returned to the Peninsula in July 1811. The battalion remained in the Peninsula for just under a year as the marches and counter-marches undertaken by it during operations on the Spanish-Portuguese border took their toll, many of the men still suffering from the effects of the Walcheren campaign. 'I never saw any army so unhealthy', wrote Wellington of his army on November 8th 1811 and two months later the 1/26th, one of the weakest battalions, just 200 strong, was sent back to Lisbon. On June 2nd 1812 the battalion left Lisbon bound for garrison duty in Gibraltar.

27th (Inniskilling) Foot

The 27th Regiment had three battalions between 1808 and 1815, all of which saw service in the Peninsula, the 1st Battalion going on to serve at Waterloo. The 1st and 2nd Battalions landed in Spain at Alicante in December 1812 where they remained until the following March. During 1813 the battalions saw action at Alcoy, Alfafara, Biar and at Castalla, where Captain Waldron engaged a French officer in single combat. After the unsuccessful siege of Tarragona the two battalions returned to Alicante but on September 12th fought at the battle of Ordal where the 2nd Battalion suffered 8 officers and 300 men killed and wounded. The battalions next saw action during the siege of Barcelona in February 1814 until the end of the war came in April of that year. The 1st Battalion was then despatched to America whilst the 2nd Battalion returned to Ireland. Fortunately, the 1st Battalion returned to Europe in time to take part in the Waterloo campaign where it served with great distinction, suffering grievous losses whilst standing in square at one of the hottest places on the battlefield. The 1/27th yielded not an inch of ground for which it paid a shocking price. Of 15 officers present 14 became casualties whilst of the 670 other ranks 498 were either killed or wounded. Such was the price of glory. The battalion remained in France until March 1817 when it departed for home. The 3rd Battalion of the 27th had landed in Spain at Corunna on October 14th 1808. The battalion remained behind in Portugal under Sir John Craddock whilst the bulk of the army marched into Spain under Sir John Moore. The battalion was thus spared the retreat to Corunna. The battalion suffered severely from a bout of fever and was withdrawn into Portugal during 1809 and so missed the Talavera campaign. Although present at Busaco in September 1810 it played no direct part in the battle and it was not until Albuera, on May 16th 1811, that the 3/27th fought its first battle, suffering 77 casualties. The battalion was part of Lowry Cole's 4th Division and next saw action at the siege of Badajoz in 1812 during which it sustained 303 casualties. Its next battle honour was that of Salamanca, fought on July 22nd 1812, where the battalion suffered only slight losses. The 3/27th played no part in the abortive siege of Burgos as it was attached to Hill's force further south and it was not until June the following year, at the battle of Vittoria, that it next saw action. The battalion was one of the heaviest engaged during the battles of the Pyrenees in July 1813 during which it lost 300 men, principally at Sorauren where the battalion made several fierce bayonet charges to push back the enemy. A detachment of the battalion was present at the storming of San Sebastian on August 31st 1813 and in November of that year the entire battalion took part in the battle of the Nivelle which saw the Allied army press on into France. The battalion was not involved during the four day battle of the Nive and next saw action at Orthes on February 27th 1814 where it suffered only light casualties. The battalion's last action came at Toulouse on April 10th 1814. After this the 3rd Battalion was despatched to America.

28th (North Gloucestershire) Foot

The 28th (North Gloucestershire) Regiment at the battle of Waterloo, June 18th 1815.

The 1/28th first saw action in the Peninsula during the retreat to Corunna in 1808-09. The battalion subsequently fought there on January 16th before embarking for England which it reached on January 26th. Five months later the battalion was sent to Walcheren where it took part in the campaign there. When Moore's army sailed from Corunna a large number of men remained behind in hospitals in Lisbon, amongst whom were six officers and 200 men of the 1/28th. These men were formed into a battalion of detachments and fought at the crossing of the Douro and two months later fought again at the battle of Talavera on July 28th 1809. Following Wellesley's retreat into Portugal following the battle the 2/28th arrived in the Peninsula as a reinforcement and in September the following year both the detachment of the 1/28th and the whole of the 2/28th were present at Busaco. In March 1810, the remainder of the 1/28th had sailed to Gibraltar and at the battle of Barrosa on March 5th the following year the battalion fought and sustained 195 casualties. During the battle the 1/28th was commanded by Lieutenant Colonel John Frederick Browne, who had joined the regiment in 1781. As Browne led his men against overwhelming French numbers he broke into his favourite song, 'Hearts of Oak.' Just over two months later, farther north, the 2/28th took part in the bloody battle of Albuera where the battalion lost 164 men in the day's fighting. 1812 saw the 28th play a minor role in Wellington's operations before it caught up with the main Allied army at Burgos in September of that year. At Vittoria on June 21st 1813 the 28th led the attack of the 2nd Division and during the day's fighting 200 of the 818 men of the 28th became casualties. During the fight at the pass of Maya on July 25th 1813 a picquet of the 28th, under Major Bradby, was surrounded by a French force ten times their number and fell back up the hill, fighting to the last until every man was either killed or wounded. At the same battle Ensign Delmar was shot through the heart whilst carrying the Colour and another young Ensign, Hill, seized it shouting, 'The Slashers shall never want a man to display their Colours to the enemy.' Hill was shot soon afterwards also but by the time the bullet passed through the thirteen folds of his handkerchief it had lost its force and he survived. The 28th next saw action at the battle of the Nivelle on November 10th 1813 and the following month lost 147 men killed or wounded at the battle of the Nive. The 28th's last action in the Peninsula came at Toulouse on April 10th 1814 where it lost 31 men. At the end of the war the 28th left for Ireland but was back on the Continent in May 1815 at the start of the Waterloo campaign. The regiment covered itself with glory first at Quatre Bras on June 16th, where it lost 75 men, and at Waterloo on the 18th where the regiment lost 177 men. On July 10th the regiment entered Paris and returned home four months later.

29th (Worcestershire) Foot

The 29th disembarked at Cadiz on July 3rd 1808 and claims to have been the first British unit to land in the Peninsula. The regiment fought at the first battle of the war, at Roliça on August 17th, when it formed part of Nightingale's 3rd Infantry Brigade. Led by Colonel Lake, the 29th saw fierce fighting during the day suffering 151 casualties, the highest figure in Wellesley's army. Apparently, Colonel Lake went into battle wearing a brand new uniform, boots, hat, epaulettes, sash, etc, and even had his hair powdered and queued, even though these last two practices had recently been abolished. Unfortunately, Lake was killed due to an error on his own part. Four days later the 29th fought at Vimeiro where casualties were much lighter, just 14 in fact. The regiment took no part in the Corunna campaign but remained in Portugal under the command of Sir John Craddock. At the crossing of the Douro, in May 1809, the light companies of the 29th saw action and two months later the whole regiment fought with distinction at Talavera. During this battle the 29th made a charge and captured two enemy colours although the eagles which had stood on top of them had been unscrewed and removed prior to their being taken, otherwise the honour of taking the first French eagle would have fallen to the regiment. The 29th suffered 183 casualties in the day's fighting. Following the battle Wellington withdrew to the Portuguese border and on September 12th 1809 he wrote, "I wish very much that some measures could be adopted to get some recruits for the 29th Regiment. It is the best Regiment in this Army." It was to be almost two years before the 29th saw action again, this time at Albuera on May 16th 1811, on which occasion the regiment suffered 324 casualties. Indeed, such were the casualties suffered by several battalions at Albuera that the 29th, 3rd, 31st 57th and 66th were formed into one Provisional Battalion under the command of Sir John Colborne. On October 3rd 1811 the Duke of York issued orders for the 29th to return to England to recover and on November 2nd the regiment embarked, under the command of Major Tucker, on HMS Agincourt, arriving at Portsmouth on December 1st. The 29th was ordered to the Netherlands in April 1815 in order to take part in the Waterloo campaign. The regiment landed at Ostend on June 13th but in spite of being rushed up by boat along the canal to Ghent, which was reached on June 15th, the regiment arrived too late to take part in the battle itself.

Ensign Furnace, of the 29th Regiment, at the battle of Albuera, May 16th 1811. During the battle the 29th suffered heavy losses; two Colour Sergeants had been killed and Ensign Furnace wounded. The remaining Colour Sergeant propped up Furnace, carrying the King's Colour, while another officer offered to take it from him. Furnace refused, however, while Ensign Vance, carrying the Regimental Colour, was mortally wounded. The last Colour Sergeant was killed soon afterwards and the Colour Party virtually ceased to exist. In an effort to save the Regimental Colour from the French, Vance ripped the flag from its staff and wrapped it round his body. That night both Vance and Furnace were found dead on the battlefield but the two Colours were safe, hidden by their guardians before they had died.

30th (Cambridgeshire) Foot

The 2nd Battalion 30th Regiment sailed from Cork on March 12th 1809, under the command of Lieutenant Colonel Minet. The battalion arrived at Lisbon two weeks later and remained there on garrison duty until the following year. In March 1810 four companies were sent to Tarifa to assist in the defence of the place but rejoined the main Allied army in November 1810, just as Wellington was about to emerge from the Lines of Torres Vedras. The 2/30th, some 507-strong, formed part of Dunlop's brigade of the 5th Division and on May 3rd-5th saw its first action, at Fuentes de Oñoro, although the battalion was positioned in front of Fort Conception, where no fighting occurred. The battalion saw no further action in 1811 and indeed were rather inactive until March 1812 when it took part in the siege of Badajoz. At the storming of the town on April 6th, the 30th formed part of Leith's division which escaladed the walls of the San Vincente bastion. 130 men were either killed or wounded during the storming, including Lieutenant Colonel Gray, who

was killed. Gray was later mentioned by Wellington in his despatch. The battalion's last action of the Peninsular War came on July 22nd 1812 at Salamanca. The battalion's strength on this day was just 349 and it formed part of Pringle's brigade, again with the 5th Division. The division was launched against the French shortly after Pakenham's devastating attack on the leading French columns. The 2/30th found itself in the second line advancing south to attack Maucune's division. The French formed in squares and were swept away with ease by the British infantry. The 2/30th suffered 27 men killed and wounded during the battle. The battalion next saw service at Burgos, although it took no part in the actual siege operations. During the retreat from Burgos, however, the battalion fought a small action at Muriel where four men were killed and seven officers and 25 men were wounded. Wellington later mentioned the gallant conduct of the battalion in his despatch. Early in December 1812 six weak companies of the

2/30th were sent home to recruit, the remaining four being formed into a Provisional Battalion with four companies of the 44th Regiment. However, in May 1813 these were also sent home. The battalion was reunited in June 1813 at Jersey. Later that same year the 2/30th sailed to the Netherlands to take part in the campaign at Bergen-op-Zoom. The battalion remained in Antwerp at the close of that particular campaign and was still there in March 1815 when news was received of Napoleon's escape from Elba. The 2/30th formed part of Halkett's 5th British Brigade, which was part of Sir Charles Alten's 3rd Infantry Division. The battalion numbered 615 men and was positioned to the left of the crossroads at Mont St Jean on June 18th 1815. The battalion played a part in the repulse of the Imperial Guard and sustained losses of 51 killed and 165 wounded. The battalion remained in France until December 31st 1815 when it sailed for Ireland, arriving there on January 29th 1816.

31st (Huntingdonshire) Foot

The 2/31st landed at Lisbon on November 5th 1808 and soon afterwards marched north to join the force under Sir John Moore. However, having received news of Moore's position the battalion returned to Lisbon and so was spared the ordeal of the Corunna campaign. The battalion's first action came at Talavera on July 27th–28th 1809 where, as part of Mackenzie's division, it was engaged in fierce fighting suffering 35 killed and 197 wounded. After the battle the 2/31st was attached to Tilson's brigade in Hill's 2nd Division. The battalion next saw action at Albuera on May 16th 1811. Once again it was heavily engaged and was one of the battalions attacked by Soult's cavalrymen who did such great damage under cover of a rain storm. The 2/31st managed to form square, however, and came through relatively unscathed. Nevertheless, the battalion lost 155 men during the day. In June 1811 the battalion took part in the abortive siege of Badajoz as part of Hill's covering force. The action at Albuera had so reduced the battalion's strength that it was formed into a provisional battalion along with men of the 66th Regiment. The battalion still formed part of Hill's force and on October 28th 1811 was present at the surprise of Girard's force at Arroyo dos Molinos. The 2/31st took no part in the sieges at Ciudad Rodrigo and Badajoz as

it again formed part of the covering army during the operations. Acting with Hill's force meant that the battalion would not be present at Salamanca or Burgos and it was not until June 21st 1813 that the 2/31st next saw action, at Vittoria. On this occasion the battalion helped drive the French from the heights of Puebla on the Allied right flank. Casualties were light, just 15 in all. Casualties were equally light, just 42, at Roncesvalles and Sorauren where the battalion fought between July 25th and 30th to gain the battle honour 'Pyrenees'. On November 10th 1813 the 2/31st took part in the battle of the Nivelle and the following month was heavily engaged at the battle of the Nive, particularly on December 13th at St Pierre during which Captain Hensworth's company captured two French guns. 7 men were killed and 2 officers and 35 men wounded during the day. The battalion earned the honour 'Orthes' on February 27th 1814 although again, as part of Hill's force, it saw little of the main fighting. While on the march towards Toulouse the battalion was engaged at Aire on March 20th and on April 10th 1814 saw only limited action at Toulouse itself, the final battle of the Peninsular War. On July 12th 1814 the 2/31st sailed for Ireland where it arrived on July 23rd.

32nd (The Cornwall) Foot

The 1/32nd formed part of the army under Sir Arthur Wellesley that landed in Portugal in August 1808. Commanded by Lieutenant Colonel Samuel Hinde, the battalion was brigaded with the 6th Regiment to be commanded by Major General Bowes. The battalion fought at Roliça and Vimeiro where the battalion came through relatively unscathed on both occasions. During the retreat to Corunna the battalion guarded the ammunition train and during the retreat and the battle itself lost 250 men. Returning to England the 1/32nd was brought up to strength and the following year sailed to Holland to take part in the campaign at Walcheren. During a French sortie at the siege of Flushing a major of the 32nd was caught in the middle of his toilet and, to the great amusement of his men, led them into the fray with his face covered with soap and an open razor in his hand. The battalion returned to England in January 1810 by which time its strength had been reduced to just 200 men. On June 24th 1811 it sailed once again for the Peninsula and on July 22nd 1812 played a part at the battle of Salamanca where it lost 137 men. It subsequently saw service at the siege of Burgos and the retreat from there to the Portuguese border. Many men were still suffering from the effects of the Walcheren campaign and the retreat of 1812 caused severe losses and reduced the battalion at one time to just 150 fit men. Reinforcements were received from the 2nd Battalion in Ireland and the 1/32nd went on to fight during the battles of the Pyrenees, at the Nivelle, the Nive and at Orthes. The battalion returned to Ireland in June 1814 following the end of the Peninsular War and both 1st and 2nd Battalions were amalgamated in readiness to proceed to America. However, when news of Napoleon's escape from Elba broke the 32nd sailed for Ostend. The 32nd was brigaded with the 28th, 79th and 95th Rifles to form Sir James Kempt's brigade, part of Picton's 5th Division. At the battle of Quatre Bras on June 16th the regiment was involved in some of the hardest fighting during the day and suffered 3 officers and 20 men killed and 12 officers and 225 men wounded. At one point a shell burst immediately over the Colours, ripping the Regimental Colour to shreds, killing an officer and one section of his company. Two ensigns were also wounded. During the battle of Waterloo on the 18th the 32nd formed part of Picton's counter-attack in the early afternoon and when he himself was shot through the head and killed, two grenadiers of the 32nd carried his body to the rear. In another melee, a French officer seized the King's Colour of the 32nd from a wounded ensign. Sergeant Switzer, of the escort, immediately thrust his pike into the Frenchman and Ensign John Birtwhistle, who was carrying the Regimental Colour, ran him through with his sword. At the end of the day the 32nd, who had gone into action at Quatre Bras some 716 strong, numbered just 130 fit men. The 32nd subsequently marched to Paris and returned to England in early 1816.

33rd (1st Yorks, West Riding) Foot

The 33rd Regiment at Waterloo, June 18th 1815.

The 33rd Regiment played no part in the Peninsular campaign but in November 1813 sailed for Holland to take part in the campaign against Bergen-op-Zoom. The battalion remained at Antwerp at the conclusion of this campaign until March 1815 when news of Napoleon's escape from Elba was received. The 33rd was assigned to the 5th British Brigade under the command of Sir Colin Halkett, the brigade in turn forming part of Sir Charles Alten's 3rd Division. The battalion got into action towards the end of the battle of Quatre Bras on June 16th, but still managed to suffer 3 officers and 16 men killed and 7 officers and 70 men wounded. Nineteen men were also reported wounded. On June 18th the battalion, along with the 2/30th, 2/73rd and 2/69th, was positioned to the right centre of the Allied army on some rising ground close to La Haye Sainte. It suffered, as did all the regiments, from French artillery fire and from their repeated cavalry attacks. The battalion also took part in the repulse of the Imperial Guard towards the close of the battle. The 33rd suffered 2 officers and 33 men killed, and 8 officers and 92 men wounded. On July 8th the 33rd entered Paris as part of the occupying army, staying there until December 23rd when the battalion returned to England.

34th (Cumberland) Foot

The 2/34th arrived in the Peninsula as Marshal Massena was pursuing Wellington towards the Lines of Torres Vedras. The battalion was present at Busaco on September 27th 1810 but played little part in the action. The battalion's first major action came at Albuera on May 16th 1811 where it suffered 3 officers and 30 men killed and 4 officers and 91 men wounded. The battalion achieved a unique feat on October 28th 1811 when it took part in the battle of Arroyo dos Molinos. The battalion took a large number of prisoners from the French 34th Regiment, including the band with its drums and the drum major with his baton. These were taken by the 2/34th and remain today as prize possessions of the regiment. The 34th Regiment is the only regiment of the British Army to hold the battle honour 'Arroyo dos Molinos'. The battalion was part of the force covering the siege operations at Badajoz in the spring of 1812 and it was to be another year before the battalion saw action again, at Vittoria on June 21st 1813, where it sustained 76 casualties. At Maya, on July 25th 1813, the battalion suffered nearly 300 casualties, including a number of prisoners, when the French surprised the British force there but three months later, having suitably recovered, it found itself fighting on French soil following the crossing of the Bidassoa. As Wellington pushed on into France the 2/34th saw action at the battles of the Nivelle and Nive, in November and December of 1813, during which casualties were light. Casualties were similarly light at Orthes where the battalion was present on February 27th 1814. On April 10th 1814 the 2/34th fought its last battle of the war at Toulouse although this was not awarded them as a battle honour. After a short spell in France the battalion embarked at Bordeaux on July 17th 1814, bound for Ireland.

36th (Herefordshire) Foot

The 1/36th Regiment formed part of the first Peninsular expedition which landed in Portugal in August 1808. The battalion fought at Roliça on August 17th as part of Ferguson's 2nd Infantry Brigade and four days later at Vimeiro, where it lost 48 men. The battalion subsequently took part in the retreat to and battle of Corunna during which it lost three men killed and one officer wounded. 156 men were taken prisoners during the campaign. The 36th saw no further service in the Peninsula until 1811 although it did take part in the Walcheren Campaign of 1809. The 1/36th returned to the Peninsula in March 1811, transported to Portugal in HMS Victory, and was soon involved in the pursuit of Massena's army from in front of the Lines of Torres Vedras. In May 1811 the 1/36th was present at Fuentes de Oñoro although it did not take part in any of the fighting. The battalion next saw action at the battle of Salamanca on July 22nd the following year. During the battle the battalion, part of Clinton's 6th Division, suffered four officers and 16 men killed and five officers and 79 men wounded. Following the battle of Salamanca the battalion went into cantonments at Cuellar but before long was on the march again, this time to take part in the abortive siege of Burgos between September and October of 1812. Following this operation the 36th, along with the rest of the Allied army, were forced to retreat to the Portuguese border which it reached in December. In May 1813 the 1/36th advanced once more with the Allied army into Spain but did not take part in the battle of Vittoria in June of that year.

The battalion did, however, see action during the battles of the Pyrenees from July to August 1813 during which it lost 46 men. The battalion suffered no casualties during the battle of the Nivelle in November 1813 and again, the following month, at the crossing of the Nive, where the battalion lost just three men wounded. The 1/36th next saw action at the battle of Orthes on February 27th 1814 and once again casualties were negligible. However, at the final action at of the war at Toulouse, on April 10th 1814, fought after the abdication of Napoleon, the battalion suffered one officer and nine men killed and 38 officers and 104 men wounded. On June 22nd 1814 the battalion embarked at Pauillac and arrived at Cork on July 11th.

37th (North Hampshire) Foot

The 1/37th Regiment saw little service during the Peninsular War. After spells of duty in the West Indies and Ireland the battalion embarked on March 25th 1812 for two years garrison duty at Gibraltar. The men spent the next twelve months kicking their heels before being despatched to Ceuta, on the African side of the Straits of Gibraltar, for yet another spell of garrison duty. Here, the 1/37th lost 4 officers and 70 men through yellow fever. On February 10th 1814 the battalion finally left for the main theatre of war to take part in the investment of Bayonne. There was little action here before the abdication of Napoleon in April 1814 and on June 4th that year the battalion embarked for service in North America.

38th (1st Staffordshire) Foot

The 1/38th sailed for Portugal in July 1808 as part of the first expedition to the Peninsula. On August 17th, as part of Hill's 1st Brigade, it fought at Roliça, the first battle of the war. Casualties were just 4 killed. Four days later the 1/38th gained its second battle honour, at Vimeiro, in spite of hardly having to fire a shot. The battalion played its part in the retreat to Corunna and at the battle there in January 1809. 143 men were lost during the Corunna campaign. The battalion was sent to take part in the Walcheren campaign in July 1809 and it was the 2/38th that returned to the Peninsula on April 2nd 1810. The battalion formed part of the Leith's 5th Division and fought its first action at Busaco suffering 5 killed and 18 wounded. The 2/38th took no part in the battles of 1811 and next saw action at the siege of Badajoz in March-April 1812. The battalion stormed the San Vincente bastion and thus drew the defenders away from

the breaches which ultimately resulted in the town's capture. The following month the 1/38th was despatched to the Peninsula to join the 2nd Battalion and arrived just in time to take part in the battle of Salamanca on July 22nd 1812. The 1/38th lost 2 officers and 14 men killed and 12 officers and 115 men wounded. The 2/38th, by now rather a weak battalion, suffered 9 men killed and 2 officers and 40 men wounded. The retreat to Burgos resulted in the loss of more men and in December 1812 the 2/38th, having first left all fit and effective men behind with the 1st Battalion, sailed for England. At the battle of Vittoria on June 21st 1813 the 1/38th suffered low casualties of just 2 men killed and 6 wounded. The battalion played only a small part in the battle as it formed part of Sir Thomas Graham's force on the extreme left of the Allied army. On August 31st 1813 San Sebastian was finally stormed after a somewhat unhappy siege. The battalion took part in the storming losing 174 men in doing so. When the 1/38th crossed the Bidassoa in October 1813 it found itself fighting on French soil and on November 10th took part in the battle of the Nivelle although this was not awarded as a battle honour. During the battle of the Nive the battalion stormed the heights of Iruse, crossed the river and fought its way forward, driving the French defenders before

them. 12 men were killed and 4 officers and 90 men wounded during the battle which was fought on December 9th–13th. This battle was the final one of the war for the 1/38th because while Wellington pushed on towards Toulouse the battalion remained behind laying siege to Bayonne. However, on April 14th 1814 the garrison made a sortie during which the battalion was engaged. In May the 1/38th embarked at Bordeaux for Ireland.

39th (Dorsetshire) Foot

The 2/39th departed for the Peninsula on June 22nd 1809, arriving off Lisbon on July 2nd. The battalion was posted to Catlin Craufurd's division and later on that year formed part of Rowland Hill's force. It saw no direct action at Busaco on September 27th 1810, although it was present during the day. The battalion's first battle came at Albuera on May 16th 1811 where, although barely 400-strong, the battalion suffered 96 casualties. The battalion was now part of Hill's force acting independently from the main army and on October 28th 1811 took part in the surprise at Arroyo dos Molinos. One officer and ten men were wounded during the attack. Whilst the 2nd Battalion was fighting here the 1st Battalion of the regiment had arrived from Sicily under the command of Lieutenant Colonel Robert William O'Callaghan. The two battalions met at Lisbon and after transferring all of its fit men into the 1st Battalion, the 2nd Battalion, on January 27th 1812, sailed for England to recruit. The strength of the 1st Battalion, meanwhile, was now 1,200 and on December 26th 1811 it marched north to join the 2nd Division of the army under Hill. The 1/39th took no part in any of the great battles of 1812 although its light company did take part in Hill's raid on the bridge at Almaraz. In

November 1812 the battalion formed part of the rearguard of Wellington's army as it retreated to Portugal following the debacle at Burgos. On June 21st 1813 the 1/39th fought at Vittoria, acting on the right flank of the Allied army driving the French from their positions on the heights of Puebla. The 39th lost 227 men during a hard day's fighting. The battalion lost a further 2 officers and 29 men killed and 7 officers and 118 men wounded at the fight at Maya, in the Pyrenees, on July 25th 1813, when the British force there was attacked in strength by French troops in overwhelming numbers. The battalion was only lightly engaged during the battle of the Nivelle on November 10th 1813 but on December 13th, during the battle of the Nive, it lost 30 men in some hard fighting around the Chateau Larralde. The battalion's final action of the war came at Orthes on February 27th 1814 where it helped turn Soult's left flank. The 1/39th played no part in the battle of Toulouse on April 10th as it was positioned on the wrong side of the Garonne, acting against enemy outposts. Even so, one officer and a handful of men were wounded. On June 8th 1814 the battalion sailed from Bordeaux, bound for Canada.

40th (2nd Somersetshire) Foot

One of only three regiments to serve throughout the Peninsular War, the 40th Regiment landed in Portugal in August 1808 and formed part of the 2nd Brigade of Wellesley's army. The regiment fought in the first battle of the war at Roliça where it suffered light casualties of just one killed and two wounded.

Four days later the 40th fought at Vimeiro. Here, the regiment was heavily involved and suffered 38 casualties during the day. The regiment was spared the Corunna campaign and remained behind in Portugal. It next saw action at Talavera on July 27th–28th where it suffered 118 casualties. The retreat to Portugal followed and the regiment saw no further action until September 27th 1810 at Busaco. Here, however, the 40th found itself on the left of the line and was not involved in any direct action. The 40th saw no action either in any of the major battles of 1811 although one company did fight at Albuera on May 16th of that year, losing ten men killed and three wounded. The regiment was part of the force besieging Ciudad Rodrigo in January 1812 although it did not take part in the actual storming. At Badajoz, however, in March and April of 1812, the 40th suffered very severe losses, particularly during the actual storming where it led the Forlorn Hope. The 40th lost a terrible 85 officers and men killed and a further 419 wounded. The 40th, somewhat depleted, next saw action at Salamanca on July 22nd 1812 although just prior to this the regiment was involved in a minor action at the Vale of Canizal where it captured the a French Drum Major's staff. This is now a prized possession of the regiment. During the main battle the 40th fought around the Lesser Arapil, the smaller of the two hills. The regiment lost 132 killed and wounded during the day. On June 21st of the following year the 40th fought at Vittoria losing 42 men whilst attacking the flank of the French army. When Wellington crossed the Pyrenees the 40th were involved in the fighting in the mountain passes during which it lost a further 231 casualties. In October 1813 Wellington began the invasion of France and on November 10th the 40th fought at the battle of the Nivelle suffering 106 casualties. The regiment's final two actions of the Peninsular War came in 1814 at Orthes and Toulouse, the regiment being particularly involved in the latter battle, and at the close of the war the 40th returned to England. In January 1815 the 40th was sent to America but arrived too late to take part in the disastrous New Orleans campaign. The regiment then returned hurriedly to Belgium as the Waterloo campaign opened. The 40th formed part of Lambert's Brigade and was held in reserve on the Allied left. As the day wore on the regiment was brought across to reinforce the centre and soon after took place in the final charge against the Imperial Guard. The 40th lost 201 men during the day, a quarter of its strength. The battalion marched to Paris after the battle, entering the French capital on July 7th 1815, and remained in France until March 1816 when it embarked at Calais, arriving at Leith on April 25th.

42nd (The Royal Highland) Foot

The 1/42nd was sent to Gibraltar in October 1805 and so was ready to join Sir John Moore's army when called upon in September 1808. The battalion took part in the retreat to Corunna and on January 16th 1809 fought at the battle there, losing 40 men. When the battalion returned to England it was seen that just 80 men had been lost during the retreat and battle and it was said that the 42nd, along with the 50th, behaved best during both episodes. In July 1809 the 1/42nd sailed for Walcheren to take part in the campaign there, during which its numbers were decimated by fever. The following year the 2nd Battalion of the 42nd sailed to the Peninsula and on September 27th 1810 fought at Busaco where it suffered just six casualties. After spending the winter behind the Lines of Torres Vedras the battalion emerged in pursuit of Massena's army and on May 3rd-5th took part in the battle of Fuentes de Oñoro, losing 34 men killed and wounded. In January 1812 the battalion took part in the siege of Ciudad Rodrigo which was stormed on January 19th. It took no part in the siege of Badajoz but was part of the covering force. Shortly afterwards, the 1/42nd arrived in the Peninsula and after giving over its fit men the 2/42nd returned home to recruit. The 1/42nd was attached to Pack's brigade of the 6th Division and on July 22nd 1812 took part in the battle of Salamanca, losing just 12 men. In September the same year the battalion marched northeast to take part in the siege of Burgos. The siege was a complete failure although the 1/42nd fought well and suffered heavy losses of 49 killed and 248 wounded. A further 30 men were lost during the battle of the Pyrenees. On November 10th 1813 the battalion took part in the battle of the Nivelle, driving the French from their positions around Ainhoe. A further 2 officers and 10 men were killed and 16 men wounded during the battle of the Nive on December 9th-13th which marked the end of the year's campaigning. The 1/42nd saw action at the final two major battles of the Peninsular War, at Orthes and Toulouse. At Orthes the battalion saw heavy fighting and lost 158 men but this was nothing compared to the carnage at Toulouse on April 10th 1814. On this occasion the battalion swept the enemy from its positions along the Calvinet Ridge but at a tremendous cost of 27 officers and 406 men killed and wounded. It was the heaviest loss sustained by any of Wellington's regiments during the day. At the end of the war the 1/42nd sailed for Ireland but the following year returned to the Continent to join Wellington's Anglo-Dutch army at Waterloo. The battalion had landed at Ostend in May 1815 and was posted to Kemmis's brigade, part of Picton's division. The battalion was hard pressed at Quatre Bras on June 16th, particularly during one dangerous moment when it was caught in line by enemy cavalry. The Peninsular training stood the battalion in good stead, however, and the French were seen off in style. Casualties during the day were 45 killed and 243 wounded. The battalion was later praised by Wellington in his despatch. On June 18th the battalion occupied a position behind Hougoumont on the ridge to the north. It came under French artillery fire throughout the day and of 329 men who went into action that day, 50 became casualties. The battalion marched for Paris afterwards before returning to England in December 1815.

43rd (Monmouthshire Light Infantry) Regiment

The 1/43rd Light Infantry arrived in Portugal just in time to take part in the battle of Vimeiro on August 21st 1808. In October of the same year the 2/43rd arrived in the Peninsula as part of the reinforcements under Sir David Baird and together the two battalions took part in the retreat to Corunna that winter. The 1/43rd formed part of the Light Brigade under Robert Craufurd, the most famous unit of Wellington's army during the war. Upon its return to England the 1/43rd was detailed to take part in the Walcheren campaign whilst the 2/43rd returned to the Peninsula. Not long after its arrival the battalion took part in Craufurd's famous march to Talavera during which the Light Brigade marched almost sixty miles in twenty-four hours. The battalion arrived too late to take part in the battle and it was to be another year before it saw another full-pitched battle. In the meantime, the 43rd, as part of Craufurd's newly-constituted Light Division, spent the summer of 1810 on outpost duty on the river Coa, during which time it found itself involved in numerous skirmishes with the French, notably on July 24th at the combat of the Coa, when the division fought desperately to avoid being destroyed by Ney's French corps. At Busaco, on September 27th 1810, the 43rd played a great part in repulsing Loison's division at the moment of its apparent victory, appearing – along with the 52nd Light Infantry – as if from nowhere to deliver a devastating volley into the French ranks. In the spring of 1811 the 43rd fought a number of glorious actions against an numerically superior enemy, notably at Sabugal on April 3rd. The 43rd was also present at Fuentes de Oñoro. At Ciudad Rodrigo the 43rd lost 57 men during the siege and storming although this was nothing compared to the casualties at Badajoz which was stormed on April 6th 1812. The Light Division, including the 43rd, led the attack on the breaches but could make little headway against the formidable defences. The 43rd lost a total of 347 men during the siege, most of whom were lost during the storming. At Salamanca, on July 22nd 1812, the 43rd were only lightly engaged and casualties slight. Casualties were equally light at Vittoria on June 21st 1813. Whilst fighting raged in the passes in the Pyrenees the 43rd was engaged in the siege of San Sebastian which culminated in the storming of the place on August 31st 1813. When Wellington drove across the Bidassoa into France in October the 43rd was in the vanguard of the advance, clearing the French from their positions on the ridges above Vera and taking the important fort on top of the Lesser Rhune prior to the battle of the Nivelle. The capture of this fort was later called one of the finest exploits of any unit during the entire war. 77 men were lost during the fighting on the Nivelle on November 10th 1813 and a further 34 lost between December 9–13th during the battle of the Nive. During this battle the 43rd engaged twelve French guns from the church-yard at Arcangues in one of the strangest encounters of the war, driving them off with sustained, accurate fire. The 43rd took no part in the battle of Orthes on February 27th 1814 and was held mainly in reserve at the final bat- tle of the Peninsular War, at Toulouse, on April 10th 1814. At the end of the war the battalion was despatched to America where it took part in the ill-fated attack on New Orleans. Upon the close of that war the 43rd returned to Europe but arrived a day late to take part in the battle of Waterloo.

Sergeant Newman, of the 43rd Light Infantry, organising troops during the retreat to Corunna, during the winter of 1808–09.

44th (East Essex) Foot

On March 20th 1810 the 44th embarked for Cadiz, arriving there on April 4th. It remained here until September 24th when it sailed for Portugal, where it arrived on October 4th. The battalion was commanded by Lieutenant Colonel Charles Bulkeley and towards the end of December 1810 it marched to join the main British army inside the Lines of Torres Vedras. The battalion was present at Fuentes de Oñoro on May 3rd-5th 1811 although only the light company was engaged. The 2/44th played no part in the storming of Ciudad Rodrigo in January 1812 but on April 6th, as part of Leith's 5th Division, it was called upon to take part in the storming of Badajoz. The 44th escaladed the walls of the San Vincente bastion and its colours were the first to be planted on top of the bastion's walls. The battalion suf- fered casualties of 2 officers and 37 men killed and 7 officers and 88 men wounded. Indeed, of the 3 officers and 53 men of the battalion's light company only one officer and 19 men were left to answer the roll the next morning.

The 2/44th next saw action at Salamanca on July 22nd 1812. During the battle Lieutenant Pearce took an eagle from the French 62nd Regiment of the Line which was then placed on a sergeant's halberd, the men giving three cheers at the same time. Casualties during the day were 6 dead and 23 wounded. The battal- ion entered Madrid in August 1812 and afterwards marched north to Burgos to take part in the disastrous siege there from September to October. On October 25th, dur- ing the retreat from Burgos, the Allied army was attacked at Villa Muriel, a minor action in which the 44th was engaged throughout the day and lost three officers killed and wounded. By now the strength of the 2/44th had been reduced to just 42 men of all ranks, such were the rigours of the retreat. A draft of 40 officers and men brought the strength up to 455 but just 130 were fit for duty. Therefore, on December 6th 1812 Wellington ordered the fit men to form four companies, which would remain in Portugal as part of a Provisional

Battalion. The remains of the other six companies would return to England to recruit. And so, on February 13th 1813, 6 officers and 76 men sailed from Lisbon, arriving in England eleven days later. The four companies that remained in Portugal eventually returned to England on July 13th 1813. The 2/44th did not remain long in England, however, for soon afterwards it departed for Holland to take part in the campaign against Bergen-op-Zoom. At the conclusion of this campaign the battalion remained in quarters at Ostend until April 1815 when news was received of Napoleon's escape from Elba. The 2/44th was posted to the 9th British Infantry Brigade under the command of Sir Denis Pack. It suffered 165 casualties during the Waterloo campaign and was particularly hard-pressed at Quatre Bras on June 16th. During the battle a French lancer made for the battalion's Regimental Colour and in the ensuing melee Ensign Christie, carrying it, was speared by the lance which entered his left eye and penetrated to the lower jaw. In spite of his wound Christie managed to save the Colour and the Frenchman was shot dead. After the battle of June 18th the 44th marched to Paris. It returned to England in January 1816.

45th (1st Nottinghamshire) Foot

The 1/45th Regiment was one of the great regiments of the Peninsular War and its 1st Battalion fought in nearly every battle from Roliça to Toulouse. The 1/45th, some 767-strong, was commanded by Lieutenant Colonel Guard, and sailed from Cork on July 12th 1808 as part of the first Peninsular expedition under Sir Arthur Wellesley. The battalion did not get ashore, however, until August 6th whereupon it was attached to Catlin Craufurd's 5th Infantry Brigade. The battalion fought at the first British battle of the war, at Roliça on August 17th 1808, and at Vimeiro four days later. Following the Convention of Cintra the 45th remained in Lisbon and was thus spared the retreat to Corunna in the winter of 1808–09. When Wellesley returned to the Peninsula in April 1809 the 1/45th was brigaded with the 3/27th and 2/31st under Major General Mackenzie and on July 27th-28th fought at Talavera where the battalion played a major part in throwing back the French attacks. The 45th lost 182 men here. It was not until September 27th 1810 that the battalion fought its next action, at Busaco where, together with the 88th, the battalion launched a ferocious bayonet charge to defeat one of the attacking French columns. Picton, commanding the 3rd Division, mentioned the charge in his report to Wellington. After a spell within the Lines of Torres Vedras the 45th next fought at Fuentes de Oñoro on May 3rd-5th. On this occasion the battalion was not heavily engaged but it did receive several French cavalry charges. In January 1812 Wellington marched to lay siege to Ciudad Rodrigo which was stormed on January 19th. During the storming Picton's 3rd Division, including the 45th, was given the task of storming the Great Breach. The 45th lost 48 men in doing so. At the storming of Badajoz, on April 6th 1812, the 45th scaled the castle walls at a cost of 25 killed and 72 wounded. The battalion claims to have been the first to enter Badajoz, Corporal Kelly being the first man to jump down from the ramparts, killing a French colonel as he did so. Lieutenant Macpherson was one of the first up and succeeded in hauling down the French flag. Not having a British flag to hoist up in its place, Macpherson took off his jacket and ran that up instead. At Salamanca, the 45th, as part of Brisbane's brigade of the 3rd Division, took part in Pakenham's attack on Thomieres' division. Commanded by Lieutenant Colonel Ridgewood, the battalion lost 55 men during the battle. Sir Thomas Picton had returned to command the 3rd Division when the 45th next saw action, at Vittoria on June 21st 1813. The battalion attacked the French centre after storming across the Mendoza bridge. Lieutenant Colonel Ridgewood was wounded during the battle and died the next day. During the battle at Sorauren on July 30th 1813, the 45th charged and took over 300 French prisoners. On November 10th 1813 the 1/45th took part in the battle of the Nivelle, assisting in the capture of the bridge at Amotz which cut the French army in two. During the battle of the Nive, on December 9th–13th 1813, the 1/45th found itself away on the right of the Allied position and took no active part in the fighting. During the battle of Orthes, on February 27th 1814, the battalion lost 130 men in some fierce fighting as the 3rd Division attacked the French position. The last battle of the war came at Toulouse, on April 10th 1814, an unsatisfactory one in which the 45th lost a further 87 men. On June 24th the 1/45th sailed for Ireland, disembarking at Monkstown between July 23rd and 24th. The battalion took no part in the Waterloo campaign.

47th (Lancashire) Foot

The 2/47th left Ireland in October 1809 bound for Gibraltar. Soon afterwards, the flank companies of the battalion were sent to assist the garrison of Tarifa which was under siege from the French. By the end of February 1811 the entire battalion was present. On March 5th 1811 the flank companies fought at Barrosa losing 71 men. The siege of Tarifa itself lasted through the whole of 1811 and ended in January 1812. On December 1st 1812 the 2/47th was posted to the 2nd Brigade of the 5th Division and in January 1813 had an effective strength of 447 men. Its first major action came on June 21st at Vittoria where the battalion formed part of Graham's force operating to the north of the battlefield. The 2/47th helped clear the village of Gamara Mayor which was carried after heavy fighting. 2 officers and 18 men were killed and 4 officers and 88 men wounded. On August 31st 1813 the battalion took part in the storming of San Sebastian, assaulting the breaches in the face of strong resistance. The battalion lost 249 men in both the siege and storming. After taking part in the operations to pass the Bidassoa and the Nivelle the 2/47th saw action during the battle of the Nive on December 9th-13th. Soult's troops attacked the 5th Division, in which the battalion found itself, in great strength and it was only after some difficulty that the British troops drove them back. The 2/47th lost 67 men during the battle. It proved to be the last action of the war for the battalion for while Wellington's main army marched on towards Toulouse, the 2/47th remained behind as part of the force blockading Bayonne. During the French sortie on April 14th 1814 the battalion lost 3 men killed and 2 officers and 11 men wounded. Ten men were also taken prisoner. The 2/47th sailed for England from Bordeaux on August 24th 1814.

48th (Northamptonshire) Foot

The 48th fielded two battalions during the Peninsular War. The 2/48th was first in the field at the crossing of the Douro in May 1809 where, as part of Hill's brigade, the battalion seized and held a bridgehead across the river, drawing Soult's force away from the best crossing place where Wellesley's army crossed relatively unmolested. The battalion also served at Talavera as part of Hill's 2nd Division, in which the 1/48th was also serving. Between them the regiment suffered 326 casualties, a figure only surpassed by the 83rd Regiment. The 2/48th was equally hard pressed at Albuera in May 1811 losing a further 422 men either killed or wounded. The regimental strength of the two battalions prior to the battle was 62 officers and 887 men and the losses were so great that they could no longer maintain two battalions afterwards and the survivors of the 2/48th were transferred to the 1st Battalion whilst the cadre of the 2/48th returned home. The 2/48th was disbanded in 1814. The 1/48th had joined Wellesley's field army from the garrison in Gibraltar and almost immediately after were thrown into the battle of Talavera on July 27th–28th 1809. This remains the chief battle honour of the 48th. When the second, very strong French attack went in a gaping hole was made in the British line into which Wellesley threw his only available battalion, the 1/48th. The gap was closed with extreme gallantry and the line held. Afterwards, Wellesley wrote, "The battle was certainly saved by the advance, position and steady conduct of the 48th Regiment." The battalion next took part in the battle of Albuera, the losses at which, as we have seen, forced the

The 48th (Northamptonshire) Regiment at the crossing of the Douro, May 12th 1809.

2/48th to return home after first transferring its effective men into the 1/48th. The battalion was present at the siege and storming of Ciudad Rodrigo losing 62 men and again at the storming of Badajoz where, as part of the 4th Division, it took part in the heroic but unsuccessful assault on the breaches, losing 173 men. In July 1812 the 1/48th fought at Salamanca but following the abortive siege of Burgos retreated, with the rest of the army, to Portugal. The battalion saw action next at Vittoria where it was only slightly engaged suffering just 19 casualties but the following month, at Sorauren, the battalion did fine work at the crucial point of the battle. During the late autumn of 1813 Wellington pushed into France and the 1/48th was present at the battle of the Nivelle losing 68 men. In 1814, the battalion saw action at both of the final actions of the war at Orthes and Toulouse, both of which were awarded as battle honours. After the peace of 1814 the battalion returned to Ireland.

50th (West Kent) Foot

The British Army under Sir Arthur Wellesley that landed in Portugal in August 1808 included the 50th (The Queen's Own) Regiment. During the battle of Vimeiro on August 21st the 50th made some brilliant bayonet charges which helped win the day for Wellesley. After the Convention of Cintra, the 50th made its way to Lisbon where it arrived on September 28th. At the end of October it rejoined the army under Sir John Moore and by the end of November had reached Salamanca. By mid-December the battalion was involved in the retreat to Corunna. During the battle there on January 16th the village of Elvina, a critical position, fell to the French but was retaken by the 50th in a spirited bayonet charge. Sir John Moore, seeing the charge, cried, 'Well done, 50th! Well done, my majors!' The front was held and the regiment embarked safely for England the next day. The two majors Moore referred to were Charles Napier and Stanhope, who was killed in the battle, one of whose epaulettes can be seen in the regimental museum today. It is still the custom of the regiment to drink to the memory of 'The Corunna Majors' on the anniversary of the battle. After taking part in the ill-fated Walcheren campaign in 1809 the 50th returned to the Peninsula in September 1810 and were present at the battles of Busaco, Fuentes de Oñoro and Arroyo dos Molinos, although none of these appear on the battle honours of the regiment. In May 1812 it formed two of the three columns which assaulted Fort Napoleon, one of several forts guarding a bridge of boats at Almaraz on the River Tagus. These columns brought up scaling ladders and after hand-to-hand fighting the French fled across the river. During the spring of 1813 Wellington advanced into Spain once again following the retreat of 1812. The 50th played a prominent part at the battle of Vittoria on June 21st 1813. Following up, the 50th fought in the battles of the Pyrenees. On December 9th Wellington forced the passage of the Nive during which the 50th forded the river breast high in a rapid current under a heavy fire of musketry. The 50th finally saw action at Orthes on February 27th 1814. During the Peninsular War the 50th were given the nickname, 'The Dirty Half Hundred', on account of the fact that the dye came off their black cuffs when the troops wiped the perspiration from their faces in 'sweating times.' "Not a good-looking regiment," said Wellesley in 1808, "but devilish steady." The battalion embarked at Pauillac on July 20th 1814 and arrived at Cork on July 31st.

51st (2nd Yorkshire, West Riding, Light Infantry) Regiment

The 51st sailed from Falmouth on October 8th 1808 as part of the reinforcements under Sir David Baird. The battalion took part in the retreat to Corunna and fought in the battle there on January 16th 1809 when it occupied a position in the British second line. The 51st disembarked in England between the 20th and 25th of January. The battalion took part in the Walcheren campaign of 1809 and did not return to the Peninsula until February 19th 1811. The 51st, 650-strong, was commanded by Lieutenant Colonel Mainwaring and was attached to Houston's 7th Division. The 51st saw its first major battle at Fuentes de Oñoro on May 3rd-5th 1811 although it was never seriously engaged. Later the same month the battalion marched south to take part in the abortive siege of Badajoz. Here, the 51st lost 96 men, mainly in the attack on the Fort San Christobal. The 51st took no part in the sieges of Ciudad Rodrigo and Badajoz in January and April 1812 and was only lightly engaged at Salamanca on July 22nd 1812. On August 12th 1812 the battalion entered Madrid and in October the same year formed part of the force covering the siege of Burgos. At Vittoria, on June 21st 1813, the battalion took part in the attack on the French centre. The 7th Division was now commanded by Lord Dalhousie who led it against the enemy-held villages of La Hermandad and Margarita. The battalion saw much skirmishing in the Pyrenees and following the action at Sorauren on July 30th 1813 the 51st was mentioned in Wellington's despatch. On August 31st the battalion was heavily engaged on the Bidassoa, close to Vera. During a fierce fight the 51st lost 85 men. The battalion next saw action on November 10th 1813 at the battle of the Nivelle where it played a part in the capture of the Louis XIV and Herastaguia redoubts. The battalion's last action of the Peninsular War came at Orthes on February 27th 1814, following which it marched north to Bordeaux with Marshal Beresford. It took no part in the battle of Toulouse and sailed for England on June 17th 1814, disembarking at Plymouth on June 25th. When news of Napoleon's escape from Elba was received the 51st, under the command of Lieutenant Colonel Rice, was ordered to Belgium, disembarking at Ostend on March 30th 1815. The battalion, some 539-strong, formed part of Mitchell's brigade and took no part in the battle of Quatre Bras on June 16th. On June 18th, however, the 51st occupied a position about 400 yards behind Hougoumont and spent the day skirmishing, under artillery fire and under attack from French cavalry. 8 men were killed and 3 officers and 20 men wounded. The 51st formed part of the Army of Occupation and remained in France until January 2nd 1816 when it embarked for Dover, disembarking the following day.

52nd (Oxford Light Infantry) Regiment

The 52nd Light Infantry had two battalions serving throughout the Peninsular War. First to arrive was the 2nd Battalion which fought at Vimeiro, while the 1/52nd arrived in October 1808. Together, the two battalions served throughout the Corunna campaign during which both formed part of the rearguards under Robert Craufurd and Edward Paget. Whilst the 2/52nd was despatched to Walcheren in June 1809 the 1st Battalion returned to the Peninsula where it formed part of Craufurd's famous Light Brigade. It arrived too late to take part in the battle of Talavera having marched a staggering sixty miles in just twenty-six hours in trying to do so. In February 1810 the Light Brigade became a Division and the 52nd spent the summer of 1810 on outpost duties on the River Coa, taking part in the infamous action there on July 24th. At the battle of Busaco on September 27th that year the battalion lost just fifteen men playing a major part in the battle. When, having failed to enter the Lines of Torres Vedras, Massena's army began its retreat back towards Spain in the winter of 1810–11 the Light Division, including the 52nd, was in the vanguard of the pursuit, fighting a number of actions in the spring of 1811, notably at Sabugal on April 3rd. On May 3rd–5th the 1/52nd took part in the battle of Fuentes de Oñoro suffering very light casualties. In

January 1812 the battalion took part in the siege and storming of Ciudad Rodrigo where it played a decisive role in storming the Lesser Breach along with its fellow battalions of the Light Division. The 52nd lost 65 on this occasion but lost 382 men during the terrible storming of Badajoz on April 6th the same year when the Light Division attempted – in vain – to storm one of the breaches there. By comparison the battle of Salamanca, on July 22nd, was a quiet affair for the 52nd, suffering just two men wounded. At Vittoria, on June 21st 1813, the 52nd enjoyed a similarly quiet battle sustaining just 23 casualties. The 52nd took no part in the battles of the Pyrenees in July and August 1813 as it was engaged at San Sebastian which was stormed on August 31st. With its comrades of the Light Division the 52nd played an important role in the invasion of France both at the crossing of the Bidassoa, clearing the heights above Vera, and during the battle of the Nivelle on November 10th 1813 when the 52nd helped storm the formidable defences high on the Lesser Rhune mountain. The battle cost the 52nd 242 casualties, the heaviest figure in the Allied army. The following month the 52nd saw action at the battle of the Nive and on February 27th 1814 played a prominent role in the battle of Orthes, suffering 89 casualties during the day. The last action fought by the 52nd in the

The capture of a French battery at Waterloo, by the 52nd Light Infantry.

Peninsula came at Toulouse on April 10th although by this time the regiment's 2nd Battalion had sailed for Holland to take part in the attack on Bergen-op-Zoom. Meanwhile, the 1/52nd, having ended the Peninsular War in France, was placed under orders for North America but fortunately ill weather prevented them sailing and by the time favourable winds arrived news of Napoleon's escape from Elba was received and the battalion sailed for Ostend instead, arriving on March 31st 1815.

Commanded by Sir John Colborne, the 1/52nd formed part of Clinton's 2nd Division. The battalion played no part in the battle of Quatre Bras but on the great day of June 18th it occupied a position away on the right flank of the Allied army. The 52nd played a crucial part in the defeat of the Imperial Guard at the end of the day, a day which cost the battalion 199 men. The 52nd remained in France until November 23rd 1818, it being the last British battalion to leave the country.

53rd (Shropshire) Foot

The 2/53rd Regiment sailed from England in March 1809, disembarking in Portugal the following month. The battalion, under the command of Lieutenant Colonel Bingham, first saw action at Talavera, suffering 44 casualties. The battalion played no part in the battle of Busaco during the retreat to the Lines of Torres Vedras and next saw action at Fuentes de Oñoro where casualties were just three men slightly wounded. The 2/53rd, part of the 6th Division, played no part in the sieges of Ciudad Rodrigo and Badajoz and had to wait until the battle of Salamanca for its next action. During the battle Colonel Bingham rallied the battalion by grabbing the King's Colour and waving it at the head of his men. The battalion suffered 142 casualties, mainly as a result of flanking enemy artillery fire from the Greater Arapil, and after the battle the 2/53rd was reduced to a weak shadow of that which had arrived some three years earlier. The battalion took part in the abortive siege of Burgos from September to October 1812 and suffered once more – as did all of Wellington's army – during the subsequent retreat to Portugal in the winter of 1812. By the beginning of 1813 the battalion had become so depleted that six skeleton compa-

nies were sent home whilst the remaining four merged with the 2nd Regiment to form a Provisional Battalion in the 4th Division. The four companies of the 2/53rd subsequently saw action at Vittoria where, although not heavily engaged, the battalion earned another Battle Honour. During the battles of the Pyrenees a single company of the 2/53rd, under Captain Fehrzen, won the distinction of forcing two battalions of French infantry to surrender, an action which won an immediate brevet majority for Fehrzen. In November 1813 the 2/53rd took part in the battle of the Nivelle, during which it took part in the storming of La Sarre redoubt. At the beginning of 1814 the six companies of the 2/53rd that had been sent home to England returned, this time up to full strength, and with the four companies already in France took part in the final battle of the war at Toulouse, during which it suffered just 21 casualties. The 2/53rd played no part in the battle of Waterloo but did, however, accompany Napoleon to St Helena. During this spell of duty the exiled emperor often dined with the officers of the 2/53rd, preferring the company of old soldiers to the governor, Sir Hudson Lowe.

57th (West Middlesex) Foot

The 1/57th arrived in the Peninsula on July 15th 1809 and the following month joined the force under Beresford. On September 7th the battalion was placed in the 2nd Division under Hill. The 57th saw no major action until almost a year later at Busaco, although it took no part in the actual fighting. The next

month was spent inside the lines of Torres Vedras but in the spring of 1811 the 57th were sent south, as part of Beresford's force, to lay siege to Badajoz. The siege there began on May 6th but just six days later Beresford marched south to meet Soult at Albuera, which battle was fought on May 16th. The

57th formed part of Hoghton's brigade of the 2nd Division. The 57th suffered grievous losses during the battle, some 318 killed and wounded. The commanding officer, Colonel Inglis, was himself wounded and as he was carried off the field shouted to his men, "Die Hard, 57th! Die Hard!" and so gave the regiment its immortal nickname. After the battle the battalion was sent to Villa Vicosa to rest. In August 1811 the battalion, now commanded by Lieutenant Colonel Macdonald, received a draft from the 2nd Battalion to make good the losses sustained at Albuera. The 1/57th saw no further action until June 21st 1813 at Vittoria where it suffered 28 casualties. The battalion saw further action during the battles of the Pyrenees, notably at Roncesvalles. 75 men of the battalion became casualties during the fighting between July 25th–30th. For the next three months the 1/57th guarded the pass at Roncesvalles until on November 10th the battalion took part in the battle of the Nivelle, during which the battalion lost 64 men including Major Ackland who was killed leading the light companies into action. On December 13th 1813 the battalion was involved in fierce fighting at the battle of St Pierre, which battle formed part of the battle of the Nive. The 1/57th, part of Byng's brigade, suffered 127 casualties during the battle. The battalion saw no further major battles although it was present at Toulouse on April 10th 1814. On this occasion, however, it took no part in any direct fighting. In May 1814 the 1/57th marched to Bordeaux and the following month sailed for Canada.

58th (Rutlandshire) Foot

The 2/58th Regiment joined Wellington's army in 1812 in time to take part in the battle of Salamanca on July 22nd 1812 where it suffered just three casualties. The battalion subsequently took part in the unsuccessful siege of Burgos in September-October 1812 and the retreat to Portugal in November that year. As a result of these actions, and of that of Vittoria on June 21st 1813, the battalion, along with the 2/24th, formed the 3rd Provisional Battalion as part of Barnes's brigade of the 7th Division. This practice was a result of Wellington's insistence on keeping seasoned troops with him, even if it meant forming them into Provisional battalions, rather than send them home to be replaced by 'green' troops. During the battles of the Pyrenees the battalion, along with the 6th Foot, charged unsupported against two French divisions and drove them from some heights, prompting Wellington to write that the charge was made with a 'regularity and gallantry' which he had seldom seen equalled. Indeed, the great historian of the British Army, Sir John Fortescue, wrote, that of the various battles in the Pyrenees, "the 4th Division and Barnes's brigade were the heroes of the fights." The 2/58th was present at the battle of the Nivelle on November 10th 1813 suffering only slight casualties and fought its last action of the war at Orthes on February 27th 1814 where it lost 31 men. The battalion returned to England at the end of the war and took no part in the Waterloo campaign. The 2/58th was disbanded in December 1815. The 1/58th saw no action with Wellington's main field army but did see action during the operations along the east coast of Spain, notably at Castalla in April 1813.

59th (2nd Nottinghamshire) Foot

The 2/59th landed at Corunna on October 30th 1808 from where it marched to join the army of Sir John Moore. However, by the time it joined him he was already retreating to Corunna and the 2/59th found itself heading back where it had come from. When the 59th reached Corunna there were just 300 fit men left who fought in the battle there on January 16th 1809. During the battle the battalion suffered 60 killed and wounded and when night fell the grenadier and 1st Companies of the battalion still found themselves fighting and can claim to be the last troops to have actually engaged Soult's French troops. When the battalion set sail it was discovered that the ship was sinking and the troops were immediately evacuated. However, with the ship about to go down Sergeant Major Perkins went below to rescue the battalion's Colours which were still on board and saved them. After a short spell at home in England the battalion was sent to take part in the Walcheren campaign of 1809. It was to be three years before the 2/59th returned to the Peninsula, arriving in Spain to find the army on the Portuguese border following its retreat from Burgos. In the spring of 1813 the 2/59th were brigaded with the 4th and 47th Regiments to form part of Oswald's 5th Division. During Wellington's advance into Spain the battalion was rebuked for bringing along such a large amount of private baggage in carts which were piled high. On June 21st 1813 the battalion fought at Vittoria where it lost 144 killed and wounded. Lieutenant Colonel Fane was mortally wounded by a cannon ball during the fighting. On July 25th, at San Sebastian, the battalion suffered 30 casualties during an assault in which it never even left its trenches. On August 31st the town was stormed and

the light company of the battalion formed part of the initial wave of Allied troops. It was virtually annihilated and when the main body of the 59th came up shortly afterwards it too suffered heavy casualties. The town was won, however, but at a cost to the 2/59th of 350 men killed or wounded. In October of 1813 the 2/59th crossed into southern France with the Allied army and in December was heavily engaged in the battle of the Nive at which it suffered 165 killed or wounded, mainly in fierce fighting around the village of Anglet. While Wellington pushed on towards Toulouse in pursuit of Soult in early 1814 the 2/59th were left behind as part of the force covering Bayonne and it was here that the battalion finished the Peninsular War. In May 1815, after a spell in Ireland the 2/59th sailed to Ostend to take part in the Waterloo campaign. However, it saw no fighting on June 18th as it was ordered to occupy the village of Hal on the extreme right of Wellington's position. It did, however, take part in the assault on Cambrai on June 24th where the battalion lost five men. Finally, on July 5th the battalion entered Paris.

60th (Royal American) Foot

The 5/60th rarely fought as a unit, and apart from Roliça and Vimeiro spent the entire Peninsular campaign split into companies which were divided between the various divisions of Wellington's army. The battalion landed in August 1808 as part of Sir Arthur Wellesley's initial force and fought at both Roliça and Vimeiro. At Corunna, the 5/60th were joined by the regiment's 2nd Battalion which defended the town during the actual battle on January 16th 1809. The 5/60th next fought at Talavera on July 28th 1809 where the battalion lost 7 officers and 44 men. A year later at Busaco, on September 27th 1810, the five companies of the battalion which were engaged in the battle played their part losing 5 officers and 24 men. Here, the battalion was under the command of Colonel Williams who distinguished himself at the battle of Fuentes de Oñoro on May 3rd-5th 1811. On this occasion, he led three companies of the battalion in repeated counter-attacks against the French who were trying to gain possession of the village. During the fighting Williams was badly

wounded whilst the three companies engaged lost 25 men. Captain John Galiffe and Rifleman David Loochstadt, of the 5/60th, gained an unusual distinction just over a week later when they fought at the battle of Albuera. Not many men claimed the distinction of fighting both at Fuentes and at Albuera. Some rifle companies were present at Arroyo dos Molinos in October of 1811 and again, when Wellington laid siege to Ciudad Rodrigo and Badajoz in early 1812, companies of the 5/60th played a part covering the siege operations. At Badajoz the battalion lost 6 officers and 44 men, mainly during the assault on April 6th. The battalion next distinguished itself at Salamanca on July 22nd 1812 where 3 officers and 33 men were killed or wounded. Colonel Williams was again wounded here. The 5/60th withdrew to the Portuguese border in the late autumn of 1812 following the retreat from Burgos and were again present with Wellington's army when he advanced the following spring to fight at Vittoria. During the battle Colonel Fitzgerald commanded a

battalion consisting of three companies of the 5/60th as well as other light companies. There was fierce fighting at Vittoria during which Major Galiffe led the assault on the village of Ariñez which finally ended French resistance in the centre. The battalion suffered 51 casualties during the day. During the battles of the Pyrenees from July 25th to August 2nd the 5/60th suffered a further 88 casualties. The battalion was present at the battles of the Nivelle, and the Nive and when Wellington advanced into France the 5/60th fought in the two final battles of the Peninsular War at Orthes and Toulouse. In all, not including minor engagements, the 5/60th had gained sixteen battle honours at a cost of 68 officers and 767 men, as well as 2 officers and 228 men missing. Testimony to the part played by the 5/60th during the war comes from Marshal Soult, no less, who in 1813 complained of the high proportion of officer casualties caused by the 5/60th's riflemen, adding that, "this mode of war is very detrimental to us."

Riflemen of the 5/60th and the 95th, c.1812.

61st (South Gloucestershire) Foot

The 1/61st, under the command of Lieutenant Colonel Saunders, arrived in the Peninsula in April 1809 and fought its first action at Talavera on July 28th that year, sustaining 256 casualties. A year later the battalion fought at Busaco where it came through unscathed. The battalion took no part in any major action until almost two years later at Salamanca on July 22nd 1812. Here, however, it certainly made up for its previous absences when it was involved in the hardest fighting of the day. Brigaded with the 11th Regiment in the 6th Division, the 61st were thrown forward to halt a French counter-attack close to the village of Los Arapiles at the crucial moment of the battle. In the fierce fighting that followed the battalion suffered 365 men killed and wounded and when the battalion halted that night only 3 officers and 78 men were able to answer the roll call. No wonder an old soldiers' song went, 'The 61st and 11th Foot great numbers they had slain, They got their jackets dusted well on Salamanca's Plain.' In

the first company every officer and man was either killed or wounded except one, Private Chipchase. The Colours were carried by two private soldiers at the end of the battle, as six officers and sergeants had been shot previously whilst carrying them. So few remained of both the 61st and the 11th that they were formed into one battalion. In September 1812 the battalion, 208 strong, was present at the siege of Burgos and during the subsequent retreat from there the men lived off acorns when supplies ran out. At Vittoria, on June 21st 1813 the 1/61st were present but had to watch the battle from the rear as it was detailed to look after ammunition supplies. During the battles of the Pyrenees the 1/61st lost 45 men, mainly at Sorauren where the battalion was involved in a race against a French battalion to the top of a hill. The 61st won and turned round to unleash a volley of musketry into the French, throwing them back down again. At the battle of the Nivelle on November 10th 1813 the battalion lost 49 men but came through the battle of the Nive the following month with just 6 wounded. At Orthes, on February 27th 1814, the 1/61st smashed two French battalions by charging them at 'running pace.' Their last battle of the Peninsular War came at Toulouse where the battalion served with great distinction at a cost of 174 killed and wounded, including their commanding officer, Lieutenant Colonel Coghlan who was killed leading his men. In fact, the 1/61st left so many men on the battlefield that it was given the nickname, 'The Flowers of Toulouse.' The battalion was also known as 'The Silver-tailed Dandies', on account of the long skirts of the jackets which were longer than any other regiment and decorated with silver skirt ornaments. At the close of the war the battalion returned to garrison duty in Ireland and took no part in the Waterloo campaign of 1815.

62nd (Wiltshire) Foot

The 2/62nd arrived in Spain on October 6th 1813, disembarking at Passages. The battalion, a strong one of nearly 1,000 men, was placed in Lord Aylmer's unattached brigade, and fought out the remainder of the Peninsular War as part of the left wing of the army. On November 10th 1813 the battalion crossed the river Nivelle, coming through unscathed. The following month the 62nd took part in the battle of the Nive, engaging the French in some heavy fighting around the Mayor's House at Barrouillet. During the fighting the battalion lost three men wounded, all of whom died later. The Nive was later awarded to the 62nd as its only battle honour of the war. Following the battle of the Nive the battalion pushed on to take part in the operations around Bayonne, although it was sent back to Vera soon afterwards. The battalion returned to Bayonne in time to assist in the repulse of the French sortie on April 14th. The 2/62nd returned to Ireland at the close of the war.

66th (Berkshire) Foot

The 2/66th Regiment arrived in the Peninsula in April 1809, numbering some 772 men. Its first action came in May of that year at the crossing of the Douro at Oporto. Here, the battalion suffered 38 casualties during the successful operation, a small number but the highest figure of the units involved. The battalion was involved in much harder fighting two months later at the battle of Talavera on July 28th 1809 where 16 men were killed and 99 officers and men wounded during the battle. The Allied army was to see no more serious action for almost another year and during this long period of inactivity two officers of the regiment were killed in duels, something which Wellington had expressly forbidden. At Busaco, on September 27th 1810, the 2/66th occupied a position on the right flank and so saw little fighting during the day. Following this the battalion withdrew with the rest of the army to the Lines of Torres Vedras. In 1811 the 2/66th found itself with the force under the command of William Beresford who had been laying siege to the fortress of Badajoz. Forced to raised the siege in the face of a threat from the French under Soult, Beresford headed south and on May 16th 1811 he fought the bloody battle of Albuera. The 2/66th formed part of Colborne's Brigade and it was this brigade that suffered perhaps the worst catastrophe of the entire war when, still fighting in line, a tremendous storm broke and under cover of the torrential rain and smoke of battle, a brigade of French cavalry, mainly Polish lancers, attacked and virtually annihilated them. The 66th lost both its Colours and lost 272 men killed, wounded or taken prisoner out of a total strength of 441. During the attack Ensign Hay was speared by a lance, the point of which came protruding through his back. He rose, but was run through a second time by the Poles who gave no quarter. Hay survived and was found later in the evening sitting up to his waist in mud and water. Unfortunately, he died two years later from a lung complaint, almost certainly caused by the terrible wounds sustained at Albuera. Such were the losses of the 66th after the battle that it was amalgamated with the 31st Regiment as the 1st Provisional Battalion, and as such it remained for the next three years until the end of the war. To be placed in a provisional battalion was seen as quite a compliment because usually a decimated battalion would be sent home to recruit. In the Peninsula, however, Wellington preferred to keep his seasoned veterans with him and form them into provisional battal-ions rather then replace them with new 'green' battalions. In spite of its amalgamated status the 2/66th still went on to distinguish itself and added Vittoria, the Pyrenees, Nivelle, Nive and Orthes to their list of battle honours. In 1816 the battalion sailed for St Helena to join the 1st Battalion of the regiment. The regiment remained here guarding Napoleon until his death in 1821.

67th (South Hampshire) Foot

On September 24th 1810 six companies of the 2/67th Regiment commanded by Lieutenant Colonel William Prevost arrived at Gibraltar before proceeding on to Cadiz, then under siege by the French. The six companies of the battalion formed part of the force under Sir Thomas Graham that defeated Victor's French at Barrosa on March 5th 1811. During the battle, the battalion was divided in half, three companies serving in Wheatley's Brigade and the other three with Dilkes's brigade. These latter companies of the 2/67th joined the Guards in their advance up the hill which played a major part in the defeat of the French.

Casualties amongst the 2/67th were ten killed and 34 wounded. In 1812 the six companies were joined by two more of the battalion and for the next two years were involved in operations along the east coast of Spain fighting more like Marines than infantry. The 2/67th saw service at Carthagena, Alicante, Onil, the Col de Balaguer, San Phillipe, Tarragona and finally at Barcelona. These moves denied Soult the opportunity of success at Valencia. On May 25th 1814 the battalion arrived back at Gibraltar where it remained on garrison duties until April 1817. The battalion was disbanded in May of that year.

68th (Durham Light Infantry)

Captain J.U.M. Leith, 68th Light Infantry, killed at Oeyregave, February 23rd 1814.

After being decimated by Walcheren fever during the 1809 campaign in Holland the 68th returned home to recover and by June 1811 was strong enough to embark for the Peninsula sailing from Portsmouth on the 18th of that month. The strength of the regiment a month later is shown as 808 all ranks. Between January and April 1812 the 68th was involved in the operations covering the main Allied army as it lay siege to Ciudad Rodrigo and Badajoz. Unfortunately, the 68th seem to have obtained a reputation for bad behaviour as an inspection report at the time remarks that several instances of looting had occurred since the men had been in the country. The regiment was also noted as being 'not so clean and healthy' and having no colours. However, on June 20th 1812, during the preliminary operations before Salamanca the 68th distinguished itself by ejecting a strong French force from the village of Moriscos. The 68th was eventually obliged to retire in the face of extreme pressure but not before some bitter hand-to-hand fighting during which Captain Mackay received 22 bayonet wounds as well as several blows from the butt of a musket. He recovered however. The 68th was attached to the 7th Division which played a part in the battle of Salamanca on July 22nd where Major Miller was mortally wounded. The 68th pushed on to Madrid where it acquired new shirts, socks and shoes, left behind by the French and it is said that the men ate the gold-fish in the fountains in the Retiro gardens! The regiment was back on the Portuguese border by the end of the year following the retreat from Burgos which had put no less than 247 of its number in hospital. By the spring of 1813 the 68th was ready for the advance back into Spain and on June 21st 1813 covered itself with glory at Vittoria where it sustained heavy losses – 24 killed and 100 wounded – including Colonel Johnson who was wounded twice. At the siege of San Sebastian in August that year the 68th provided several volunteers for the storming and soon afterwards the regiment as a whole saw action during the

battle of the Pyrenees. At Sorauren on July 30th the 68th broke two French regiments which moved Wellington to call it, 'the finest thing he ever witnessed.' During the crossing of the Nivelle the 68th took three strong redoubts but at a cost, for by the end of the operation the battalion was reduced to just 197 fit men. The war pushed on into France and on February 23rd the 68th captured the important bridge over the river Adour at the village of Oeyregave. Captain Leith was killed during this successful attack. The last battle of the war for the 68th was fought on 27th February at Orthes. Here, the 68th, as part of the 7th Division, was sent forward after an attack by the 4th Division had floundered. Its attack was successful and the battle ended in an allied victory. The 68th played no part in the battle of Toulouse and remained in France until July 1814 when it embarked for Ireland. During their period of service in the Peninsula the 68th lost no fewer than 364 men all ranks killed in action or died of wounds or sickness.

Captain Leith's uniform and 1803 pattern sword.

69th (South Lincolnshire) Foot

The 2/69th was already in Europe when Napoleon escaped from Elba in February 1815. The battalion had taken no part in the Peninsular War but had been engaged during Graham's campaign in Holland in 1813 and 1814. The 2/69th numbered 30 officers and 580 men at the beginning of the campaign and was commanded by Colonel Charles Morrice. It formed part of the 5th British Brigade under Major General Sir Colin Halkett. During the battle of Quatre Bras, on June 16th 1815, the battalion was badly mauled by French cavalry after the Prince of Orange ordered it into line in spite of their

presence. During the ensuing fight the battalion lost the King's Colour and 5 officers and 147 men were killed or wounded. Two days later, at Waterloo, the battalion occupied a position about 250 yards to the north of Hougoumont and spent the day under French artillery fire and under attack from enemy cavalry. The battalion played a part in the repulse of the Imperial Guard. By the end of the day the 2/69th had sustained losses of 4 officers and 15 men killed, and 3 officers and 50 men wounded. Colonel Morrice was among the dead. The battalion remained in France until January 1816 when it returned to England.

71st (Glasgow Highland Light Infantry) Regiment

The 1/71st sailed from Ireland on July 12th 1808, and arrived off Mondego Bay, Portugal on August 1st. The battalion was present at Roliça on August 17th as part of Fergusson's 2nd Infantry Brigade, although only the light infantry company was engaged. Four days later, however, the whole battalion was in

action, this time at Vimeiro where the 71st sustained 112 casualties. During the battle Piper George Clark sat bleeding from a severe wound as he sat on the ground but played his pipes regardless. As his comrades went forward he played 'Up and waur them aa, Willie.' During the retreat to Corunna the 71st was

The 71st Highlanders at the battle of Vittoria, June 21st 1813.

major action, at Fuentes de Oñoro, during which the 71st saw a great deal of hard fighting and did fine work with both bayonet and musket, although at a cost to the battalion of some 144 casualties. For the remainder of 1811 the 71st found itself as part of the force under Rowland Hill which was operating independently against the French forces in Andalucia. On October 28th Hill's force surprised a French force under General Girard at Arroyo dos Molinos capturing 1,300 French prisoners and killing a further 800. In May 1812 the 71st saw further action, again as part of Hill's force, during the attack on the bridge and the works at Almaraz, a short but nevertheless sharp affair which cost the 71st nine killed and 34 wounded. The 71st next saw action at Vittoria on June 21st 1813. With the pipers playing, 'Johnnie Cope', the 71st claimed the honour of being the first British regiment to draw enemy blood that day, a day that cost the 71st fourteen officers and 301 men killed or wounded, such was its contribution to the victory. A further eight officers and 200 men became casualties at Maya on July 25th 1813 and a further 24 men killed and 36 wounded two days later at Sorauren. On the final day of the battle of the Nive, on December 13th 1813, the 71st lost another 130 men in hard fighting around the heights of Mouguerre. The 71st also took part in the final battles of the war at Orthes and Toulouse in 1814 before returning to Ireland in July 1814. In January 1815 orders were issued for the 71st to sail for America but bad weather prevented the battalion from sailing for two months by which time Napoleon had escaped from Elba and the 71st was ordered to sail instead for Ostend. The 71st played no part in the battle of Quatre Bras but did do excellent service two days later at Waterloo where the battalion lost 16 officers and 198 men killed and wounded. The battalion marched on to Paris after the battle and remained in France until the end of October 1818 when it embarked at Calais for Dover which was reached on October 29th.

brigaded with the 36th Regiment and the 92nd Highlanders in Catlin Craufurd's brigade. The battalion was placed on the left wing of the army at the battle of Corunna on January 16th before finally being re-embarked upon ships bound for England at about 8pm that night. Shortly after its return to England the 71st became a Light Infantry regiment and in July that year sailed to Walcheren as part of the force under the Earl of Chatham. On September 15th 1810 the battalion sailed for Portugal once more, disembarking at Lisbon on the 26th of that month. By the time the 71st joined Wellington's Field Army it was just beginning to take up its positions inside the Lines of Torres Vedras and it was not to be until May 1811 that the battalion saw another

The 71st Highlanders on the march during the Napoleonic Wars. The man in the bottom right hand corner of the painting appears to have found himself a bottle.

73rd Foot

Like the 2/69th Regiment, the 2/73rd had taken no part in the Peninsular War but having served under Sir Thomas Graham in Holland in 1813–14 it found itself already on the Continent when the news of Napoleon's escape from Elba broke in 1815. The battalion was attached to Halkett's brigade which formed part of Alten's division. After having marched from Soignies on June 16th the battalion was immediately thrown into the battle of Quatre Bras where it lost 53 men. On June 18th the 2/73rd occupied a position on the ridge about 250 yards behind Hougoumont. Most of the day was spent under French artillery fire or under attack from enemy cavalry. Towards the end of the day the battalion helped repulse the Imperial Guard. Out of 489 men who were with the battalion that morning some 289 became casualties. The 2/73rd marched to Paris after the battle and returned to England at the end of December 1815.

74th (Highland) Foot

The 1/74th Regiment sailed for Portugal from Cork on January 18th 1810, arriving in the Tagus on February 5th. The battalion was attached to Henry Mackinnon's brigade of the 3rd Division under Sir Thomas Picton. Its first action came at Busaco on September 27th 1810 when it helped repulse the attack on the British centre by Reynier's division. The battalion suffered two officers and 25 men killed and wounded during the day's fighting. The 74th's next major action came on May 3rd-5th 1811 at Fuentes de Oñoro during which the battalion was involved in fierce fighting in and around the village there. Four officers and 69 men were lost here. In January 1812 the 74th crossed over into Spain to take part in the siege of Ciudad Rodrigo which was stormed on January 19th. During the storming the 74th attacked the Great Breach although casualties were light, just 26 killed and wounded. Two months later the 74th took part in the siege and storming of Badajoz which was assaulted on the night of April 6th. The battalion scaled the walls of the Castle, along with the rest of Picton's 3rd Division, which decided the town's fate. During the storming the 74th lost 16 officers and 120 men. From Badajoz the 74th headed north-east to

Salamanca, where the 3rd Division, now under the command of Edward Pakenham, played the major part in the initial attack on the French army. 2 officers and 47 men were lost by the 74th during the battle which was the regiment's fifth battle-honour. The 1/74th also had the honour to enter Madrid behind Wellington himself when he entered the Spanish capital on August 12th. The battalion remained close to Madrid until October 20th and in so doing missed, fortunately, the abortive siege of Burgos and it was not to be until June 21st 1813 that the 1/74th next saw action, this time at Vittoria where, as part of Brisbane's brigade of the 3rd Division, the battalion helped sweep the French from the knoll of Arinez. 82 casualties were sustained by the 1/74th during the battle. At the second battle of Sorauren the 74th distinguished itself by attacking a French unit and inflicting losses of around fifteen hundred. During the battle

of the Nivelle the 74th made an attack on the important French front line works around the village of Sarre following which the battalion pressed on an assisted in the capture of the vital bridge at Amotz. The battalion lost 6 officers and 69 men killed and wounded during the day. Although present during the battle of the Nive the 1/74th never took part in any of the main fighting and it was not to be until February 27th 1814, at Orthes, that the battalion fought its next action. The 74th also took part in the action at Tarbes on March 20th which cost it sixteen men. Three weeks later the battalion fought in the last action of the war, at Toulouse on April 10th, which cost the 74th nine officers and 132 men during a day of severe fighting. On July 4th 1814 the 74th embarked at Pauillac for Cork, which was reached on July 25th. The battalion took no part in the Waterloo Campaign of 1815.

76th (Hindoostan) Foot

The 76th Regiment embarked at Harwich on September 14th 1808 and arrived at Corunna on October 13th. The regiment, commanded by Lieutenant Colonel Symes, formed part of the reinforcements under Sir David Baird and upon arrival was brigaded with the 51st and 59th Regiments under Major General James Leith, part of Sir John Hope's 1st Division. The retreat to Corunna began soon afterwards and on January 3rd 1809, at Lugo, the 76th found itself posted on the British left flank where, according to Napier, 'Moore had posted the flower of his troops.' During the fight the light company, under Lieutenant Hamilton, was heavily engaged, clearing the road leading to Villa Franca of French troops. During this clash both sides closed with each other and there was a great deal of bayonet fighting. In fact, at one point a French soldier was just about to push his bayonet into Lieutenant Hutch's face when Private Cramer came forward and brought the man to the ground. During the battle of Corunna on January 16th the 76th saw little fighting although one man was killed and six wounded. The 76th arrived back in England on January 26th having lost 170 during the whole campaign. Lieutenant Colonel Symes died on board ship, mainly due

to the rigours of the retreat. The 76th next saw service during the Walcheren Campaign of 1809 but such were the ill-effects of the campaign that it was not until 1813 that the regiment was fit for any further service. The regiment sailed from Ireland on August 5th 1813, bound for the Peninsula once again, and landed at Passages on September 15th. The regiment was commanded by Lieutenant Colonel Wardlaw and was part of Major General Aylmer's unattached British brigade. The 76th took part in the battle of the Nivelle on November 10th 1813 and although it did come under fire from French artillery it was not involved in any direct fighting. The regiment suffered sixteen casualties during the battle of the Nive from December 9th-13th, during which it saw much skirmishing with the enemy. The regiment spent the first two months of 1814 in cantonments south of Bayonne and spent the remainder of the war as part of the force blockading the place. The regiment marched to St Jean de Luz on May 8th and remained there in camp before departing the following day for Bordeaux. On June 4th the 76th sailed for Canada and consequently saw service in the war with the America.

77th (East Middlesex) Foot

The 77th had taken part in the Walcheren campaign of 1809 and did not arrive in the Peninsula until July 1811. The battalion, some 850-strong, formed part of Picton's 3rd Division and fought its first action on September 25th 1811 at El Bodon. The action was a fierce one but it was never awarded a battle honour. In January 1812 the 77th marched to Ciudad Rodrigo to take part in the siege of that place. On the 19th of the same month the town was stormed but the battalion was kept in reserve during the actual storming. Casualties during the siege itself were 14 men killed and 5 officers and 31 men wounded. The 77th did, however, take part in the storming of Badajoz on April 6th 1812, during which casualties were relatively light, just 33 killed and wounded. The storming of Badajoz effectively marked the end of the battalion's service in the Peninsular War for in late April it was sent back to Lisbon for garrison duty. By the end of 1813 it had recovered sufficiently and in 1814 moved forward to join in the operations around Bayonne. On August 24th 1814 the battalion marched to Passages where, on September 8th, it embarked aboard ships bound for Ireland, the 77th being the last British battalion to leave France.

79th Foot, or Cameron Highlanders

The 1/79th sailed from Spithead on July 31st 1808 and landed at Maceira Bay on August 26th. The battalion was attached to Major General Fane's brigade and took part in the retreat to Corunna in the winter of 1808-09. The 79th was not engaged during the battle of Corunna on January 16th although the light company did see some skirmishing. In June 1809 the 1/79th, having received a draft from the 2nd Battalion, was brought up to strength and saw service during the Walcheren campaign later that year. A small contingent of the 1st Battalion, 5 officers and 49 men, had remained sick in Lisbon, while the rest of the battalion marched to Corunna and this handful of men fought at Talavera on July 27th-28th 1809, suffering 14 killed and 28 wounded. On January 31st 1810 the 1/79th returned to Portugal and was almost immediately sent to assist in the defence of Cadiz. The battalion remained here until August 16th 1810 when it returned to Lisbon. It joined

The 79th Highlanders in square formation at Waterloo, June 18th 1815.

Piper Kenneth Mackay, of the 79th, at Waterloo, marching round the Camerons' square playing the Pibroch Cognathna Sith.

Wellington's main field army in time to fight at Busaco on September 27th 1810 after which it retreated with the rest of the army to the Lines of Torres Vedras. It remained here until November 14th 1810 when Massena withdrew. The 1/79th was engaged several times with the French rearguard, notably at Foz d'Arouce on March 15th 1811. Its next major action came on May 3rd–5th 1811 at Fuentes de Oñoro. The battalion was heavily engaged in the fierce fight for the village itself, during which its commanding officer, Colonel Cameron, was mortally wounded. As well as Cameron, the 1/79th lost one officer and 31 men killed and 10 officers and 138 men wounded. The battalion took no part in either of the great sieges of 1812, at Ciudad Rodrigo and Badajoz and did not fight again until July 22nd 1812 when, as part of Campbell's division, it fought at Salamanca, although it only saw direct action during the later stages of the battle. In September and October 1812 the 1/79th was engaged in the siege of Burgos, during which Major Edward Charles Cocks, a highly promising officer of the 79th, was killed. His loss was deeply felt, particularly by Wellington, who is said to have wept at his funeral. Throughout the winter of 1812 and the spring of 1813 several drafts from the 2/79th arrived to bolster the 1st Battalion's numbers. It played no part in the battle of Vittoria as it remained at Medina del Pomar, covering the magazines and stores. The 1/79th formed part of the 6th Division at this time and on July 28th 1813 fought at Sorauren, losing 58 men. The battalion, commanded by Lieutenant Colonel Neil Douglas, next saw action during the battle of the Nivelle on November 10th 1813 and the following month fought at the battle of the Nive. In February 1814 the 1/79th marched to St Jean de Luz for a new issue of clothing and so missed the battle of Orthes. It did, however, fight at the final battle of the war, at Toulouse on April 10th 1814, where it suffered severely. Of 494 men present some 221 became casualties. On July 3rd 1814 the 1/79th embarked at Pauillac and disembarked at Cork on the 26th. The 1/79th actually sailed for North America on February 8th 1815 but bad weather forced it back to port. This was fortunate, for while at Cork news was received of Napoleon's escape from Elba. The 1/79th was immediately despatched to Ostend and having marched to Brussels was brigaded with the 28th and 32nd Regiments under Major General Sir James Kempt, part of Picton's 5th Division. The battalion fought at both Quatre Bras and Waterloo, losing heavily at the former battle. On July 8th the 1/79th arrived at Paris where it remained until 1818. On October 29th of that year it embarked at Calais, disembarking at Dover the next day.

81st Foot

The 81st Regiment saw only limited service during the Peninsular war. The 2/81st Regiment sailed to Portugal as part of the British reinforcements sent there in October 1808. The battalion soon found itself embroiled in the retreat to Corunna, however, and suffered 154 casualties during the battle there on January 16th 1809. During the battle the 2/81st formed part of Manningham's 3rd Infantry Brigade and was heavily engaged throughout the day. The battalion's casualty figure is one of the few to be recorded from the battle. Another of the Walcheren battalions, it saw no further service with the Allied army in the Peninsula. The battalion subsequently saw service under Wellington during the Waterloo campaign of 1815 as part of Lambert's 10th British Brigade. However, the battalion was not present during the battle as it remained behind at Brussels, guarding the military chest. It did, however, march to Paris in July 1815 and remained in France until January 9th 1816 when it marched north to Calais for England, arriving at Dover on January 18th. The 1st Battalion of the regiment saw action as part of the British force operating on the east coast of Spain from mid-1812 until the end of the war. Most of this period was spent in campaigning between Alicante and Tarragona where the battalion took part in only minor actions against the French. At the end of the war the 1/81st marched to Pauillac where it embarked on June 16th 1814 for Canada, arriving there on August 8th.

82nd (The Prince of Wales's Volunteers) Foot

The 1/82nd Regiment arrived in Portugal in August 1808 and took part in the first two battles of the war, at Roliça, on August 17th and Vimeiro on August 21st where the battalion was one of the heaviest engaged. The battalion formed part of Nightingall's 3rd Infantry Brigade and suffered 86 casualties during the four days' fighting. Following the battle of Corunna on January 16th 1809 the 1/82nd returned to England from where, in July 1809, it sailed to Walcheren in order to take part in the abortive campaign there. The 1/82nd was not to see any further action in the Peninsula until June 1813 when it took part in the battle of Vittoria. The battalion formed part of Grant's Brigade, in Dalhousie's 7th Division, and suffered 31 casualties during the battle. The battalion next saw action at the battles of the Pyrenees in July and August 1813 during which it suffered 173 casualties all ranks. The battalion was equally busy on November 10th 1813 at the battle of the Nivelle during which it had a hard time taking its objective which ultimately cost the battalion a further 73 casualties. The final battle of the war for the 1/82nd came on February 27th 1814 at Orthes where the battalion lost 28 men. At the end of the war the 1/82nd sailed for Canada. A detachment of the 2/82nd served at Tarfia and Barossa.

83rd Foot

The 2/83rd sailed from Cove, Ireland, on March 29th 1809, some 970-strong under the command of Lieutenant Alexander Gordon. The battalion saw its first action on May 12th at the crossing of the Douro and four days later took part in the attack on the French rearguard at Salamonde. The battalion's first major battle came on July 27th-28th at Talavera. The 83rd formed part of Cameron's brigade and on the 28th was heavily engaged, losing 4 officers and 38 men killed, and 11 officers and 202 men wounded. Among the dead was Lieutenant Colonel Gordon, who was killed early on in the day. He had been wounded and was blown apart by a French shell while being carried from the field. The battalion next saw action at Busaco on September 27th 1810. The 2/83rd was commanded by Lieutenant Colonel Collins and was attached to Picton's 3rd Division. At Busaco the 83rd saw little direct fighting and casualties were light. The battalion clashed frequently with Massena's rearguard following his withdrawal from in front of the Lines of Torres Vedras and on May 3rd-5th fought at Fuentes de Oñoro where it remained in support behind the village. The 83rd did a spell of duty in the trenches before Badajoz in June 1811 but retired when the siege was lifted. In January 1812 the battalion marched to Ciudad Rodrigo where it took part in the storming of the place on January 19th. The battalion withstood a much tougher test on April 6th at the storming of Badajoz. The 83rd had already seen action during the taking of one of the outworks, Fort Picurina, and on the night of the actual storming lost 69 men out of 400 engaged. The battalion next saw action at Salamanca on July 22nd 1812. Command of the 'Fighting' 3rd Division had passed to Pakenham, Picton having gone home wounded. During the battle the 83rd, part of Colville's brigade of the 3rd Division, was in the forefront of Pakenham's attack on Thomieres' division. After a period in Madrid

The 83rd Regiment at the storming of Badajoz, April 6th 1812. Note the spiked planks on the ramparts and the savage, tigerish expressions of the combatants.

the 83rd retreated to Portugal with the rest of the Allied army following the failed siege of Burgos in September and October 1812. The 83rd was heavily engaged at Vittoria on June 21st 1813 where Colville, impressed with the battalion's conduct, directed the 83rd's adjutant to take down the names of the men who had been at the front of its attack which had cleared the enemy from the village of La Hermandad. The next day he sent them all one guinea each. The battalion was in the Pyrenees at the time of Soult's offensive in July 1813 but took little part in the fighting. The 83rd did see action, however, on November 10th 1813, at the battle of the Nivelle, where the battalion helped drive the enemy from the

Louis XVIth redoubt and assisted in the capture of the bridge at Amotz. On February 27th 1814 the 83rd fought at Orthes where it was in the thick of the fighting, losing 50 men. The battalion's last action of the war came on April 10th 1814 at Toulouse where it was only partially engaged and casualties light. On June 1st 1814 the 83rd embarked at Bordeaux for England. Of all the 2nd Battalions which served in the Peninsula which already had their 1st Battalions serving overseas, and which had joined Wellington's army in 1809, the 2/83rd was the only one to serve throughout as a complete unit, the others being formed, at some time, into Provisional Battalions or being sent home to recruit.

84th (York and Lancaster) Foot

Although the 2/84th served during the Walcheren campaign in 1809 it did not arrive in Spain until August 16th 1813, landing at Passages in the north of the country. It was brigaded with the 76th and 85th Regiments under the command of Major General Lord Aylmer. Soon after its arrival in the Peninsula the battalion found itself occupying the village of Oyerzum, covering the siege of San Sebastian. On October 7th the battalion crossed the Bidassoa into French territory and took up a position near St Jean de Luz. The battalion was now attached to the 5th

Division and on November 10th 1813 fought at the battle of the Nivelle. The 2/84th attacked a strong position on the French right flank which was carried by the light company of the battalion. The following morning the light company assembled to receive the thanks of the brigade commander, General Robinson. 2 men were killed and five wounded during this action. The 2/84th then remained in the village of Bidart until December 9th when the battle and passage of the Nive commenced. The battalion took part in the attacks on the French positions in front of Bayonne and suffered 6 dead and 40 wounded during the day. The following day saw the French counter-attack and during fierce fighting the brigade's piquets were overrun and many prisoners taken including two officers and 18 men of the 2/84th. Repeated attacks were made on the 84th during the 10th but the battalion held on in spite of losing Lieutenant Colonel Lloyd who was shot in the breast by a musket and died instantly. The battalion fought on until their ammunition ran out upon which it was relieved by the 4th Regiment. During the day the 2/84th suffered 17 killed and 57 wounded. On December 11th the enemy made yet another attack on the Allied positions and at one point during the fighting the 2/84th came under the direct orders of Wellington himself who ordered the battalion into line from close column. He later remarked upon the coolness and steadiness with which the movement was executed. This day's fighting cost the battalion another 13 killed and 19 wounded. On January 8th 1814 the battalion was sent to Hendaye to recover having been hit by a serious outbreak of fever. Here, the battalion buried nearly 300 of their men. After a draft of fresh troops was received from England the 2/84th were employed in the blockade of Bayonne, where it remained until the end of the war in April of that year. The battalion left France in August 1814, sailing for Ireland on the 27th of that month and disembarking at Cove on September 2nd.

Lieutenant Colonel Richard Lloyd, 2/84th Regiment, killed in action at the battle of the Nive, December 11th 1813. Lloyd is buried standing upright in the churchyard of the small village of Bidart.

85th (Bucks Volunteers) Light Infantry Regiment

Having taken part in the Walcheren Campaign of 1809 the 85th Regiment did not arrive in the Peninsula until January 1811. The regiment numbered some 936 men and formed part of the 7th Division. Its first action came at Fuentes de Oñoro on may 3rd-5th 1811 where the 85th suffered 53 casualties. After the battle Wellington praised the 85th for its splendid conduct. In June of the same year, the 85th took part in the first siege of Badajoz. During the assault on the Fort San Christobal the 85th suffered heavy casualties, so severe in fact, that the regiment was sent home to England to recruit. The 85th returned to the Peninsula in July 1813, disembarking close to San Sebastian. The regiment were thrown straight into action as part of the force laying siege to that place which eventually fell on August 31st. The 85th next saw action during the battle of the Nivelle on November 10th 1813, during which it suffered just 14 casualties. During the battle the 85th was ordered to hold the village of Urugne, which it accomplished with distinction, holding off numerous enemy attacks. At the battle of the Nive the 85th, at a crucial moment, were commanded by Wellington in person, who came forward crying, "You must keep your ground, my lads.....charge! charge!", after which the regiment let loose a shattering volley and charged, scattering the French before them. The 85th remained behind laying siege to Bayonne whilst the main part of the army pressed on towards Toulouse and it was at Bayonne that the regiment finished the war in April 1814. On May 31st 1814 the battalion embarked at Bordeaux for North America.

87th (Prince of Wales's Irish) Foot

The 2/87th arrived in Portugal in March 1809 and four months later on July 27th, fought first at Casa des Salinas, the preliminary fight at Talavera, and then on the following day at the battle of Talavera itself where the battalion suffered over 40% casualties, largely whilst standing in position in the face of a heavy enemy barrage. After receiving fresh drafts the battalion recovered and in 1810 was sent to Cadiz in the south of Spain which was under siege by French forces under Marshal Soult. In March the following year the battalion was part of a force of 4,000 British troops under the command of Sir Thomas Graham which sailed up the coast from to Cadiz to Algeciras. From here the battalion marched back towards Cadiz in order to attack the French from the rear. On March 5th 1811 Graham's force clashed with the French under Victor at Barrosa. Emerging from thick pine woods the

2/87th, along with the Coldstream Guards, attacked the French with the men shouting their old battle cry of 'Faugh-au-Ballagh'. As the 87th closed with the French the enemy's eagles became the centre of fierce fighting and Ensign Edward Keogh was cut down whilst trying to take the eagle of the French 8th Regiment. However, Sergeant Masterson grabbed the eagle, slew the French officer holding it and took it back in triumph. After the battle, which resulted in a British victory, Graham wrote to the Colonel of the 87th, 'Your regiment has covered itself with glory; too much cannot be done for it.' As a result of the conduct of the 87th at Barrosa the Prince Regent ordered that the regiment in future be known as the Prince of Wales' Own Irish Regiment and that it should bear an eagle with a laurel wreath upon its Colours. That same year the 2/87th were ordered to Tarifa to assist in the defence of the place and when, in December 1811, the walls were breached and attacked by the French, the 87th played a major part in repulsing the French attacks, the men fighting to the sounds of the fifes and drums playing 'Garryowen' and 'Patrick's Day'. After their adventures in the south of Spain, the 2/87th was ordered north to join the main Allied army under Wellington which it did in the summer of 1812. The 2/87th spent the spring of 1813 on the Portuguese border, recovering from the retreat of the army in November 1812. In May 1813 the battalion fought at Vittoria where it sustained 269 casualties. During the rout afterwards, Marshal Jourdan's baton was captured by a drummer of the battalion. The 2/87th next saw action at the crossing of the Nivelle where, after its attack on a fortified position, its divisional commander called it the 'Gallant 87th'. At the battle of Orthes on February 27th 1814 the battalion suffered 264 casualties, which, apart from the 268 suffered by the 88th, was the highest casualty figure in the army. Their final action of the Peninsular War came at Toulouse on April 10th 1814. On July 7th 1814 the battalion embarked at Pauillac and arrived at Cork on the 20th of the same month.

88th (Connaught Rangers) Foot

The 1/88th embarked for Cadiz on December 28th 1808 but bad weather forced it into Cork, where the battalion remained until February 21st 1809. The 88th finally disembarked at Lisbon on April 13th 1809 and its first action came at Talavera on July 27th-28th 1809 where the battalion lost 136 men in heavy fighting. In February 1810 the 3rd Division, in which the 88th was brigaded, came under the command of Thomas Picton, under whose leadership the 88th was to establish a reputation as one of the most fearsome battalions in Wellington's army. On September 27th 1810 the 88th fought at Busaco where, under the command of Lieutenant Colonel Wallace, the battalion distinguished itself with a fierce bayonet charge, prompting Wellington to say, "Wallace, I never saw a more gallant charge than that just made by your regiment." Its next major action came at Fuentes de Oñoro on May 3rd-5th 1811. Once again the battalion did great execution with the bayonet and at one point trapped about a hundred Frenchmen in an alleyway, none of whom survived the 88th's attack. The battalion was in the forefront of the stormings of both Ciudad Rodrigo and Badajoz, which were taken in January and April 1812. During the latter storming the 88th escaladed the walls of the castle and fought with the French 88th Regiment which defended the ramparts. On July 22nd 1812, at Salamanca, the 88th achieved a notable feat when it captured the 'Jingling Johnny' of the French 101st Regiment. The instrument was carried in triumph for the rest of the war. After the retreat from Burgos in October 1812 the 1/88th received a draft of men from the 2nd Battalion, making good the losses sustained that year. At Vittoria, on June 21st 1813, the 1/88th lost one officer and 34 men killed and 4 officers and 197 men wounded during some fierce fighting when, prompted once again by the colourful language of Sir Thomas Picton, the battalion made several bayonet charges against the French centre. The battalion earned the honour 'Pyrenees' for its actions between July 25th and 30th 1813. The battalion did not take part in the storming of San Sebastian and was only slightly engaged at the battle of the Nivelle on November 10th 1813. Its next action, in fact, came at Orthes on February 27th 1814 where it suffered 277 casualties, many of which were caused when French cavalry got in amongst the leading companies during a charge. When the 88th opened fire in return only a few of its assailants made it back to their lines. The 88th's final battle of the war came at Toulouse on April 10th 1814 where only three companies were actually engaged. Nevertheless, 86 men were lost. On June 15th 1814 the 1/88th embarked for Canada and did not return in time to take part in the Waterloo campaign. It did, however, march to Paris as part of the Army of Occupation, remaining there until 1817 whereupon it returned to England.

91st Foot

The 1/91st landed in Portugal on August 4th 1808 as part of Wellesley's original expedition to the Peninsula. That same month the battalion saw action at the first British battles of the war at Roliça and Vimeiro where it formed part of the reserve on both occasions. Before the year was out the 91st found itself on the retreat to Corunna and in January 1809 took part in the battle of Corunna. No accurate casualty figures are available for the actual battle but when the battalion arrived home in England it numbered just 534 men having lost 164 men during the battle and retreat. By March of 1809 there were just 337 men fit for duty as a further 144 men had gone into hospital suffering from the effects of the campaign. When the 91st returned to full strength it was ordered to Walcheren where it took part in the ill-fated campaign there. 218 men of the 91st died there from fever. By the time the 91st had recovered for active service once again, Wellington was poised to cross the Pyrenees. The 91st took part in the fighting here and in the subsequent battles of the Nivelle, the Nive, Orthes and Toulouse. On June 24th 1814 the battalion sailed for England. Following Napoleon's escape from Elba the regiment, already having embarked for America, was diverted instead to Ostend where it disembarked on April 11th 1815 but although the 91st arrived in time it did not take part in the actual battle, occupying the extreme right of Wellington's line instead. The regiment later took part in the advance on and occupation of Paris, which it entered on July 7th 1815. The 91st remained in France until November 1st 1818 when it embarked at Calais, arriving at Dover the following day.

92nd (Highland) Regiment

The 1/92nd sailed for Portugal on July 31st 1808 and on August 19th arrived off Mondego Bay. The battalion did not come ashore until August 27th and so missed the battle of Vimeiro. On October 26th 1808 the 92nd was attached to Sir John Hope's division and subsequently took part in the retreat to Corunna. During the battle there on January 16th 1809 the 92nd occupied a position on the left flank of the army and during the fighting its commanding officer, Lieutenant Colonel Alexander Napier, was killed. On January 26th the battalion disembarked at Portsmouth and in July the same year took part in the Walcheren campaign. The 1/92nd returned to the Peninsula in 1810, arriving at Lisbon on October 8th. The battalion was commanded by Lieutenant Colonel John Cameron and was brigaded with the 50th and 71st, in Howard's brigade of the 1st Division. The 92nd's first action upon its return to the Peninsula came at Fuentes de Oñoro on May 3rd–5th 1811. 55 men were lost here. Later that same month the battalion was posted to Hill's 2nd Division which formed part of the force covering the siege operations at Badajoz in June 1811. On October 28th 1811 the 92nd took part in Hill's action at Arroyo dos Molinos, where a French force was surprised and routed. The 92nd was one of the first battalions to enter the village. Lieutenant Colonel Cameron was amongst the wounded here. The 92nd remained with Hill's force in 1812 and so missed both the great sieges at Ciudad Rodrigo and Badajoz and also the battle of Salamanca. However, two months before the

The 'Jingling Johnny', captured at Salamanca by the 88th (Connaught Rangers). Reputed to have been carried in battle by the Moors the instrument found its way into the possession of the French Army and was surmounted by an Imperial Eagle. The instrument was carried at Salamanca by the French 101st Regiment which was practically annihilated during the battle. The instrument was subsequently damaged on two occasions during the 19th century and was sent, ironically, to Paris to be repaired.

division. The men of the 92nd were eventually forced back having sustained terrible losses of 320 killed and wounded. It was said afterwards that the 92nd's valour 'would have graced Thermopylae.' It was, perhaps, the 92nd's finest moment of the war. Once again, Lieutenant Colonel Cameron was amongst the wounded. Further skirmishing followed in the Pyrenees which reduced the 92nd to just 362 men. On November 10th 1813 Cameron led his men against the redoubts at Ainhoa during the battle of the Nivelle and the following month led them at the battle of the Nive. During this latter battle, on December 13th 1813, the 92nd were attacked in strength and suffered 184 casualties. On February 17th 1814 the battalion distinguished itself in a minor action at Arriverete, where it secured a bridge over the Gave de Mauleon. Wellington recommended that the 92nd be allowed to bear the word 'Arriverete' on its Colours. The 92nd fought its last major action of the war on February 27th 1814, at Orthes, although it did see action at the combat at Aire on March 2nd. The battalion was not engaged at Toulouse and on July 17th 1814 it embarked at Pauillac, arriving at Cork on the 26th. On May 10th 1815 the 1/92nd landed at Ostend to take part in the Waterloo campaign. It was attached to Pack's brigade, part of Picton's 5th Division. The 92nd suffered severe losses at Quatre Bras on June 16th 1815 where 286 men were lost. Amongst the dead was Lieutenant Colonel Cameron, who had led his men in the Peninsula. His death was mentioned by Wellington in his despatch. On June 18th the 92nd joined the charge of the Scots Greys, many of the men grabbing the stirrups of the cavalrymen. Another 116 men were lost on this great day. On July 3rd the 92nd camped near Paris, where it remained until October 28th 1815 when it marched north to Calais, embarking there on December 17th. It disembarked at Margate the following day.

With enemy cavalry hot on his tail Wellington takes cover in dramatic style amongst the 92nd Highlanders during the battle of Quatre Bras, June 16th 1815.

latter battle, the 92nd saw action during Hill's raid on the bridge at Almaraz, carried out on May 19th 1812. The battalion distinguished itself during the fighting and was awarded the honour 'Almaraz', the 92nd becoming one of the few regiments to hold that particular honour. It was to be another year before the 92nd saw any further action, at Vittoria on June 21st 1813 where casualties were light. On July 25th 1813 the 92nd formed part of the small force holding the pass at Maya. The pass was later attacked by a French force vastly outnumbering the British and half a battalion of the 92nd formed up in line across the crest of a ridge and held back an entire French

94th (Scotch Brigade) Foot

The 94th embarked at Jersey on January 19th 1810 and disembarked at Lisbon on the 31st. The battalion, 970-strong, did not remain long, however, for on February 6th it sailed for Cadiz. The battalion remained here, assisting

in the defence of the place, until September 9th 1810, when it sailed back to Lisbon in order to join Wellington's main field army. The 94th was attached to the 2nd Brigade of Picton's 3rd Division and after a spell within the Lines of Torres Vedras saw its first action at Redinha on March 12th 1811, whilst in pursuit of Massena's retreating army. On May 3rd-5th, at Fuentes de Oñoro, the 94th's light company was engaged, the remainder of the battalion occupying a position on the ridge behind the village. The 94th next saw action at the storming of Ciudad Rodrigo on January 19th 1812. The battalion stormed the Great Breach and suffered 69 casualties in doing so. A further 65 men were lost by the 94th on April 6th at the storming of Badajoz. By the time the 94th fought at Salamanca, on July 22nd 1812, the battalion had been reduced to just 24 officers and 323 men. Nevertheless, it formed part of Pakenham's 3rd Division which smashed Thomieres' division and so began the defeat of Marmont's army. On August 12th 1812 the 94th entered Madrid amidst great rejoicing by its inhabitants. The battalion remained here until October 24th when it marched to join the main Allied army, retreating from Burgos. The 94th was now commanded by Major Thomas Lloyd, as a Brevet Lieutenant Colonel and on June 21st 1813 he led the battalion into battle at Vittoria, driving the French from the village of La Hermandad. The battalion held off several enemy cavalry charges during the latter stages of the battle before it reached Vittoria itself where, along with the rest of Wellington's army, it stopped to plunder Joseph's baggage train. The 94th suffered 66 casualties during the day. On July 28th 1813 the 94th fought at Sorauren and after crossing the French border next saw action at the battle of the Nivelle. The 94th, part of Colville's brigade, took the bridge at Amotz but during the fighting Lieutenant Colonel Lloyd, much loved by his men, was killed whilst leading the battalion into action. He was just 30 years old. The 94th took no part in the battle of the Nive but did see action at the last two battles of the war, at Orthes and Toulouse. The 94th embarked at Pauillac in late May 1814 and disembarked at Cork on June 14th.

97th (Queen's Germans)

The 97th Regiment, the re-numbered 96th, arrived in Portugal on the evening of August 19th 1808 and came up in time to join Wellesley's army at Vimeiro the following day. It was part of the 7th Infantry Brigade under Anstruther. The regiment was not heavily involved in the battle on August 21st but did, however, lose 22 men. The commanding officer, Lieutenant Colonel Lyon, was praised by Wellesley in his despatches afterwards. The regiment remained in Portugal after the Convention of Cintra and did not take part in the Corunna campaign of 1808-09. During the Talavera campaign of 1809 the 97th was placed in Sontag's brigade which was part of the 4th Division, although he was later succeeded by Kemmis. On July 27th-28th the 97th fought at Talavera losing 37 men. It was to be another year before the 97th saw any further action, at Busaco on September 27th 1810, although Kemmis's brigade was not involved in any direct fighting. Following the battle Wellington's army fell back to the Lines of Torres Vedras and the 4th Division went into quarters at Azambuja. The 97th next saw action at the first siege of Badajoz in May 1811. The siege was unsuccessful and the regiment lost 106 officers and men killed and wounded. When Beresford marched south Kemmis's brigade went too but the rising waters of the Guadiana prevented Kemmis from reaching Albuera in time to take part in the battle there on May 16th 1811, although two companies of the 97th did arrive and lost 20 men there. On October 3rd 1811 a General Order was issued recalling the regiment back to England and it took no further part in the war.

95th (Rifle) Regiment

Perhaps the most famous British regiment of the period, the 95th Rifles served throughout the entire Peninsular campaign, fighting in almost every major battle from Roliça to Toulouse and was present at Waterloo. The 95th was much feared by the French who nicknamed them 'Grasshoppers', on account of their green uniforms. The 95th fired the first

A rifleman of the 95th. Nicknamed 'grasshoppers' by the French on account of their green uniforms, the 95th proved one of the great successes of the Peninsular War. Armed with the Baker rifle – slower to load but more accurate than the musket – the riflemen of the 95th were a constant thorn in the side of the enemy.
During the retreat to Corunna Rifleman Tom Plunkett shot the French general, Colbert, through the forehead after deliberately taking aim.

British shots of the Peninsular War, at Obidos, on August 15th 1808, and in Lieutenant Ralph Bunbury, who was killed during the skirmish, the 95th suffered the first officer casualty. The 95th arrived in Portugal piecemeal, four companies of the 2/95th arriving at Lisbon on August 1st 1808, two companies of the 1/95th arriving on August 20th. For the sake of simplicity we will look at the 95th as a whole, rather than break the regiment down into its individual battalions. As already stated the regiment fired the first British shots of the war at Obidos on August 15th 1808. On the 17th and 21st of the same month the 95th fought at both Roliça and Vimeiro before playing a major part in the retreat to Corunna, during which it formed part of the rearguard. During this latter occasion the 1st Battalion served in Paget's division whilst the 2nd Battalion marched to Vigo with Craufurd's Light Brigade. When Wellesley returned to Portugal in April 1809 a single company of the 95th, that had remained at Lisbon during the retreat to Corunna, served with him and took part in the crossing of the Douro. The 1st Battalion of the regiment, however, did not return to Portugal until June that year and, as part of Craufurd's Light Brigade, took part in the famous march to Talavera the following month, covering forty-two miles in sixteen and a half hours. The 95th had to wait over a year before its next major action, at Busaco on September 27th 1810, but saw a great deal of fighting during the summer of that year as part of Craufurd's Light Division, operating on the Portuguese border opposite Ciudad Rodrigo. The actions at Barba del Puerco and on the River Coa are the more memorable of these fights. After the battle of Busaco the 95th retired to within the lines of Torres Vedras and while there was joined by the 3rd Battalion of the regiment. Six companies of the 95th were present with Graham at Barrosa on March 5th 1811, suffering 66 casualties. There were several skirmishes involving the 95th when Massena withdrew from in front of the Lines of Torres Vedras, notably at Pombal, Redinha, Condeixa and Foz d'Arouce, in March 1811, culminating in the action at Sabugal on April 3rd. The 95th suffered relatively light casualties at Fuentes de Oñoro on May 3rd–5th 1811 and casualties were equally light amongst the detachment of the 3/95th that took part in the defence of Tarifa from

December 1811 to January 1812. When Wellington stormed Ciudad Rodrigo and Badajoz in January and April 1812 the Light Division was at the forefront on each occasion and the 95th suffered accordingly. 62 men were lost at Rodrigo with another 382 at the siege and storming of Badajoz. The 95th saw little fighting at Salamanca on July 22nd 1812 and entered Madrid on August 12th. The regiment took no part in the siege operations at Burgos but did lose a number of men during the subsequent retreat to Portugal afterwards. The 95th next saw action at Vittoria on June 21st 1813, losing 79 men and was afterwards engaged in the Pyrenees and at the siege of San Sebastian. The green-jacketed riflemen were in their element during the operations to invade southern France and made considerable contributions to the fighting on the Bidassoa, Nivelle and Nive rivers. The regiment saw only limited service at Orthes on February 27th 1814 but was engaged in what was called, 'the sharpest action of the war,' at Tarbes on March 20th 1814, where the regiment lost 93 men. A further 86 riflemen were lost at the final battle of the war at Toulouse on April 10th during which some of the 3/95th pushed on too far and having suffered from enemy fire had to jump into an open sewer for cover! On July 13th 1814 the 1/95th and 2/95th embarked at Pauillac for Portsmouth, arriving there on July 22nd while the 3rd Battalion sailed a few days earlier and arrived at Plymouth on July 18th. The 95th served under Graham in Holland in 1813-14 and in the ill-fated attack on New Orleans in January 1815. The regiment returned to Europe in 1815 to join Wellington's army in Belgium. Only the 1st Battalion saw serious fighting at Quatre Bras, losing 64 men, while all three battalions of the regiment, albeit only six companies of the 2nd and two companies of the 3rd Battalion, served with great distinction at Waterloo on June 18th, losing a combined total of nearly 400 men. When the Allied army entered Paris on July 7th the 2/95th had the honour of being the first to enter the city. The contingent of the 3/95th returned to England in December 1815 with the 1/95th and 2/95th remaining in France until October and November 1818, by which time the regiment was called The Rifle Brigade, by virtue of an order dated February 16th 1816.

BIBLIOGRAPHY

The Napoleonic Wars marked the beginning of a great age of military literature, prompted largely by an increase in literacy and partly by the successful campaigns fought by Wellington's army. The Peninsular War in particular produced a flood of memoirs which continued years after the campaign had ended and still continues today.

It was only natural, of course, that so many of the participants should want to tell their story and scores of diaries, memoirs, journals and letters found their way into print. Some were written during the campaigns themselves whilst others were written afterwards or were edited by a member of the diarist's family. Others, were dictated by illiterates to those who could write. These memoirs vary in the degree of reliability and realism. Those written at the time are often the most reliable with regard to accuracy and truth whereas those written years afterwards, although having the edge in style and entertainment, were done so with the benefit of hindsight with the diarist often only too keen to stress or play up his own part in the war. Another problem with these latter memoirs is that few of the writers were willing to criticise Wellington which is not the case with some of the contemporary letters which are often quite scathing, Wellington himself having yet to have attained his lofty status as saviour of Europe.

The Peninsular War produced one of the great works of English literature in William Napier's *History of the War in the Peninsula and in the South of France*. Having served with the 43rd Light Infantry, Napier was ideally placed to witness the events of the war and this, combined with his unique ability to recapture them in vivid and brilliant prose, makes his work an absolute must for any student of the war.

The number of regimental histories also runs into hundreds and again are of varying use to historians. Some merely give lists of officers or medal rolls, whilst others, such as Wylly's *XVth (The King's Hussars), 1759 to 1913*, are quite massive works. Colonel Daniel Mackinnon of the Coldstream Guards had served in the Peninsula and was one of the defenders of Hougoumont at Waterloo. His *Origin and Services of the Coldstream Guards* was one of the earliest detailed works to appear. In the middle of the 19th century Richard Cannon produced a remarkable series of regimental histories which, although often scorned by historians today, provided much of the groundwork for many of the deeper and more professional histories that appeared later. But it was the late Victorian era that ushered in the age of the great regimental histories, a tradition which flourished into the early years of this century. The works of C.T. Atkinson and Colonel H.C Wylly, in particular, stand out as some of the best works of the period. One feature of these histories is the extensive use of contemporary material, the letters and journals of the officers and men of the regiments, much of which has disappeared since.

In the late 1960s, in a hark back to Cannon's series of histories, Leo Cooper published his Famous Regiments series which consisted of short accounts of numerous British Army regiments. Each book certainly gives a flavour of the regiment concerned but they are very general and have limited worth to the serious military historian. There has, however, been a return to the scholarly approach adopted by Atkinson and Wylly. Robinson's superb *The Bloody Eleventh: History of the Devonshire Regiment*, is certainly amongst the finest regimental histories to have been produced and has set a new bench-mark for those who follow. Michael Glover's *That Astonishing Infantry: The History of the Royal Welch Fusiliers, 1689–1989*, is another fine modern history.

Several unit histories of individual campaigns have also appeared over the years. Charles Cadell's *Narrative of the Campaigns of the Twenty-Eighth Regiment since their Return from Egypt in 1802*, published in 1835, was one of the earliest while William Leeke's *The History of Lord Seaton's Regiment (The 52nd Light Infantry) at the Battle of Waterloo*, ranks not only as one of the better regimental campaign histories but is also a prime source relating to the Waterloo Campaign itself. Willoughby Verner's *History and Campaigns of the Rifle Brigade*, published in 1919, although ending at the Vittoria campaign of 1813, probably

ranks as the best in the regimental campaign history category. In recent years these regimental campaign histories have continued with Alan Lagden's *The 2/73rd at Waterloo*, Caldwell and Cooper's *Rifle Green at Waterloo*, Michael Mann's *And They Rode On: The King's Dragoon Guards at Waterloo*, and Fletcher and Poulter's *Gentlemen's Sons: The Foot Guards in the Peninsula and at Waterloo, 1808–15*.

The following bibliography is by no means a complete one. There are literally hundreds of books on the Peninsular War and the battle of Waterloo, in the form of diaries, memoirs and journals etc., while the number of regimental histories is equally great. However, space precludes an inclusion of a bibliography featuring histories of each regiment mentioned in this book. Therefore, the reader is directed to Arthur White's *Bibliography of Regimental Histories of the British Army*. The following short bibliography lists just a few of the books covering Wellington and his army between 1808 and 1815.

General Bibliography

Ascoli, David. *A Companion to the British Army*. London, 1983.

Brett-James, Anthony. *Life in Wellington's Army*. London, 1972.

Chandler, David. *The Hundred Days*. London, 1984.

Fletcher, I. *Craufurd's Light Division*. Tunbridge Wells, 1992.

Fletcher, I. *Fields of Fire: Battlefields of the Peninsular War*. Staplehurst, 1994.

Fortescue, Sir John. *History of the British Army*. 13 Vols. London, 1899–1920.

Glover, Michael. *The Peninsular War, 1807–14*. Newton Abbot, 1974.

Glover, Michael. *Wellington as Military Commander*. London, 1968.

Glover, Michael. *Wellington's Army in the Peninsula*. Newton Abbot, 1977.

Haythornthwaite, Philip J. *Wellington's Military Machine*. Tunbridge Wells, 1989.

Jones, J.T. *Journal of the Sieges* undertaken by the Allies in Spain. London, 1814.

Longford, Elizabeth. *Wellington: The Years of the Sword*. London, 1969.

Myatt, F. *British Sieges of the Peninsular War*. Tunbridge Wells, 1987.

Napier, William. *History of the War in the Peninsula and in the South of France, from the Year 1807 to Year 1814*. 6 Vols. London, 1889.

Norman, C.B. *Battle Honours of the British Army*. London, 1911.

Oman, Sir Charles. *History of the Peninsular War*. 7 Vols. Oxford, 1902–30.

Oman, Sir Charles. *Wellington's Army, 1809–14*. London, 1912.

Ward, S.G.P. *Wellington's Headquarters*. London, 1957.

Weller, Jac. *Wellington in the Peninsula*. London, 1962.

Weller, Jac. *Wellington at Waterloo*. London, 1967.

White, Arthur S. *A Bibliography of Regimental Histories of the British Army*. London, 1965.

INDEX